BICYCLE!

A REPAIR & MAINTENANCE
MANIFESTO

BICYCLE!

A REPAIR & MAINTENANCE
MANIFESTO

by Sam Tracy

speck press

denver

Copyright 2006 © Sam Tracy
Published by: *speck press*, speckpress.com

ISBN 1-933108-01-0, ISBN13 978-1-933108-01-8

Photo copyrights by ©Seng Chen, ©Nancy McBride, ©Dan Osterud, ©Sam Tracy, ©ShutterStock, ©iStock. For individual image credits please contact the publisher.

This publication is provided for informational and educational purposes. The information herein contained is true and complete to the best of our knowledge.

Book layout and design by CPG
corvuspublishinggroup.com

Printed and bound in the United States of America

Library of Congress Cataloging-in-Publication Data

Tracy, Sam.
  Bicycle! : a repair and maintenance manifesto / by Sam Tracy.
    p. cm.
  Includes index.
  ISBN-13: 978-1-933108-01-8
  ISBN-10: 1-933108-01-0
  1. Bicycles--Maintenance and repair. I. Title.

TL430.T727 2005
629.28'772--dc22

                                        2005021835

10 9 8 7 6 5 4 3 2 1

Acknowledgments

This volume might never have appeared were it not for Bill Michalski and Genevieve Munsey at Black Kettle Graphics, who were brave enough to publish its predecessor in 2000. And Xara Lindstrom, Dan Osterud, Seng Chen, and my mother, Nancy McBride, were all gracious enough to help capture more of the action this time through. Needless to say, we should not presume that any of the viewpoints expressed herein are necessarily shared by anyone beyond myself.

Left to my own devices, odds are good I am listening to ska. My best ideas often came Saturday mornings in Minneapolis, listening to Rude Radio on 770, Radio K. But I should thank Jordan Gray for introducing me to Snog and the Flying Lizards, which with Crass remain some of the clearest and most inspirational bands I've heard. Mike Robertson from the Quincy Punks got me in to that last band long ago, whether meaning to or not. We both went to school with some of Saint Paul's Blind Approach, which was the first real band I ever saw. Matt Stofflet was eventually able to direct me towards the Upright Citizens, and later the Cows; Oak out in Arcata hipped me to the Coup. And it was Randy Neckolaishen, one of the best drummers the Midwest has ever known, who got me in to Scratch Acid and the Cherubs and so many others. Steve Post in Minneapolis enlightened me about In Flames, as well as to many details on the singlespeeds, and Xara let me know about Sublimation. Kari Petersen tuned me in to County Z and the Knotwells and that whole trip, and it was Jim Kolles who let me know about Resolve and Contravene. I don't recall who told me about Danger Boy and the Road Vultures, but they also get a mention. Nor can I remember who told me about Submission Hold, but theirs might have been my favorite show in 2002. And the Calhoun Rental band of the year for 2003 was Peru's amazing Autonomia … great stuff. Some of these others I've been lucky to see at the Bedlam Theater in Minneapolis, which deserves our enthusiastic support.

On leaving, Kerri Spindler-Ranta really brought the song into my life. And I remain grateful for conversations with Dan Ditty, Jon Londres, Travis T., and all the other mechanics I've worked with over the years, the sum of which strengthened this project to a considerable degree.

TABLE OF CONTENTS

Introduction

This is for the little bike that wants to roar: the bike with earnest potential that has, for reasons both complicated and obscure, been kept far too long in a space much too small. Because suspense, necessarily, cannot carry forever!

As the proudly disingenuous ad men and their attendant mystics fade into the twilight—together with the endless noise about various smog machines and bottle rockets—the incredible bicycle can only be made more free.

And it is here, rising from the pits, that our story begins. The cursed mutants squeezed from big department stores can't easily be considered bicycles, let alone incredible, but still this leaves legions of candidates. More, the means to make your own bike soar will trace back to a patient series of rituals, the sum of which will embrace your own ride, your kid's bike, and the one after that. It is holistic.

This manual, my second, concerns itself with explaining things in a more reliable way. I've come into a number of new secrets over the years, most of which I can share with you. We also have the ceaseless white noise of what is called "technical development." But cycling was already an amazing privilege before experiments began: we will dip our toes in the new electric water, for the sake of its occasionally worthwhile revelations, but this leaves plenty of time for those pursuits we know to work well enough already.

It may become possible to strip everything away; to better trust cycling's charms to simply explain themselves. Home-builders and clubs like the Hard Times take the opportunity to define the leading edge of bike design, but the dispassionate and well-capitalized pretenders presuming to dominate the cycling "industry" still find excuses to rely on the vapor trails of perpetual novelty to make a shady buck on something that should, by right, belong to public will and desire. The pretense itself is only crude, reductionist farce.

Rather than share, those mechanically sound ideas emerging from the desperate fogbank of failed hype are instead privatized and patented, imprisoned in the silly money-zoo. Rarely, even, do the industry's various hucksters and prophets pause long enough to plainly except the ideas that are good from those that really don't seem to be. It takes a special bending of the light to appreciate how the hell some of this shit is even supposed to work in the first place—the folding or even the collapsing of the space-time continuum, as the case may be.

My wrenches fly like zodiacs, lately: I maintain a vast fleet of rental bikes by day, and often enough I'm overhauling old courier bikes or projects for The Hub after that. There must be time to fix everything at once, so that is what I do. It is that time of year; the regeneration points in the best direction. Just as cycling itself can become a brilliant refusal to participate, so too can bike mechanistry's readily accessible ways move us towards a better place.

There is nothing sacrosanct about bike repair. Its pursuit only requires the will to learn. I really believe that. Mechanical aptitude need be neither blessing nor curse; too often it is only so much shopworn cultural shorthand. Circumstance can lead us to become more or less mechanically inclined, but that's really all it is. Fate seems to concern itself with certain larger projects. Let *Bicycle!* become another proud and unabashed testimonial toward the inherent value of broad and inclusive public education.

1: TOOLS

*We begin with the tools. An understanding of their
selection, use, and care will start us out in the right
direction.*

*Cone wrenches, with
offset brake wrench*

The natural place to start is with the tools. A good number of bike repair scenarios do involve garden variety hand tools—more wrenches and screwdrivers than hammers and chisels, hopefully—but there's also a wide raft of other tools that were designed to be bicycle-friendly.

You will find that it's generally easier to fix things if you have one particular spot for such purposes—where you can afford the luxury of time; where your tools are gathered together as one; where it's at least bright enough to illuminate how dirty the floor gets to be. But you might also put down a big piece of cardboard, a bike box for example, to keep shit off the marble floors. It's also much nicer to stand on; your feet don't get all dreary so fast.

Roadside repairs, by nature, breed the tendency to rush. It is possible to wreck just about anything, if you do it fast enough. Sudden fixes also lend themselves toward more forceful sorts of persuasion, which can easily

become just as counterproductive. Your bike may be strong enough to support your weight and more, but many of its individual parts respond best to a more delicate touch. The latter becomes a point to which we'll return liberally, in the coming pages.

The first things we'll look at are **BIKE REPAIR STANDS**. Their firm and helpful presence echoes through all the established bike shops, like a solid and reliable chorus. They accomplish the useful trick of removing the wheels from the ground, which greatly simplifies our work on the brakes and drivetrain. But the improved vantage is also precious in its own right, in that we're better able to reach for things. It's best if you have things where you can easily move them. The worthwhile stands are spendy, but they're worth it. Maybe you can go in on one with your friends.

The stands we use at work, together with a good number of our bike-specific tools, are made by the Park Tool Company. They make heavy-duty shop models, simpler home-repair versions, and folding stands as well, together with just about every other bike tool you might look for.

Our shop variety is the ubiquitous workhorse. It is a sturdy steel pole, bolted to a heavy metal base. The package becomes massive enough to absorb the serious torque bike mechanistry sometimes requires. This is the ideal, to have the means to hold the bike very securely.

And just a tip, tie a strap from an old toe clip to the base somewhere, if you do have a stand. It is occasionally useful to make sure the fork does not exit its frame; wrapping the strap from down tube to fork crown lets this be so.

The repair stand's most successful alternative finds you flipping the bike upside-down, to take advantage of the gravity. This also leaves the bottom bracket sitting right up high, where you can easily address its various concerns. This junction, to occasionally include the pedals, is where you most likely need to apply heavier force.

Useful bike repair stands work around rubber-lined jaws, which clamp to the bike's frame. The best place to grab is usually on the bike's seat post. You might have to loosen the bolt and raise it a little—the original position might be noted with electrical tape, of course—but that's cool, because the effort can very easily save you all kinds of hassle. Certain kinds of people tend to get all pissy if you manage to scuff up their decals or stickers, of course, but it can actually go south from there. Some frame materials can be damaged by repair stands.

Do not wrap a clamp around a carbon fiber tube. The material is markedly vulnerable to compression pressure; always clamp to the seat post instead. Unless the seat post is also carbon, in which case you need to borrow a dummy seatpost to put the bike in the repair stand. And you want to exercise the very same cautions with lightweight aluminum tubing, for similar reasons.

The stand's jaws arrive to us in several varieties. The two most common examples, both from Park, are cam-activated clamps. The simpler consumer version is built around a spring. The breadth of its bite is not adjustable, but it actually works well enough. The shop model can be adjusted to fit a general range of frame tubing diameters. Ultimate Bicycle Support also makes an adjustable clamp to fit its own or Park stand bases; a dial on the end opens the jaws a bit wider yet. Park also makes a more adjustable heavier-duty version of the same, the Extreme Range Clamp.

You will probably want one of these last two if you're working on a fat-tubed recumbent bicycle. It's often easiest to clamp to the bike first, in the case of the 'bents, before hoisting the whole package in to the stand. They're lower and heavier; this can make a big difference. Some short wheelbase recumbents such as Bacchetta will respond better to one of the traditional Park clamp jaws, however, wrapped tightly around the neutral side chainstay.

Your bent wheels are best straightened within the helpful context of a **TRUING STAND**. That made by Park Tool is easy to operate, sturdy as hell, and reliable like eternity. The business version costs a couple bills; you might consider some kind of collective acquisition. I bartered for mine! Life is good like that.

Real stands like the Park invariably work better than those lesser attempts toward the truth more cheaply available, simply because they're able to hold the wheel quite securely. Those items euphemistically termed "consumer" truing stands tend to be plastic. Flimsy! You might go ahead and conserve your resources, if you can't spring for the real deal.

The wheels might be trued to a basic accuracy within the frame and fork, of course, using the brake pads or similar as calipers. This is easiest with lots and lots of light, but it's all the more so in a bona fide truing stand. That our wheels come in various dimensions is the only thing to complicate the truing stands. Cheap little wannabe stands struggle to make both arms and calipers highly adjustable, through the economist's dreary haze of inferior materials and shoddy construction. But you might have some luck clamping these cheap truing stands in a bench vise.

Our mounts might well have a range of different needs, in terms of the various hand tools, but this concern has been tamed with the thickness of time. A fair number of curious toolage protocols were cycled through in the early years; only the most enterprising among them have been carried through to the present. The rest can only fall in to the dustbin; they're forgotten a little more each year.

The more modern your bike happens to be, the more it will correspond with the increasingly standardized parameters of bike tools. "Standard" is good in this sense; it means we can more easily talk to each other, and you have fewer tools to buy. The small bolts holding things in place, for example, have increasingly been finding some common ground. Having experimented with a number of possibilities, the great thinkers among us have more recently focused in upon the **ALLEN WRENCHES**. These are the six-sided hex keys, of course, whose bolts are more adept at handling their torque. Basically, they're less inclined to strip out.

Stripping finds the tool slipping off target, wearing down those useful angles we might otherwise rely upon to turn things around. The wider the hex, the deeper its target, the more you can comfortably lever on it.

The threads featuring on these hex screws are almost always lined up in accordance with the metric system. The old clutter about inches and feet and their obtuse fractions is increasingly useless. It still haunts my speech, by virtue of the tremendous force of its habits, but I yearn to be free.

The most common are easily 5 and 6 millimeters. The screws associated with modern racks, shifter bosses, water bottle cages, and the like are 5 millimeter; those securing brakes to the frame are 6 millimeter. The size distinction quickly becomes obvious; you start to recognize it.

Both the bolts' thread dimensions and the wrench sizes used to turn them are commonly described in terms of millimeters. It can be momentarily confusing, but that's just how we talk. The particular Allen keys used to turn our 5-millimeter and 6-millimeter bolts vary some, for example; they generally fall between 3 and 5 millimeters. The 5 is preferable, because it's the sturdiest. This wrench should probably be your first acquisition, if you don't already have one. Every mobile bike repair kit features one; they're also found in sets with their peers.

The wrenches are L-shaped, because each end has its own ambitions. Those among these with ball-ends to them are even better, because they can be spun at useful angles. Ball is only on the long end; its opposite is more useful in delivering the final torque. So my first advice is to score a full set, from 2 to 10 millimeters. The T-handled or 3-headed Allens are better for some applications, but they can come later.

BOX WRENCHES in the range of 8 to 17 millimeters are also pretty central to bike repair. Most hub adjustments, axle locknuts, some pedals, and all manner of accessories are best moved by their efforts. An adjustable wrench can usually fill in for the job, but it's more cumbersome, and also more inclined to lose focus and strip things out. You have to kind of keep an eye on the wrench, while you're working on something, and this becomes a distraction. I'd much rather throw down a few extra bones for the full set of box wrenches. It's not that much more.

Start here: Allen wrenches

The exception I make is for a big old **CRESCENT WRENCH**. Its relatively large measures will more reliably stay within useful adjustments; its considerable heft can make positive contributions in torque. Three sets of **PLIERS** are also particularly useful: the basic box, the needlenose, and the larger channellocks. The dreaded vice-grip pliers, rarely called upon in professional adjustment applications, can best be considered a tool of last resort.

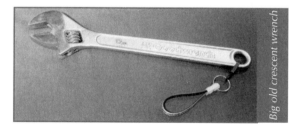

Big old crescent wrench

You will also want **SCREWDRIVERS.** You might get away with only a pair, to start: a larger Phillips-head and a smaller regular one. The longer their handles, the more leverage you will earn. The Phillips is for many derailleur and brake adjustment screws, as well as those found on many handlebarmounted accessories. These are all pretty small, but most often carve out pretty well. And the little regular one might be most often misused, actually, as a sort of miniature

pry bar. And you might eventually pick up one of Park's wide-nosed T-handle screwdrivers, which is very useful when working with various older handlebar control levers.

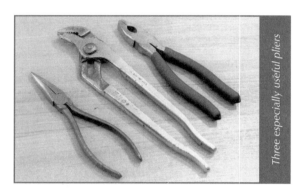

Three especially useful pliers

You can find quality sidecutters that will slice bike cables, but for such purposes your cash is better dispatched on a pair of dedicated **CABLE CUTTERS.** Those made by Park, Shimano, Pedros, and others can shear pairs of wicked little half-moons across each other, slicing cables and cable housing with predictable ease.

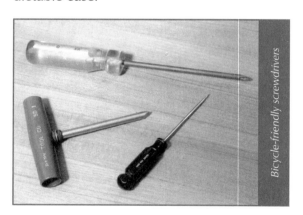

Bicycle-friendly screwdrivers

Bicycle cables are tightly wrapped braids of zinc or stainless wire. They're pretty tough. Lower-quality sidecutters—the greater number of those available—will simply shrink away in fear from their tight and serpentine demeanor. The cutting angle is less than ideal in the first place; the cheap jaws are not hard enough. Tool manufacturers enlist methods in making some steel implements considerably harder than others—this is why it's so difficult to drill holes in the wrench—and with the cutters, you're paying for hardness.

The cable cutters' mighty jaws may break if you try to sic them on stainless fender struts, but they're more inclined to loosen than wear out. They do need to be nice and tight to spring into action. The arms pivot on a stout little screw, which passes through the one side and threads into the other, before being capped with a nut to hold things in place. Don't be messing with this unless you need to; its proper resolution might take a few. You want to end up with the jaws just barely loose enough to pivot freely, with the nut tightened down nice and sturdy.

Your special new cable cutters are pointedly bike-specific; they will only coincide with the outside world at their leisure. Following on the heels of this opening is the amazing **FOURTH HAND** cable tool, which is basically pliers, held in tension by a small spring. The stronger springs found in brakes can make it difficult to secure cables in particular positions; the fourth hand steps in to sort things out. The cable is gripped in one slot and passed through another; squeezing the tool's handle effectively tightens the cable.

The fourth hand earns its name by replacing something called the third hand. This was basically a bent-up strip of metal, bearing a profile something like an imaginary teacup, which simply held the brake pads in place against the rim. Don't worry; it was nothing special in the first place.

There will arrive occasions when there's just not the space to fit a fourth hand into any good position—racks or other fixed accessories might be in the way, for example—and so you might introduce a small accessory.

Cut yourself a few short centimeters of brake cable housing, as described on page 72, and fit each end of this with a housing cap. Slide this down the cable you're working on; the fourth hand tool can now lever itself off this device, rather than the component. In keeping with our theme I propose we call these **SPARE FINGERS**.

Our work with the cable housing requires a small sharp stick to reopen the thin plastic liners within freshly cut slices. You can go buy one of these, but it's cheaper to sharpen up a dead spoke. Hold one against somebody's bench grinder and rotate, slowly; it takes all of a minute. The bike cables themselves are inclined to fray, poking at the plastic. New or soldered cables do not, but they are not sharp enough to do the job either.

You may also want to score some **SPANNERS**—maybe, if your bike is old enough, or cheap enough. There are several distinct spanners associated with cycle repair, the pins of which correspond to matching holes on the parts they're charged with turning. I have this hunch that one at least moonlights in freewheel deconstruction—the Park's red-handled model, methinks—but this really doesn't come up anymore. Their green is meant for the older three-piece adjustable cups; the yellow goes with the big one-piece units. These are all light and wispy creatures; they do not handle torque well. Component manufacturers have long since moved on to more reliable arrangements.

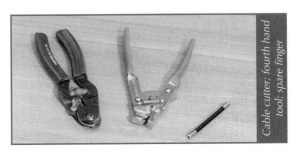

Cable cutter; fourth hand tool; spare finger

Where the spanners end, the **LOCKRING TOOLS** soon begin. Their functions are roughly parallel, but the lockrings only surround more central elements, and so most all will approach cautiously from the sides. Your track hubs, bottom brackets, and a tiny group of ancient headsets may require their various and specialized services.

Traditional threaded headsets—those bearing wrench flats across their foreheads—are adjusted with the curiously broad and flat **HEADSET WRENCHES**. A bearing cup is counter-tightened against its locknut to achieve the proper adjustment; there is no room to fit a big old crescent wrench in both positions at once. The flats range in size from 30 to 40 millimeters, dependent upon age and manufacturer. Far and away, 32 and 36 millimeters are the most common.

Especially old headsets will only feature knurled edges on that upper bearing cup, rather than any useful flats. These are adjusted with the big **CHANNEL LOCK PLIERS**. (Loosen that locknut up top first though, the task becomes much easier.) The top locknuts on all of these threaded headsets are best served by the big old crescent wrench.

The 36-millimeter headset wrench may also have another use. Look at the edges of the drive-side bottom bracket cup: does it feature a pair of wrench flats? These will *almost* always measure 36 millimeters. There is a specific bottom bracket tool that fits it best, because it catches their rounded edges as well, but your 36-millimeter headset wrench can fill in if it needs to.

The pedals on most bikes can be installed and removed with a regular 15-millimeter box wrench. But the clumsy old wrench flats are also losing favor, among some of the newer clipless pedal sets, which replace them with

stylish metric sockets in the axle bases. You need an Allen wrench. But it's far more common that we see 15-millimeter flats too narrow to accept the usual box wrenches, which is why we have the **PEDAL WRENCH**. It is burly, but also thin.

The **CONE WRENCHES,** of which a 15-millimeter is available, are even thinner. So thin, in fact, you probably don't want to use them for the pedals. The torque you want to apply down there will threaten to damage the tool. They are meant for the hub bearing cones. Situations vary, but the 13, 15, and maybe 17 millimeter are most common. You'll like two of these, in the ideal, and one each of their even sizes.

The cone wrenches remind me to mention Park Tool's offset **BRAKE WRENCHES**. These are of similar dimensions, but the wrench heads are offset 90 degrees. They're meant for the road bike caliper brakes; we find situations where nothing else will really work. These are ambidextrous, with distinct wrench flats at either end, in sizes from 10 to 14 millimeters. And there's also an odd one that only grips the caliper's spring, now that I think about it.

One other oddball you want to pick up is known as the **CRANK EXTRACTOR**. The great majority of modern crank arms will only be removed with these tools. The tool is threaded all the way down in to the crank's interior center, and only thus might it pry the suckers loose. Your cranks are supposed to be press-fit quite tightly around the bottom bracket spindle; the alternative method finds you hammering the hell out of them. It is, unfortunately, all too easy to accidentally put yourself in just such a position. *Make sure to see what's said on crank pulling,* pages 137-138, *before you start.* Three-piece bottom brackets feature either the old tapered or the new splined spindles, to put it in a nutshell, and it is supremely important you select the correct tool.

Old school: headset wrench, bottom bracket wrench

You also have some choice as to the tool's particular style, beyond this point, and this is really up to preference. The extractor threads down into the crank; a handle threaded into the extractor itself comes to push against the bottom bracket spindle. The more common consumer version is built around a simple metal handle; the shop tool supplies only wrench flats. The original Park consumer models featured a second, shorter stack of threads opposite the usual ones, which were meant for some older cranks made by Stronglight. A rare handful of older Campagnolo cranks makes use for a wholly distinct extractor with left-handed threads, and for the obvious reasons I would imagine these become less common each year.

You should also grab a **CRANK BACKER**. This is an odd little spanner, meant to hold the backs of the chainring bolts as you tighten them.

Prior to pulling your three-piece cranks, you must remove the bolts pinning them in place. If you have a really old bike and its ancient steel cranks feature obtuse nuts to their sides, you want to check out the rundown on cottered cranks, (see page 133.) More modern spindles are capped with sturdy nuts or bolts, either of which answer to 14- or 15-millimeter sockets, dependent on age and manufacturer. These are supposed to hide beneath dust caps, which might be threaded out or pried from the cranks, depending. The original crank bolts (or nuts) are only removed with **SOCKETS**. Park Tool makes wrenches bearing 14-, 15-, and 16-millimeter sockets. Ratcheting or fixed versions are available; either is a totally welcome addition to your set. They have two on opposite sides at one end, and just the one at the other; the larger sizes are useful for dealing with bolt-on wheels. More common are the three-way "Y" wrenches. The 8/9/10-millimeter socket is damned near ubiquitous—it earns its keep quite well—but the larger 12/13/14-millimeter Y-wrench is not nearly as special. These larger sizes will generally require more torque than this relatively small tool can offer.

Crank backer, tapered spindle crank extractor

The better and more recent a crankset is, the more likely its crank bolts will be surrendered to an Allen wrench instead. The size, depending upon circumstances, will be 5, 6, 7, 8, or 10 millimeters. You did get the full set, right? It does not come with the 7, but don't sweat it; that shit's rare.

The **EXTRACTION TOOLS** are distinct from the crank extractors. They are more similar to the sockets, being small attachments used to grip and turn things, but everything else is quite new: no sequence, no pattern, no simple six-sided hollow. They channel the force required to accomplish important and worthwhile tasks with precision, without necessarily relying on the usual truncated conceptions of "order." Practical anarchists.

Extraction tools feature various circles of *splines* or teeth. They're gripped in vises or wrenches, to remove specific components of matching dimensions. There exist maybe twenty such tools. Most are meant to plug into freewheels, which are what we call the gear clusters found on cheaper or older bikes. The more modern extraction tools will remove cassettes—the more recent gear clusters—as well as newer bottom brackets and some crank parts.

You also need a **CHAIN TOOL**. Here again, I have to recommend Park. Every shop I've worked for uses their burly professional model; the smaller consumer version is also good, its design is better. While the saddles in lesser units will break easily, under the slightest misuse, those in Park Compact Chain Tools are relatively thicker and less pronounced, sturdier. If you are working on chains more frequently, you really should get the business version, the CT-3. Whichever the case, don't forget to oil the threads now and again.

Chain whip with extraction tools

Following, of course, comes the **CHAIN WHIP**, whose focus narrows to better appreciate the gear clusters, or, failing that, the cog. Every track bike should have one, at the least. And you do have a **FLOOR PUMP**, right? The smaller portable jobs get to be kind of stupid, after a while. You also want

some **TIRE LEVERS**, of course, as well as a **PATCH KIT.** The glueless patch kits are worthless; get a real one.

If you do make a practice of repairing bikes, your work will be declared all the more precise with the introduction of certain reliable assistants. The **TENSIOMETER** provides exacting readings of a wheel's spoke tension, for example, lending our corrections unrivaled precision. Several models are available; their particulars are described on page 188.

More central to our diverse repair tasks is the **TORQUE WRENCH.** It is a long thin metal wishbone, joined by a socket fitting. One digit forms a sturdy handle, augmented with a short ruler-like gauge, while the other merely sprouts from the base. The very tip of this beanpole traces a course across the gauge as we press the handle, measuring the torque in either foot-pounds of pressure or Newton meters of force or perhaps even both.

Bicycle component manufacturers tend to suggest specific torque ranges, with regards to the installation and adjustment of their wares, and the only way we're able to actually report back on our findings is to use the torque wrench. The parts commonly arrive with paper instructions, when first they're born at least; these list any torque recommendations.

When it is here suggested that a given part is tightened to greater or lesser degrees, the reader should understand this fulfills only the most general of descriptions. If a given component manual cannot be tracked down, solutions might be pursued through the manufacturer's website. You might also check one of Shimano's annual component manuals, for details on their products. If you were in the position to warranty a given piece of equipment, any shop or manufacturer can quite reasonably ask if you followed the directions, and the torque wrench may well provide your best proof.

And we're almost done! We could do it in one gulp, in fact: the **HAMMERS** and **RULERS** are alternately most crucial, but a small **MAGNET** and some **FILES** are quite handy as well, and of course we need our **SPOKE WRENCHES** and some kind of **LEVER**. Got it?

At work we have these awesome hybrid-hammers, with the steel at one end and hard rubber at the other. The option is a nice one to have. I just have some rusty old claw hammer at home; I have not gotten around to scoring myself a rubber mallet. We also have specific spoke rulers at work, but I suppose anything will do. Get a **METRIC CALIPER** as well, if you're doing a lot of work.

The magnet's sole purpose is to collect the hub bearings during overhauls. Luke at Calhoun Cycle hipped me to this; it ends up saving a good piece of time. And my files are none too specific; I own a small round one and a larger, rougher one. Spoke wrenches? You just get the Park ones; you can find them anywhere. There is the red, the green, and the black—big, middle, and small. (Yellow and blue sizes are also available; in eleven years I've never called on either.) And your lever is probably a hollow pipe of some kind, snipped from a dead bike frame for example, and it's at least 30 or 40 millimeters across on the inside, maybe most of a meter long. It steps in when you need some extra leverage. And that's it; you're all set with your standard tools.

As for care, whatever it is you do, your tools will greatly prefer a dry climate, as opposed to humidity. Maybe you can score a dehumidifier for your basement, or some slightly oily rags, failing that. Your hex wrenches can be expected to lose their bite, as time goes

on. The top edges wear down; the tool slips off target, threatening to strip out your screws. This won't happen to occasional tools, only over the months to everyday equipment. But don't throw them away. Track down somebody with a grinder wheel; get in the habit of filing a new edge on your wrenches every now and again.

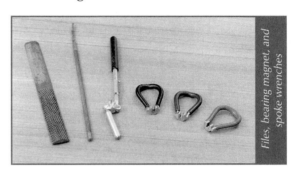

Files, bearing magnet, and spoke wrenches

Ancillary Tools

Our discussion to this point forms a context from which to appraise the various **MULTI-TOOLS**. These are the compact amalgamations of those tools most often called upon, meant for portable roadside repairs. Their trade off comes in leverage and maneuverability. You can generally get down to business, from a svelte package no less, but everything will likely take a bit longer. Asking one of these devices to fill in for the chores of more regular, specific bike tools on any persistent basis gets annoying.

Park Tool might have the best mobile kit. It is a small collection of solid implements. Nothing is hinged together in unlikely combinations; everything simply happens to fit together in a pouch—less gee-whiz factor; more natural handling. I've worked at least a couple of these into rotation.

Bike chains are best fed with an **OIL DROPPER**. You don't get the after-spray all over the living room furniture; nobody gets in trouble. Imagine the pressurized can brims with forceful National Police Radio cheezwhiz; it will only be a short time before we prefer to support the more measured and insightful Pacifica Network instead. Which, to follow the example, is the svelte and accurate dropper bottle. Gel lubes are displacing their Teflon forebears, just as the first dry lubes rendered the wet ones obsolete, and of what we've seen so far I really have to say the Rock and Roll goods are just the shit.

The outside world seems gripped by a powerful delusion, which suggests that any mechanical detailing on a bike must inevitably bear down to pour copious volumes of any available oil upon the chain. "The more, the better." But a wet chain picks up more grit, and this makes for that nasty gunk all over your leg. The oil and grit complement each other to form a sort of liquid sandpaper, which wears your drivetrain parts down to tortured nubs, and the sooner your periodic parts bill come due, which is really too bad because after a point chain lubrication becomes entirely secondary to shifting performance. All the chain lube left in creation will not resolve maladjusted parts, nor ease the tortured travels of rusted-out cables.

The oil droppers can also be refilled, incidentally. Is that cool or what? Grip the tip with your pliers and pull it out. Pop! This flattens out the hole therein; rotate the pliers and give it a little squeeze. Most chain oils can be found in bulk quantities.

Always, always, always wipe the chain down when you finish with the oil. OK? The old-style wet lube is best saved for the heavy winter, when they bust out the road salt, just before you take the drivetrain down for spring cleaning.

Some people seem to think the spray cans will carry the oil into every crevice where it might be useful. I'm thinking of all the bikes I've ever seen with that embarrassing build-up of supplementary road grit right exactly where you don't want it, close to the bearing seals. It means somebody has been squirting oil at the hubs. But the dust caps sealing bearings from the outside world are designed to keep this very grit away; drawing it in with the oil is a bad idea. The sand gets in between the balls and the races, and it fucks shit up. You've heard about how pearls are made, when an oyster gets obsessed with a grain of sand? The hubs have not yet learned this trick.

Besides, bearings run on grease, not oil. Oil is thinner. It will break down and disperse the grease if it gets in. I use oil whenever I do a bearing overhaul, to clean the old grease out of the way.

The thing we want for the hubs is a **GREASE GUN**. These you can find at the bike shops. The consumer versions are sold with tubes of the manufacturers' grease. It threads in; you squeeze. You roll up the tube as you go, just as you are supposed to do with the toothpaste. The grease tube does not stay rolled up, so you need to hold the end in some kind of binder clip.

The refillable grease guns, such as the Dualco pictured herein, can be fed with a tub of grease. You spoon it in. This takes more time, but it will prove to be a lot cheaper. A tub of worthy bike grease might cost you all of five bones, and it will last a really long time.

The coolest thing about any of these is the pinpoint nozzle. It helps you become precise and disciplined in your work; you don't end up with slop all over the place. You can just paint in some grease right out of a tub, if you really need to, but this is not a good idea. Grease tends to accumulate grit, if it's left out in the open, and of course this is easily transferred right down to the bearings. Grime will simply clog up the nozzle on grease guns; just clear it with a pin, or blow it clean with an air gun.

It's well enough that the grease has its guns, because it also has enemies. At the far, opposite end of our elemental spectrum sit the thread-locking compounds. The more a particular threading is stressed or otherwise pulled upon, the more it will appreciate some help.

Oil droppers with grease guns

There are several ways the thread locking might be pursued. We can see examples of the no-nonsense mechanical method with the hubs, where the bearing cones and their locknuts are counter-tightened against each other. And of course it works out well enough when we tighten things sincerely. But not every situation is meant for such finality—the quick-release components, for example—so people have done different things.

The old-fashioned approach to thread locking uses special washers to hold things down. Serrated washers create a friction bond beneath the screw's nut; small spring-like washers force the nut against its threads. You still see this sometimes, with the toe clip hardware for example.

Liquid thread-locking compounds such as Loctite have since become broadly available—in differing strengths, no less—but it is far more common that we see the **NYLOCK NUTS.** Spell it out with me: the nut is equipped with a nylon insert, which grips itself around the bolt's threads. The nuts holding your rack hardware together should be nylock, together with those fixtures capping all but the oldest quick-release skewers.

2: FRAMES

The bicycle begins with the frame. It joins the wheels to their kindred elements, marshalling each to the fore.

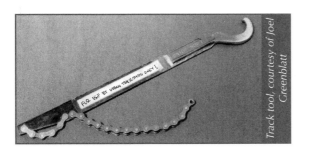

Track tool, courtesy of Joel Greenblatt

A given frame's composition and construction will invariably impact upon its relative quality. These considerations are first glimpsed through the bike's **FRAME TUBING DECALS**. These are small and meticulous notes, usually found on the seat tubes or down tubes, and perhaps a fork blade as well. And just as the acupuncturist can see so much from so little, so too can the mechanic read from a decal. They let us know how well a given bike has kept pace with advances in the metallurgical sciences.

Right about any bike may acquire a fancy demeanor, by sporting the flash parts, but the frame tubing decal exercises a veto power over any such presumptions. Things are expected to line up and match, essentially, unless somebody has been doing some ill-advised upgrading. With the steel bikes, the signal we first like to see is a reference to "cro-mo" or similar. But lo, there have come the inevitable attempts to trade in cromoly's worthy name! Small print on the decal will disclose that only the seat tube or the main triangle are made with the proudly advertised cromoly,

for example; the rest is hi-ten or something. And the high-tensile steel, at this point, is no longer worthy of our serious consideration in terms of frame construction.

The decals are also expected to disclose whether or not the tubes are butted, and this is another important consideration. The interior dimensions of quality tubesets will be slightly reduced through their midsections, such that their ends become slightly thicker in comparison. Butted. We like the lengths of tubing to be as thin as we can manage, to further enhance the steel's vaunted riding characteristics. And the stress tends to accumulate at the joints, where the tubes are left somewhat thicker, so the whole thing works out pretty well. This internal reduction will be spread across the tube's wall thickness in two or three distinct levels; we read this as double- or triple-butted on the decal.

Butted cromoly tubing draws the steel's inherent resilience to its fullest potential, and this helps to take the edge off the bumps and vibrations. Everything is still contingent on a good frame design, of course—the bike needs to be flexible in some ways and quite rigid in others; the essential art is in balancing the two—but the tubes are the beginning.

Titanium, aluminum, carbon fiber, and combinations thereof have also been used to make bike frames. You might even track down a wood frame, to match the dusty old wooden rims. But let's save these other things for the eternally helpful sales staff down at the shop, OK? Barring the occasional ill-advised upgrades, the frame's design and construction should be the most relevant features of any bike. The wisest and most worldly amongst their lot will skillfully balance a carefully refined strength within a light and tightly disciplined mass. But this clarion dynamic might be considered from a number of perspectives, and so does the debate continue. The longer you listen, the more cash you wish you had. Our decisions might only be made contingent upon the particular sequencing of our priorities. And so what about it then? Is it straight sex appeal you're shooting for? Or more of a jaded, rock-and-roll effect?

Frame tubing decal. This one means good stuff

It is easy enough for any of us to dump on the original metal, from the dispassionate scientific viewpoint, but real metal always has a visceral and romantic appeal, which may be buttressed with a judicious reading of the elemental considerations, depending. Has steel weathered through the centuries, or was it

these other devices? Once the factories begin to crumble, which is more easily coaxed toward continuing on?

As yet, of course, we haven't even cracked next week. Certain other, more happening frame materials win the weight-loss competition, hands-down. But I wonder if they're not flying too close to the sun. As with the dominant culture's cloying old narcissism more generally, the reigning consumerist cross-valuations trip has only become more diversionary. I tell you what, though, once the vastly more crucial work of the Intergovernmental Panel on Climate Change is afforded the immediate relevance it should rightfully command, I'll get to testing out the carbon. And once America moves beyond implementing drastic emissions reductions programs to developing truly social transportation, I will *like* it. I promise.

The material itself is famously resilient. The newest generations can be made at once more firm and responsive, while still providing for a remarkably supple riding experience by achieving a heretofore unrivaled strength-to-weight ratio. Did I get that right, guys?

A logical place for a sticker

The carbon forks have really become standard with the road bikes. But the material is also starting to hit up the cross bikes' forks as well, and this is arguably more alarming. The carbon forks' brake bosses tend to vibrate a little more, to my experience, and this means the brakes they wear are more likely to squeak.

Small matters such as this last point may be resolved some day, in theory at least. Carbon's central cancer is more damning. It will not take a hit well from the wrong angle. Might splinter! Nor can it reliably endure the simple compression of our ubiquitous repair stand, or be tapped with threads, or repaired with the frame tools. Much as with foreign policy, you fuck up the once and it's gone.

Frame Damage

Take a hacksaw to a dead carbon frame some time, and see how long it takes you. The frozen epoxy stew, against the true metal? Shit. If sloppy derailleur adjustments let the chain fall down there enough times, it too will begin the quick and efficient work of steady mechanical attrition.

But bike frames are mortal, just like us. All are vulnerable to damage, to one degree or another. It is only sometimes clear that anything has even happened. Problems with the bottom bracket threads are not unusual, for example. Older models become more vulnerable to rust-related problems; any of them might be damaged if the bottom bracket is not installed correctly. It is best to get the threads re-tapped, in such circumstances. Most shops have the equipment to tap most bottom bracket shells, here in the developed world, at least.

The threads inside the rear derailleur hanger are also sometimes stripped. They may be brought back to health with a 10-meter tap, if we're lucky. Replacement thread inserts are available for use with many older bikes—the hanger only needs to be wide enough to accept them—but newer bikes tend to use replaceable dropouts instead.

Bad things are always happening to rear derailleur hangers. They become levers of sorts, if the bike takes it on the drive side, bending their hanger tabs in toward the frame. You can spot this problem pretty easily, looking down from the rear of the bike. The derailleur's cage will no longer be parallel with the wheel.

Park and Campagnolo both make decent hanger alignment tools, meaning to resolve this very dilemma. A huge lever is threaded in to the hanger tab, allowing us to bend it back in plane with the rear wheel. But you may be able to do something roughly similar with your Allen key, if you're not so equipped. Slot its short end in to the derailleur's mounting bolt, gripping the body with your other hand, and see if you can gradually straighten things out. Do not yank! Move slowly. *This is especially important with aluminum.*

Aluminum's particular qualities leave it less inclined towards negotiation, comparing with the more conciliatory steel, and so the smarter alloy frames have been showing up with **REPLACEABLE DROPOUTS**. Cannondale was the first to popularize these, but at this point their mounting details vary from company to company, year by year. The derailleur tab itself needs to end up in its fixed position, of course, but the bolt hole(s) and the mounting plate dimensions above it are somewhat more whimsical. There is not yet any standard replacement dropout, as far as I know. I'm not sure when we can expect to see one.

On-the-road hanger alignment

Those riding alloy frames born before all this replaceable business would do well to pick up a Sinner derailleur supporter from Therapy Components, a sharp update on the clumsy old chrome derailleur guards.

It should go without saying that I can not advise you to ride any frames afflicted with crimps, buckles, or wayward bends. This is especially crucial with the head tube, the down tube, and the fork. Your best choice is to abandon the project in question. Bikes ramming into fixed objects commonly stub their forks, for example: if you are left with any questions at all about its integrity, you need to take it in to your friendly local independent bike shop.

FRAME ALIGNMENT is the larger issue here. Crashes will sometimes leave the frames less than straight. These kinds of alignment issues are rarely obvious to the eye, but a good shop will have the means and methods to answer such questions definitively. It is smart to get the frame checked out if ever you're hit by a car, for example, especially if you're riding something nicer. So if your ride suddenly pulls to one side or something, you know what to do.

Creaks

It may be possible, in the course of your travels, that your bike will pick up a **CREAK.** This may or may not mean anything in itself—we need to track it down and see what was up, basically—but even the more innocuous sorts of groaning too often presume to pass a special judgment ... their mad echo proudly announces to the world that your bike is afflicted with some kind of loud and annoying problem.

The creak exists to mock us. There might be other, more immediate considerations involved—these annoying ghosts do not simply spring unbidden, from the midst—but their patient subversion invariably claims the last word. You may be all up there claiming you know the score, or whatever the hell it is, but it sure as hell won't sound like it.

The creak is not going to sit down and have a drink with you. Nor will its unfathomable requests be salved by the passage of time. Odds are better it convinces its creepy friends to merrily croak along instead. So you need to track the little fucker down, because you need to grease it.

It is in the creak's nature to become eternally mysterious, and it is this very tendency that allows for their stubborn persistence. I have to stop short of calling them clever; their motives suggest more of a raw cunning. Their earnest pursuit tends to involve a good deal of careful hunting—for hours at a time, as the case may be—and this requires a more disciplined approach. You first need to isolate the sound as best you can, and then attend to every possible remedy to the situation, testing the results of each. But there is one important thing to remember: you should never apply any grease to carbon fiber, because it may weaken or damage the material.

Creaks are born within the endless intersections of common mechanistry, where metal is faced against anything else at all. And the bicycles, straining beneath, allow for a splendid range of opportunities. I have known water bottle cages to squeak, straining against their wispy cages, or even the slightest flex arriving through their frame tubes.

The first thing you need to do is locate your target. Does the creak arrive when pedaling or coasting? Sitting or standing? Clutching tightly to the handlebars or chasing some more daring ambition? With your hands resting atop the brake hoods, with or without stomping on the pedals?

Older drop bars often incorporate sleeves to accommodate the stems, and these in themselves can sometimes creak, which is one reason the drops go for bugle sections instead these days. The stem clamp is particularly famous for its noxious sounds; you will want to get some grease up in there. The brake lever clamps can creak as well; they have to get the same treatment. More of a hassle. And lather yet more grease inside or around the steerer tube, depending on the arrangements. But the headset cups can creak as well, which is why we want to make sure they are installed in to fields of grease. Even some of the actual headsets will manage to creak, in the final analysis, and might themselves need replacement.

Creaks haunting the bottom bracket can be just as entertaining. The unit itself will need to enjoy grease both inside and outside its cups, on the bolts, and perhaps the spindle as well. But the chainring bolts will also need to be greased and tightened, together with the pedal axles, and perhaps even the screws holding the pedal cages. Then we do the water bottle screws, front derailleur clamp and bolt, and of course any damned suspension pivot points.

Did that get it? What about the seat? Grease all the bolts you find there—the pinch, the mounting hardware, anything—and also get the rails, right around where they are clamped in the post.

Creaks crafty enough to survive this awesome barrage might well indicate structural damage, but this is fairly rare, and it's well worth your time to consider the situation first.

Homemade speed

3: FORKS

The frame is led by the fork. It is the crucial wishbone joining handlebars to front wheel, allowing them to move as one.

The **FORKS** coincide with a few basic points, to fit with a given bike. Front axle spacing is the easiest detail. Some folding bikes are born with 70-millimeter forks to match their diminutive front wheels, but all the others can be expected to share the standard 100-millimeter axle spacing. The hub might fit a little snug into the dropouts—or, with cheap and less trustworthy forks, things might be just a shade wide—but you should not need any contortions to make things work.

The **FORK RAKE** is a measure of how far it trails forward. The effect is meant to complement a given frame's geometry; it will further accent what is already there. More rake is associated with older touring bikes; less rake is found with the younger racing bikes.

Just about every fork has rake, but some are more sly about it. The angle has been already set up in the crown; the legs otherwise appear to be straight. And this has become quite stylish with the road bikes. And we need to consider the rake before deciding if a fork was bent. The contours of each leg should always precisely match the other, looking from the sides. The presence of a wheel can mute or disguise any difference between the two; take it out before you check.

Forks that are only slightly bent might be fixed, using yet more of our specialized shop tools, but most bent forks cannot be safely straightened. And I'm in no position to become more specific than this, from the present vantage; suffice it to say that anything questionable should definitely get checked out at a shop.

Steerer Tubes

The new fork needs to fit with the existing wheel, brake, headset, and frame. We first need to make sure the **STEERER TUBE** is going to work. It needs to be tall enough and just wide enough, and its top section may or may not be threaded.

The curious old 1 1/4-inch steerers have been fading fast. Our world has instead settled upon the lighter 1- and 1 1/8-inch steerers. We cross each of these sizes against the two major headset styles, threaded and threadless, and we arrive upon a grand total of six possibilities.

The steerer tube's height may simply be copied from the original, but it can also be deduced by means of an equally simple formula. For threaded headsets, we add the head tube's total length to the headset's **STACK HEIGHT**, which is the sum of its exposed pieces. You can figure about a 35-millimeter stack for 1-inch forks, or 40 millimeters for 1 1/8 inches. With the threadless headsets, the steerer must also pass through the stem and any spacers, to stop 5 millimeters short of the top. So you add the collective heights of these other features to the head tube and stack height, then subtract 5 millimeters. But we are able to work with just about anything, with enough head tube spacers.

Some shops still have the toolage required to extend fork threads down a steerer tube, if it needs to be cut, but this is becoming an outmoded operation. Threadlessness pretty well renders its forebears obsolete, essentially. The quill-style stems used with threaded headsets need to anchor themselves below the threaded section; any extra threads will limit your options in safely raising the stem.

The headset needs to be threadless, in fact, to work with any of the newer carbon or aluminum steerer tubes. An aluminum steerer's walls need to become pretty thick to support any threads; we no longer will be able to fit the prescribed quill stem down inside. And the threading process shreds the carbon fiber, of course; any quill stem inserted therein will quickly splinter the remains.

Some of the newer **SHOCK FORKS** have been arriving with the new Tullio QR system. Their legs feature novel quick-release collars, rather than the usual dropouts, which are meant to work with 20-millimeter axles. These are just more than twice as wide as those we otherwise expect to find. The idea is to enhance stiffness, so you can go be a rugged downhill racer or something like that.

Tullio is supremely lucky, in one important sense. It proved immune to the great disc brake scandal of 2003. The standard front disc brake mounting platform was suddenly found to have the effect of gradually encouraging the front skewer to loosen. Which, un-

attended, could encourage the front wheel to up and jump out of the fork. This is a function of the rotor's braking force, as it intersects with the drops. Whoops!

I wish I was more surprised. But the simple fact is the marketing imperatives do not encourage people to really think things through. The solution involves scrapping the old standard and starting over—I recommend some kind of libertarian socialism, but this is none too likely. And so it comes to pass that the unlikely Tullio fork has become the safest way to run a front disc brake, in the meantime. You have to keep a close eye on your front wheel skewer, otherwise.

You get a sense of how sudden this news was, looking over contemporary technical literature. Hayes, in their MX-2 mechanical instructions, recommends, "the use of steel, quick-release skewers only." The problem was first highlighted by James Annan, a Scottish mountain biking enthusiast working in Japan. He published his findings at www. ne.jp/asahi/julesandjames/home/disc_and_ quick_release/.

4: HEADSETS

The fork pivots in its frame by means of the headset, which aligns two circles of bearings along their steering axis.

Modern headsets appear in one of three distinct styles. The threaded and threadless are far and away the most common. It was decided more recently that we also need an additional mish-mash of frame-specific "integrated" headsets. The head tube is made bigger and carved out in novel ways, to better swallow one of a few distinct happy meals.

The 1-inch, 1 1/8-inch, and 1-inch **HEADSETS** have each been available in both threaded and threadless versions. One-inch threaded headsets were the norm for a very long time, but the consensus has shifted toward 1 1/8 inch, for the threaded and threadless styles both. The integrated headsets all use cartridge bearings, in arrangements mimicking the threadless format; their discussion should carry you through.

One thing to understand about any of the standardized headsets is that they're meant to work as cohesive systems. The frame fittings and adjustment parameters will coincide with one of our few standards, to be sure, but the measurements associated with individual pieces will set each apart. We replace them as complete packages. I ended up compiling a respectable collection of headset debris, over the years, but in all that time I think I pieced together all of one complete set.

The loose headset is easy to spot. When you lift the handlebars and drop, the bike rattles.

It is an annoying, obvious problem. Things rarely become too tight up there, but this too you notice. You can *really* feel the bearings, as you hold the frame and turn its fork, as if they are almost ratcheting in to position. The worst cases among these develop to become a sort of indexed steering: the bearings wear slight hollows in their races, from which they only move reluctantly.

Threaded

The **THREADED HEADSETS**, being more traditional, prefer to do things one at a time. They are first concerned with attaching the fork to the frame, and it is only then that we can talk about securing the stem and handlebars. The two tasks use vastly different toolage; there is little mistaking the one for the other.

Threaded headset

The threaded and threadless headsets may look at least vaguely similar, but the originals wear more exciting collars. There are almost always at least two distinct layers to these turtlenecks, each of which may be turned, and *this* is our cue. There are wrench flats, or at least a knurled surface to turn, to suggest threads.

The two pieces are counter tightened against each other, to set the appropriate bearing adjustment, just as we do with the hubs or the old school bottom brackets. The locknut flats measure 30, 31, 32, 36, or 40 millimeters, here in the developed world; and 30 and 31 are very old and fading fast. The 40 is in nearly as precarious a position, while 32 and 36 both still enjoy active use, for 1-inch and 1 1/8-inch headsets respectively.

The bearing cones beneath this lockring also face 32- or 36-millimeter flats, if we're lucky. Again, 40 millimeters is less and less common, and neither the 30 or 31 millimeters are used in this application. But we may instead find basic knurled collars, with very old 1-inch stacks. These are lame! They were the first draft; their gaps are often wide enough to almost see the bearings. So grit gets in there; it fucks things up. More to the point, the limited purchase offered by this old-fashioned knurling business will not lend itself to any serious torque. Squeeze tightly with your channel-locks; it's about all you can do.

There should be a washer between the locknut and the bearing cone. It eases their friction; we're better able to tighten things. These are most often "keyed," which is to say their interiors feature small nubs—or flat spots, depending—to correspond with matching features carved to the rear of the steerer tube.

Any spacers, cable guides, or other features meant for the steerer tube also need to fit in this same place, between the cone and locknut.

Tightening a threaded headset

We can find locknuts with supplementary thread-locking features, if a headset is having trouble retaining its adjustments, but I'm first curious about what else may be going on; the final adjustment probably is not being made tight enough. We don't want the nuts to be all crushing down on the bearings, but they must be tightly pressed against each other.

Mismatched parts, poorly aligned races, or missing bearings may also impact upon a headset's staying power. Such problems might leave a headset too loose at some angles, but too tight in others. You also want to make sure you don't install the headset seals upside-down or pinch them at odd angles between the other parts. The frame's head tube itself may need to be faced, in the worst case, but this will require shop tools.

The preferred headset adjustment will hover evenly in the middle distance, without binding or rattling, and its component parts will be left supremely tight against each other. It is best if you can arrange to complete your adjustment by clasping your hands over the two wrenches, to tighten them together. This makes for better leverage. More power to you, basically.

You also want to brace the front wheel between your feet, because this lets us decide whether the cup or the locknut is being turned. Loose headsets are also easier to miss, with the bike up in the stand.

We should also lay to rest the remnants of an old dispute, so long as we're here, about the precise meaning of this "one inch." Everything was sorted out prior to the arrival of threadless headsets, fortunately, so this old confusion only really haunts their threaded peers. The larger sizes are totally safe—they're truly standardized—but this only follows on the protracted slaughter of little "one inch."

A few headsets bearing slightly different measurements have each adapted this moniker, essentially. Japanese Industrial Standard (J. I. S.) features a crown race with an inner diameter of 27.0 millimeters; it was used for garbage wagons and various older bikes. But all the other 1-inch threaded headsets use 26.4 millimeter for the inner crown race diameter. The wrong race will simply slip loosely in to position, in other words, or else it will not fit at all.

We find ways around either of these situations, by milling the head tube's base or knurling its surface, but either of these will involve even more special shop tools. And the dispute extends forward from there, actually. The vast majority of 1-inch forks will accept stems bearing 22.2-millimeter stalks, but a goofy 21.5-millimeter stem will occasionally show up on older garbage wagons and the like. And the BMX "one inch," finally, features frame cups that are actually almost 3 millimeters wider than all the others.

Threadless

THREADLESS HEADSETS represent a better design. Everything is more straightforward, and usually lighter. The threadless fork's steerer tube extends up well past the top of the threadless headset, because the threadless stem clamps in place around it. Make

sure you slap some grease around the steerer tube, before installing a stem, unless either part is made of carbon fiber. The grease will ease the calculus of our adjustments, in other cases, and it may even stop a creak.

A 6-meter bolt then shoots through a big fat washer, which caps both the stem and the steerer tube. And the bolt finally threads in to a fitting, suspended in the middle of the fork's steerer tube: tightening the bolt squeezes the frame and fork together.

We call the fork's fitting the star nut. The old threaded nuts' dramatic mission is essentially miniaturized, with the threadless. Where the threaded headset tightens its external parts against the crown fork race, the threadless system tightens its diminutive bolt in the star nut.

The crowning features are the hats they wear. Threadless headsets are required to wear caps, at least as wide as the steerer tubes they cover, and these are meant to lay perfectly flat.

Quill stems will sometimes wear various headgear as well, but any of this will really be smaller. And the quill stem caps are also most usually set back, at some rakish angle. The style of a threadless headset's cap can tell us how old it is, or even its pedigree. Where the older, simpler sorts favor basic black plastic hats, a great majority of their replacements will instead sport sharp aluminum berets. And this is cool, because you can't over-tighten the bolt and accidentally sink its head down through the cap. This is easy enough to do, of course, with the chintzy plastic hats.

Where the bolt in the quill secures it within the fork, that featuring atop the threadless headset is only its **PRELOAD BOLT**. It only sets the bearing adjustment. The bolt(s) featuring immediately in front of or behind the steerer tube will tighten the threadless stem in place. These need to be loosened before you adjust the preload bolt. You also want to keep an eye out for any bolts securing cable hangers to the steerer tube, which will also need to be loosened.

The adjustment we're looking for mimics that sought with the old threaded headsets, at mid points between binding and rattling. But you should bounce the threadless bike's front wheel on the ground a few times, before finalizing a given adjustment, because its parts will take a little more convincing to settle in to position.

Loosen the cable hanger before adjusting the threadless headset

Overhauls

The threaded and threadless headsets each rely on two sets of bearings, one upstairs and one downstairs. These are usually held in nice circles by means of thin metal retainer cages. The needle bearings suspend diminutive rollers within resin bases. Loose bearing headsets are all but extinct. Most high-end manufacturers have long since moved on to the sealed bearing cartridges. These new bearings are simply replaced, if they are not moving fast enough. Things are different now; that's just how it is.

The sealed bearings are meant to be efficient, you see, and they like to be left alone. We

have no business trying to crack them open, for which I provide no guarantees. Neither will the different companies' sealed headsets mean to be cross compatible; I could no more cover you on swapping their parts around. The cartridges like to see a thin coat of grease before they go in, but that's all you can really do for them. They're supposed to be stoic, that's the whole point.

Any loose balls remaining in our curious new world can get rolled around in a rag with lightweight oil to clean up. You can do the same with the caged bearings, but it will be better to soak them in undiluted bicycle-specific citrus solvent. (I've had less luck with the generic hardware store degreasers.) Where soaking removes the grit-laden grease trapped up inside the bearing cages, the oily rag only glosses things over. Can you let them soak overnight, or a couple nights even? Cool. The citrus rinses off with water. And let them dry for a bit, OK?

The cups and cones can be cleaned up with the oily rag. You may first need to dispose of some hardened grease, with the truly old 'n crusty headsets: douse this crap with lightweight oil to break it down. Polish the bearing surfaces as best you're able to. This will also highlight any scars on their faces. The less you rely on a pitted headset, the smarter your bike will become.

The lower headset bearings see the most abuse. The **CROWN RACE**, perched beneath the bearings on the fork's crown, is left in a particularly vulnerable position. These are hammered in to place, around the slightly wider base of the fork's steerer tube, right where it meets the fork crown—the fork's fat lip. We pound them down with stout sections of pipe, known as crown race hammers. A blessedly simple tool; available in each of our three sizes.

Crown race hammer

We use a hammer and punch to remove crown races from their forks. There should be a nice slice of the race's bottom hanging over the front and rear of the fork crown; we pound on these spots to knock it off. But many suspension forks are built around fat aluminum fork crowns, which will extend well past the aforementioned ledges. The punch won't do shit. This was a passing concern of mine, where last I worked—the 'bents went largely untroubled by suspension; it just was not my problem—but then I got in at Freewheel in San Francisco, where my practiced colleague Jon Londres pointed out that the J. A. Stein company makes a tool for just such purposes.

You also want to keep an eye out for any bearing seals, which will generally seat right around the edge of the crown race, just outside the bearings. Tightening these at angles between the frame and fork will probably destroy them, or at least leave them warped beyond use. It's better to press the fork up in to the frame from beneath, when reassembling, with everything sitting just where you like it to be. Spin things a little, to be sure: hold it just like that, with the one hand, while you tighten the upper deck with your free hand.

Your headset should also have a similar seal beneath the top bearings, of course, and take similar cautions with this one. Older

or cheaper headsets are often more square; they may not be hip to the seals thing. But you can help them out, if you're feeling charitable. Go find a single dead mountain inner tube, and chop it into sections. One-inch donuts. You and all your friends now have a lifetime supply of retrofit headset seals. You have to take things apart to fit them, however. It should be snug, and there should be an overlap on to the fork: it will dampen the steering some, but not to any extent that will impact the ride. The forces present with riding more than cancel the effect; you only want to account for it when dialing in the headset adjustment.

The threadless headsets, of course, do not have any wrench flats for you to worry about. The seals charge up and over their bearings, filling the gap from bearing cup to handlebar stem; the upper bearing surfaces are incorporated to their undersides.

Directly above or immediately below these threadless seals, we find a peculiar wedge-shaped washer. Its outer face slopes down to correspond with an equally steep slope on the cup's interior, underneath. And this is the big secret; the element that allows the preload bolt to act so smooth all the time. The compression it generates translates smoothly across these slopes, from wedge to headset.

Headsets are somewhat further removed from the ever-present road grit, comparing to our other bearings in the hubs and the bottom bracket, so they can generally survive on less maintenance. The biggest risk to just letting things go might be the stem seizing in place. This is why we *grease* them, before they're installed.

If you are **REPLACING A HEADSET**, it is best to have it done at a shop. The fixed parts are all press-fit in to place, and this is not easy to simulate at home. It is important that the two sets of bearings become precisely parallel to each other; we shop rats own the best means to make this happen.

Our headset press is a long threaded rod, equipped with curiously stepped fittings, which press the cups in to the frame. And the steps, of course, consider each of our three head tube sizes. You have yourself one fuck of a jigsaw puzzle, piecing one of these together at the hardware store.

Besides, it's also possible the head tube needs to be faced. Something so simple as a buildup of paint can throw off the headset's adjustment; our facing die will shave at the head tube until its ends becomes perfectly parallel. But these things are ridiculously expensive; it's not likely somebody will just go and loan you one. We had a boxed Campagnolo frame tool set at the shop I worked at in Milwaukee; those of us allowed to peer within had our names noted on the lid.

Rounding off the proud roster of our official headset installation tools is the crown **RACE HAMMER.** It is a sturdy piece of pipe, maybe 6 inches tall: you set the race on top of the fork's crown, and you pound it in to place. The impacts will start to sound a little different, once the race touches down and goes flat. I'll go and pound it a few more times, just to make sure. You may even pick one of these up, if you find yourself doing this much; they're not so expensive. It is the other tools that will break you.

The only alternative I'm aware of for getting the cups in is still the sketchy procedure described in my first book. The two cups are installed individually, using a hammer and a wooden block. Careful! And for fuck's sake, don't even pretend to hammer on carbon fiber anything. But you don't want to hack

this on any worthy metal frames either, actually, because it will tend to flare out the head tube. This can also happen to racing bikes, of course, if they really get worked. But this is rare; I've seen it all of twice in my life. And you do not want the head tube to flare out, because the cups will lose any interest in staying put. The headset will just keep coming loose.

I did fix a flared head tube on an old RB1 once, by adding some brass to the tube's interior with a torch. And then I ran the mill through again, to clean up the excess; things firmed right the hell up. But it's far more likely that your bearing cups are stuck in there pretty well. You will have to pound them out, to remove them. The inner edges of the headset cups provide for dramatically thin ledges, which you need to pound upon to knock the cups out. We professionals have yet another unusual tool for this—I want to tell you about it, but it really defies easy description—but you can do as well with a thin steel section of tubing, something with a good edge to it.

5: STEMS

The stems sprout from our forks and reach out to greet the handlebars, joining their theory to the practices extending below.

I feel like I'm juggling a few things at once! I've introduced so many distinct features on the bicycle; their continued description begins to seem less fluid and seamless than one might hope. I want to retain some unity of purpose through the book, you see, with events lilting freely from one arena to the next—the effervescent, hypnotic rock-and-roll tour—and here the endless parade is already pulled toward Earth by the weight of its very premises. But the text has also picked up its own momentum, propelling us forward in to the void. You can imagine we're talking about some great fish, if it helps.

Considering our place in the story so far, it seems like a fine time to get in to the **STEMS**. Their very form represents a crucial union between points of special interest. They are the graceful acrobats, spanning the distance from fork to handlebar. Where other regions of the bicycle require reinforcements in their work, the stems retain the focus to concentrate their strength within a solitary beam.

Theirs is a pointedly ambitious pursuit—to provide for a sufficiently rigid interface, without being all bulky and obtuse—and it is most honest to say that some can pull it off better than others. A good stem prevents the handlebars from flexing, when you stand up and jam on the pedals, and this makes the bike more efficient.

Stems are described by their length, from the center of the steerer tube to the center of the handlebars, and by their angles of inclination. And these details, in turn, superimpose atop our other considerations. If the stems are suspended handily within the ether, the steerer tube size crosses back against its headset details and the handlebar's clamp diameter.

The stem is intended for either threaded or threadless headsets, which are built around 1-inch, 1 1/8-inch, or 1 1/4-inch steerer tubes. At the same time, the far end will feature a clamp of 25.0, 25.4, 26.0, 26.4, 28.6, 31.7, or 31.8 millimeters for the handlebars. This may already be more freedom than we really find useful, but that's how it is. Love it or leave it.

This fledgling constitution already requires a number of amendments, actually—older BMX stems, some integrated systems, a few oddballs from Cannondale. But the bikes form a democracy, and their great majority has agreed to follow these simple rules with the stems. The steerer tube size is easy enough to keep track of, as are the headset details. The clamp diameter is less obvious to the naked eye, but we can figure it out. The fit should be nice and snug. The bar should not be able to wriggle around, when the stem's clamp bolt is released. There is some leeway possible with the steel stems—their clamps can be safely pried or squeezed a bit for odd-sized handlebars—but this is not a good idea at all with the aluminum stems. The alloy has different properties; it is far less likely to simply go with the flow.

You will know if the bars are too wide for a given alloy stem, because it will have taken a hammer to set them in place. This is not a good idea, because it puts the stem in a weaker position, and you need at least as much force to get the bars back out. Sorry, you're fucked; start over. An aluminum stem is just as vulnerable, alternately, if it is clamped around a handlebar of smaller dimensions.

The old alloy stems may be quite nice. They only need the right handlebars. The drop bars are often a good match with the old aluminum stems, and not just for the clamp diameters. Their steel kin are often too square to even allow the drops to pass. Their graceful curves require half-moons cut out of the stem clamp, in order to snake through; these have always been more of an alloy thing.

Our world has witnessed the rise of the **TOP-LOADING STEMS**, more recently, and these careful diplomats are able to resolve many of these old schisms. Their firm but transient facemasks are simply bolted and un-bolted, to accept a different set of handlebars. None of the grips or control levers need to be removed, in other words, and the bars can curve as they damn well like.

Some of the new high-zoot road bars fully require top load stems, of course; their flattened wing sections will not fly through any merely circular clamps. Top-loaders may also forgive small discrepancies in size more easily, between 25.4 and 26.0 for example. I do not recommend such ventures, which will contradict all manner of technical specifications, but I can tell you I've had plenty of luck with this.

However I do ride fairly pedestrian sorts of bars and stems—used or free, for the most part—and I really do not encourage any mismatching on high-end ultra-light parts, where this will likely become a more crucial consideration.

Lugged steel stem; very precious

Quill

Stems meant for the threaded headsets, which we call the **QUILL STEMS**, reach back and slip their straws down inside the fork's head tube. The threaded headsets only happen to surround this exchange; they are not immediately involved.

The gap between the quill stem and its steerer tube must be lined with grease, lest things seize in place. This has happened before, and it secretly wants to happen again. An **EXPANDER BOLT** shoots down from the quill's crown, to thread in to an offset nut in its base. Tightening this down will brace the stem against the steerer tube. The nut will either wedge against the bottom of the stem, or it will draw up between a slit or two to expand the stem itself.

The expander bolt needs to be very tight. Under no circumstance should the stem allow the bars to move independently of the fork. You should slop some grease on the bolt's threads and under its head as well, if you're having troubles here. We also need to keep an eye out for the maximum height lines, with the quill stems. These notices, etched at mid-points across their stalks, warn us against allowing the expander bolt to press against the upper threaded section of the steerer tube, which is weaker. I've seen steerers bend and crack, for just such reasons.

Raising the bars has become an increasingly popular pursuit, among leisure cyclists, and there are already high-rise stems and handlebar options available for just about any bike. But each of these is also marked with the very same max height line, because it really is that important.

Any truly spectacular raises will also require some new cables and housing sections, because the old ones are rendered too short. Any cable that strains at any point in the bars' rotation should be replaced, because the stretching will eventually fuck it up proper.

Threadless

The **THREADLESS STEM** is also found in each of our favorite steerer sizes, but this is where the similarity ends. They wrap around the fork's steerer, rather than plumbing its depths. This may be the single best way to recognize threadless stems, at this point; they'll always be wide enough to slide down around the fork's steerer tube. They're most often clamped in place by means of two bolts strapped across their backsides, but this has not always been the case—there may only be one, and it may be hiding under a button in front of the steerer tube.

Threadless stems are found in a variety of lengths, rising to a range of different heights. Circumstance also provides them with a further trick: they can be flipped, to provide more or less rise to the bars. You may not

need a whole new stem, in other words; maybe the old one only needs to be made right side up. And it's easy enough to check, with the removable face plate.

Threaded stems

Adjustable

Threadlessness more generally is a blazingly efficient program, outlining the leading edge of all we know so far. And so we may think we're doing well enough in this respect, given the sum of our options, but apparently we're not. Certain worn-out minor industrialists have managed to present us with items described as **ADJUSTABLE STEMS**, which, mechanically, are a fucking catastrophe.

Threadless stem

The industry's more righteous engineers would have called them on this crap a decade or two ago, but the precious new whiz kids sheltering beneath the major manufacturers lent their acquiescence instead. The project has subsequently sprawled forward! It's gotten to the point that adjustable stems are nearly expected, on many of the new bikes at least. But this is totally fucked because they are a demonstrably bad idea.

The adjustable stem is only a shoddy marketing device. Their tendency was first noticed in the late 1990s; it has come to afflict both threaded and threadless stems. The adjustables usually sport the smart new face plates, but only because they had the fortune to show up at a convenient time. The gesture falls well short of any adequate compensation.

It has been my experience that people have specific inclinations about their preferred handlebar positions. You may want to be stretched-out for speed and stability, or more upright for comfort. I'm not sure I've ever known anyone to whimsically hop back and forth. Besides, those stems on hand were already simpler, lighter, and more durable. But then came the new adjustable stems, marching in like they own the place. Their arrival would not have been possible without tremendous artifice.

Any stem needs to be fairly rigid, to compensate for the inevitable stresses it will face, and the adjustables fail in this regard. Their design finds the strain concentrated on a relatively small channel, which is not secured nearly as well as it should be.

In the most common version, this adjustment hinges upon a pair of bolts. The longer of the two pierces the stem's two major parts, to form a basic pivot. Its partner lurks underneath, pressing two sets of splines together to finalize a given adjustment. The theory could have been readily saleable, based upon its gee-whiz potential, but this in itself does not necessarily provide any further validation.

The adjustable stems look kind of overbuilt, which is unfortunate, but neither does this help their case. The cross bolt needs to be made supremely tight, because the torque shooting through its intersection also strives to loosen it, and to my experience this is exactly what happens after a while.

Most of the bolts seem to have been greased back at the factory, but this has not made any meaningful difference. I really don't think a thread-locking compound will be able to help in this particular situation. And it's also a bit counterintuitive, of course.

The wrench fittings are surprisingly shallow, given the bolt's size and purpose; the heads tend to strip out fairly easily. And this starts the final process: the bolt loosens further, the stem begins to rock around, the gaps between its major parts are widened. The problem compounds itself and becomes permanent.

It is not for capricious reasons when I tell you to avoid these. I am trying to save you some trouble. They become loose, following regular use, and we are no longer able to tighten them.

The things claim to be adjustable. It is not unreasonable that aspiring mechanics check them out, and it's beyond my power or ambitions to prevent that kind of thing. It's not for me to devise some retroactive policing operation; the problem is that these things were let out in the world in the first place.

6: WHEELS

Around and around the wheels will go, churning us down the garden path, and if they do stay well and true, then we know at least we've done the math.

Tubes

You are forgiven to suppose that there exists an organized conspiracy to pop your **INNER TUBES** at precisely the wrong occasions, for diabolic and untoward reasons we dare not speculate upon. But our villains are only opportunistic! They spy an opening, and they go for it. We may have called them entrepreneurs, in another setting.

I would like to see the staples given a more prominent position in the tragic pantheon of puncture folklore, myself. The wire is just thin and sharp enough; it becomes the perfect unassuming nemesis. It is good to avoid running over debris, to the extent we're able to at least, but there's no way we can spot every last piece of it. The tire's characteristics will inevitably become relevant. Those thorns lurking to the garden path's shadowed periphery may well indeed have malicious, protracted scores to settle with your inner tubes, but something has to let them inside to begin with.

It is best to carry a spare tube, in your travels, and the easiest way to build up a stock of these is to repair the old ones. The happening On-the-Road section (page 169) will better consider your more spontaneous situations. And rather than simply cast your popped balloons by the wayside, you should make a habit of hanging them in a corner somewhere. You'll eventually be able to patch a whole loop of tubes at once, this way, and the exercise will suddenly become eminently practical and efficient.

First, grab your floor pump and see if they inflate really big. If they won't, you should be able to spot the hole with your eyes. Turn the music down, failing that, and run the tube past your ear; see if you hear the air rushing out of its dastardly little pin-prick. Otherwise you have to go and do the dunking-underwater thing. Anything you can fit a patch over can be fixed. You want like a quarter-inch overlap to each side. Tubes can and do last for decades; long blow-out gashes or holes right up by the valve stem are the only things that really kill them dead.

Your patch kit usually comes with one or two larger patches: I find myself cutting these in half or thirds for smaller projects, most of the time. All you really need to do is make sure the tube is nice and clean, and the glue is really dry. Most patching maneuvers that do fail trace back to one of these two points.

The patch kits feel obliged to present you with a little square of sandpaper to scuff the tube. And it is a nice gesture, but I cannot even remember the last time I actually used one of these. The sandpaper hangs over from the crazy old days, before they got the glue figured out. I encourage you to glue the different squares to a piece of plywood some-where, to make for a rough quilt.

Dose a good puddle of glue right over each hole, enough to surround the patch com-pletely, and let it sit like that for a good long time. This dries the glue way the hell out, which is precisely what we like.

Peel the foil and lay the patches down, press-ing firmly. I clamp the patched sections in the Easy-Grip, as a matter of fact, to press the hell out of them. You just line the patches up like pancakes and press. I think this does some good; my failure rate is very low. And our final exam inflates them fully again, to see if they hold all their air overnight.

I had hoped to present the readership with some kind of cohesive and unified flat repair theory, but as is often the case the engineers had other ideas. The **TUBELESS TIRES** explain away the inner tube, replacing it with an airy void of their own design. The tire's bead and the rim hook correspond to each other in more meaningful ways. The spoke nipples are hidden from view by means of small plugs, which thread in to place; everything stays nice and airtight. But you want to treat these eye-lets with threadlocker, before they go in.

Tubelessness allows the tires to run at low-ered air pressures. Where the stupid old in-ner tubes predictably succumb to pinch flats if you run them too low, these new space tires go with your flow. And the wider contact patch to result, in turn, scales your mountain bike right the hell up hills.

Rim Strips

The spokes are sharp metal sticks, but the inner tubes are only bags of air. Theirs is no

likely combination. The spokes are already under great tension; they're only waiting out an excuse. The hopeful tube expands out to meet them, like it wants to be friends or what-ever, and after a point they just pop the fuck-er. But the danger is no less real on the more sophisticated rims, where the spokes' nipples are recessed in to the rim. The tube will try to crawl in to each of their holes, and this little adventure ends its life just as surely.

Our prescient intermediary is the **RIM STRIP**, an eminently reasonable diplomat, which qui-etly manages to obscure their various differ-ences. Neither the pre-fab wheels nor the new tubeless tires need to ask after rim strips, for their obvious reasons, but all the other wheels should be made to put on some protection. And the wheels may favor one sort of rim strip or another, based upon their features.

The simplest are the big black rubber bands. Different sizes are available, to perhaps in-clude a choice on the width. The size may be marked somewhere, in ungainly white block lettering, listing the nominal wheel size in inches and the width in millimeters. But the rubber bands become brittle, after a while, and even the freshest ones will threaten to snap. They were associated with the bottom-feeder bikes for a pretty long time, in fact, but some wretched loser has since chanced upon a method to use strapping tape for the rim strips. The heavy plastic crap, like what we found around the newspaper bundles on our old paper routes, sucks.

Where the basic rubber rim strips may be pulled aside to replace a spoke, or even re-used on a wholly different wheel, we have no such luck with the plastic. You need to destroy it to change out a spoke nipple, and then we have to sell you a new rim strip.

The rubber one only costs a buck, but it's *so*

much smarter to just get one of the real ones instead. The bike rubbers break far too easily! And you don't even want to trust them at higher pressures, especially on rims with recessed spokes. The tube pushes the rim strip into the spoke holes, as it becomes excited, after which point the spoke holes' edges may pop it at their leisure.

Several manufacturers have produced useful updates on the old rubber bands, using thin plastics just strong and pliable enough to do the job, in the 26-inch and 700-centimeter wheel sizes at least. But the more traditional choice is the **RIM TAPE**. The first you see is probably going to be the classic Velox tape, the face of which reads *Fond de Jante*, over and over again. Nice and thick stuff, about like cardstock. It is usually sold in individual rolls, in one of three widths, each of which is long enough to cover a road-sized rim. You pare it down to fit the smaller-sized wheels, folding it to cut a tiny diamond-shaped valve hole with the very tip of the sidecutters.

The rim strips are helpful and good. I relish their discussion, in fact, because our next topic already brings the fighting bile to the back of my palate … the **SLIME**. The name is forthright, for it is an absolute shady bastard of a product. It will never, ever be a good idea to install dubious liquids to an inner tube in active use.

The slime and its clones are marketed as a "flat preventative." Its roots likely slither back toward the automobile industry. And I can scarcely imagine what manner of bitter cynic could have been so low as to inflict the slime upon innocent bicycles. But it is not relevant, because their transgression bears no potential for redemption. We only want to play and have fun with the bikes, but the slime arrived and made a horrible stinking mess, which must now be disposed. Make

good and sure you warn all your friends away from this shit.

Slime is pushed by desperate hustlers of no particular distinction. It and kindred substances will sometimes infect the new inner tubes from the time of their birth, as with some of the less fortunate new bicycles, but it is also sold openly to the unknowing passersby. This is a thick liquid, often bright green in color, meant to be introduced to the tubes through their valve stems. No more flats!

I have lost track of how many slime-filled inner tubes I have replaced on rental bikes. The shit does not even do what it is supposed to do. *Quality tires are much more effective in preventing flats.*

The slime does add some appreciable weight to your wheels, however, but there is also the chance it may spray you. The air compressor hose hits the valve, just like before, only this time a mess of green ooze spurts suddenly from the valve. Or maybe it won't; seems to be kind of random. But you never know, so you want to keep your face well back from the wheel, whenever you air the damned tire. I did this all summer long once, with every last Specialized Expedition comfort bike in the rental fleet where I worked. We were busy as hell, all the while; it was absolutely fucking ridiculous.

The slime may or may not clog up the tube's valve over time. You know if it does, because you won't be able to fill the tube anymore. But then, at least, you will not get sprayed! Based on these experiences, I encourage the reader to think of the slime and any other tube sealant products as the drainage from a great, festering pool of waste.

Tires

The **TIRE SIZE** is noted on the sidewall, at some point. It is a reliable and timeless jargon, which crosses the tire's diameter against its width. But of course this is not so simple, because people tend to look at things differently.

The tire may be measured in inches or millimeters—or even obtuse amalgamations of both, as the case may be—and any of these may reference the inside diameter, its outside, or points between. We've been left with a grand mess, in other words, of which you need to know just enough to get by.

History has provided us with no less than eight distinct wheel sizes whose names begin "26 inch," to take one favorite example, and Sutherlands' famous manual has dutifully kept track of their particulars. The metric measurements of 599, 597, 590, 585, 584, 571, 561, and 559 each refer to a distinct **BEAD DIAMETER**, used at different points in our history, but they might just as easily be listed as 26 x 1.375, 26 x 1 1/4, 26 x 1 3/8, 26 x 1 1/2, 26 x 1 3/4, 26 x 2.25, and 26 x 2.0.

Indeed, the names change and even overlap, across different national and manufacturers' standards. The smaller sizes have suffered as well. While "20 inch" may mean a bead diameter of either 406 or 451, the "16 inch" may be either 305 or 349. I'm not aware of any outstanding disputes around the 12-inch tire size, but the hairs have split again up at 24 inch. It's usually a kids' bike tire size, but a distinct high-pressure slick tire makes a very occasional appearance. Also available are 14-inch and 17-inch tires, but each is even more uncommon. The same could be said all the more emphatically for all the dozens of other different tire sizes the world has witnessed, some majority of which has

at last been laid to rest. The vast majority of bicycle wheels now answer to either the 559/26, or the 700c, which is our external-diameter shorthand for the ubiquitous 622-bead diameter.

Were this not enough, various people have also begun talking about 29-inch tires. As with the 27 or the 26, the name only approximates the outside diameter of a fully inflated example. But 29 inch is essentially another name for the 700c size; either uses the very same 622 bead diameter. The 29 inch is only the knobbier, wider big brother to the 700c hybrid tires we've known for many years. Nor is the concept entirely new, for that matter; I remember seeing a Diamond Back set up this way in the early 90s.

The famous old 27-inch road size still finds its way in, now and again. Its ISO number is 630; a few basic tires are still broadly available. These diameter measurements are the only ones that really matter. You cannot fuck around with this; it really needs to be right on. A suitable replacement only needs to be at least as wide as the rim, or just narrow enough to fit in the frame.

It should be clear enough what ambitions different tires might hold. The knobbies hide no secrets; they go for the mud. The thin road slicks at the far end of the spectrum are equally strident about their own preferences. It is in the great middle, with fat slicks and tour tires and everything else, that the changes occur.

A number of manufacturers have successfully encouraged a broad assumption that knobby mountain bike tires are somehow the best. I have no idea how this is for the trucks, but it is no rule for the bikes! The small free-standing knobs on the mountain tires mushroom out and wriggle around, as they're pressed to the pavement; the ground itself becomes blurry and indistinct. Knobbies are also meant to run on an air pressure somewhat lower than that prescribed in other scenarios, and this makes for a wider contact patch hitting the ground, which slows things yet further. The thinner the tire, and the higher its pressure, the quicker you will become. And the ride becomes somewhat less forgiving, of course.

Tire Wear

A tire's wear is most evident in terms of **DRY-ROT**. The sun and the water both have business with the soft rubber tires; their efforts will eventually affect small cracks. You can see these easily, with older and cheaper tires. You'll see them better yet, if you let the air out and squeeze the tire flat. The cracks tell us the material has become dry and brittle.

The best example of this phenomenon may be the decrepit gumwall tires on the dusty old basement bike, suddenly rescued after years of abandonment. The bike itself may have potential, but I bet the tires are toast! Their treads may even have retained their unblemished gumwall grin, all these long years, but it will not mean a thing. The rubber becomes hard, and it holds a form easily enough, that is until it's challenged by a thumbtack or the like.

"Gumwall" refers to the sidewalls, which are rendered in the same cheap compound used for the tread. The two areas may be different colors, but it will not make any difference. It's about the cheapest way to make a tire. And so we should not be surprised when the dumb gumwalls keep losing their little arguments with the glass.

More realistic tires have long since adopted distinct materials, for tread and sidewall both, because each has its own design function. This becomes a useful point of departure, in considering tire quality. The riding characteristics and durability are both functions of the materials used. Various types of basic armor plating have filtered down to the cheaper tires, but these simpler examples are also fairly heavy, and this is a drag. Sharp decals and splashy colors don't necessarily mean a thing, if the tire is heavier than your beer. There are all kinds of tires that probably do well enough, in terms of avoiding the flats, but it is only the special ones that can do this on a diet.

Truing Wheels

So you want to true the wheels, do you? Are you quite sure you're up to this ultimate challenge? Have you read the sacred texts; do you understand the meaning of the rituals; have you solemnly prepared yourself for the task? You tossed a certain special *something* into the dying embers at precisely the stroke of midnight, to summon those elements that can guide you? What have been your readings from the holy deck these last seven days?

I suppose we may begin. The first round of incantations, as we shall see, will hail the power of the Northern Star … . No, I'm kidding. It is really not so complicated. This is the big secret: you can follow through with any of the aforementioned signals, were you so inclined, but I'm not sure they're necessary to the task at hand.

You will notice, peering within, that the wheel is only held together with a lacing of thin wires. It is delicate, but it is magnificent. The Spartan, minimalist pattern joins distinct hubs and rims to their own coalitions of spokes, and their unlikely union suggests some hope for redemption.

Our wheels are battered in an endless campaign of attrition; our skills in repairing them accrue in the opposite direction. There are better and worse conditions for a wheel's elements, which we come to recognize, and these are only separated by degrees. Excluding the bleak and humorless pre-fab wheels, all the others still proceed from the original idea: our whims are translated down to the hubs, where the spokes explain our intentions out to the rims. The premise that tensioned spokes can optimize the relationship betwixt strength and weight is all things graceful and prescient. It also affords us the option to replace parts individually, which may be just as interesting.

The pre-fab wheels, of course, update the original wooden oxcart constructions. The materials have certainly evolved, from the old plastic mag wheels to our shiny new carbon ones, but still there is no theory. They arrive here from some contrived and secondary dimension, where everything is simultaneously immortal and disposable. Some may be repaired back at the factories, eventually, but this only leaves them equally expensive and pretentious—the hipster squares, among the wheels.

Some of the carbon spokes are more vulnerable to side hits. It is certainly possible to make stronger composite structures, but this adds weight, and the higher-end wheels just are not in to that. The alloy hoops glued to the outsized epoxy frisbees remain vulnerable to the problems any other wheel may encounter, of course. They can be dented, for example.

Circumstance will challenge the wheels quite randomly, but patterns appear if we are looking for them. Every wheel may crave redemption, but in the end only some will be saved! The great majority of injured wheels I've come across are in fact repairable, but this is providence, not scripture.

Our wheels are hubs, spokes, and rims. Each must remain worthy for their project to continue. The relatively vast projections the outer elements provide for the hubs are construed as a basic worship, in our example—religious ideologies, like the others, merely presume we like to orbit their central abstractions—but we should be wary of the false gods, especially here.

Are you sure the hub is cool? A loose one could throw this whole thing off; its tightening is described on page 154. What about the spokes? Are they all present and accounted for? Their pattern should be the same, the full way around—no gaps, no blank spots—and their relative tension needs to be evenly high. The spoke tension is crucial.

The truing process begins by squeezing the spokes together, to make sure nothing is secretly busted. This is how it usually happens. The spokes break up by the hubs, but their lacing and the nipples hold the shattered wands in place. And they just hang out, like there's nothing going.

The rear spokes carry most of the rider's weight, and this makes them more vulnerable, but generally we should not resign ourselves to watching them break. It is not any natural condition. Spokes pop when the wheel takes a serious hit, or when they are asked to carry more than they are meant to handle. If a wheel is losing spokes on any kind of regular basis, something very basic needs to change. The wheel may be usefully rebuilt with a stronger lacing pattern—three cross in place of radial, for example—but it's more likely that we want to get more spokes involved in the first place, and that is a different wheel.

Truing stand

Those spokes that do snap tend to go one at a time—the solitary suicides, in our ideological model—but dramatic events may also take out several at once. The most spectacular of these is the chainsaw massacre, where a poorly adjusted rear derailleur allows the chain to hop off the last cog, and our pedaling force is transferred toward chopping the spokes down. The effect is not subtle; the spokes nearest the chain get all mangled. They may not fail right away, but the carved-up ones will really want to, so you should go ahead and replace them first.

This is what the **PIE PLATES** are for, incidentally, to prevent this kind of thing. Yet pie plates have never been entirely fashionable, outside the lower reaches of the bicycle hierarchy. They are the mechanic's training-wheels, out in full public view; their presence suggests some basic uncertainty with regards to the derailleur adjustments. But a suddenly bent derailleur hanger, of course, can easily ruin the concentration of even

the most studious example. And so does the slaughter continue.

A rim's health can be harder to measure. We will certainly spot some of the more obvious casualties—the Pac Man, the potato chip—but the others are less forthright. They may be able to suck it in, just enough to pass, from a certain view at least.

It is sometimes possible to make a bent rim look straight, by playing with its spoke tension. You jack it all the way up on the one side, then loosen the others to some more noodling consistency. But this creates a weak spot, even if the wheel still looks good and true. It loses what true it has all the easier.

The hub and spokes may be reused, depending, but the rim is toast. I am not aware of any reliable method for redeeming these, at this point in time. Go ahead and recycle it.

Deconstructing a wheel is a very straightforward process, once any gears are removed. You simply take everything apart. The full extent of the rim's troubles will become more visible, as the spoke tension's soothing influence is pulled away (much like the irrepressible hangover, after the serious bender).

Tightening spokes past a useful range of tension generally means that you're loosening some number opposite them, and the slack saps away at the wheel's strength. You have accidentally thumped the apple, and so you expect to see a bad spot.

The relative size of a wheel's bad spot in itself is not necessarily indicative of anything, up to a point at least. What really matters is the spoke tension. It should even out, as you true the wheel, resolving differences between the excessively tight and the wantonly loose.

Our discussion here really transpires along a continuum; the dead rim is only the final extension of a far more common problem. Were the rim bowing out to the right, for example, we locate the center of the problem and see about tightening up the spokes on the left. But it is possible these were already as tight as we really like them to be—visiting their comrades across the left, to determine a rough average—in which case we move to loosen up some of those over on the right. And the two things might happen at once, in fact: the spoke(s) in need of tightening should be a bit loose, and those in need of loosening will be slightly tight. Tension levels on rear wheels are sometimes distinct to each side, for reasons soon to be explored, but in the ideal they both become reasonably even. This simple balancing provides the wheel its lasting strength.

The more you work on wheels, the more you will come to appreciate the relevance of spoke tension. It is best measured with a tensiometer, as described in the wheelbuilding section (see page 187). But it's not common that we whip one out for simple truing work. Wheels that were built right in the first place will have little use for its services.

The most reliable spoke tension has always been found with quality hand-built wheels, as opposed to those pieced together by machines. So track down a wheel of some upstanding reputation, and squeeze its spokes together; you want to translate this feeling over to your own wheel.

Wheels do tend to loosen up, as parts settle in to place. A good level of tension will hold up well enough on its own, but it may need to be refreshed, shortly after the build and perhaps again later in life.

A really bad hit may knock a rim out of true,

or punch a flat spot in it, or both. I have no special familiarity with astrophysics, so I can not provide any extensive detail about the characteristics of such death-blows. I could see about maybe passing along quasi-mystical suggestions, if anyone is interested in hearing about those … I'm thinking of the Campagnolo rim that I accidentally destroyed a month ago, leaving work. Right outside the door, actually, at the top of the stairs. I did the usual thing, swing the leg over to ride away and all that, but then the front wheel managed to jump off the sidewalk. I pulled it back up as soon as I realized this, and something in the exchange managed to knock the life out of that rim! Whoops. The wheel had already served the better part of a decade, so it wasn't as tragic as it might have been, but it still freaked me out.

Any **BROKEN SPOKES** will need to be replaced, before the wheel is trued. You may or may not need to replace the nipple as well, which involves removing the tire and the rim strip. You want to be careful replacing any nipples in deep-dish rims, lest they tip in to the taller rim sections, where they happily rattle away until you manage to shake them out. We have a special tool for just such purposes at work, but you can get what you need by threading the nipple on to a spare spoke, backwards. This is then stuck up a spoke hole, where the intended spoke descends from its hub to meet the nipple's top. Holding the handy surrogate in place, twist its gift up and away to the wheel.

The replacement spoke itself will mimic the pattern it finds on the wheel. Most wheels are three cross, for example, and this will find the new spoke going over two others and under a third on its way home.

This journey involves bending the spoke, which is fine because steel is so damned resilient. Spokes bearing actual crimps are less ideal, but even these may be straightened with the box pliers, if they need to be.

The hub gears will most likely need to be removed, to install the spoke. Some smaller fixed cogs and BMX freewheels make for exemptions—the incoming spokes can shoot straight over their heads—but everything else will have to go. Procedures for removing freewheels and cassettes are described down with the hubs (see pages 150-152).

The new spoke should be of the same length as its predecessor. No horseshoes; no hand grenades. It can't shoot through the nipple and stab the inner tube, but it still needs to thread at least most of the way in.

WHEEL TRUING itself is a series of three steps, repeated in succession, until we get what we want. You position the caliper, spin the rim slowly past, and finally make your adjustment. Each step is centrally important; they share responsibility for your results.

Positioning the caliper is not difficult at all with the Park stands. One dial moves it up and down, in relation to the rim, while another opens and closes its jaws. Pretty damned slick. Whichever stand you're using, you want to proceed with the same basic sequence. Spin the rim, to figure out where the biggest problem is, and adjust the caliper such that it just *barely* grazes against the mountain's top. You will be starting with this one, before working your way down through any smaller ones. It is possible the calipers will outline a broader bad spot, without any particular center. This is less common, the product usually of poor building skills. But it's resolved in much the same way, only amplified; you turn three or four spokes instead of the one or two.

You may find yourself flipping the wheel around in the truing stand, such that the prob-

lem faces against the opposite caliper, dependent on your situation. The wheel's orientation in the stand is not particularly relevant to the basic truing process; it is more important that you can see what you are doing.

Our adjustments on the spokes are made with the spoke wrenches. Park Tool's black, green, and red—for small, medium, and large—are presently the most ubiquitous in America. The correct choice fits nice and snug around the nipple. It should not be able to wiggle around. A spoke wrench too large will eventually begin stripping the nipples. Their sharp edges slump and wear down; it becomes difficult to get them doing anything at all.

The spoke nipples themselves should be kind of hard to turn. The spokes are supposed to be treated with some sort of thread-locking compound or another, and they may also be somewhat corroded. And they're supposed to be tensioned, in either case.

This said, it is also important the spokes do not wind up when turned. A dearth of lubrication can help spokes seize to their nipples, over time; they both simply move as one. And, past a certain point, the spokes simply snap. You want to deposit a drop of oil precisely atop each nipple's threads to resolve this. Hit the base of the nipple as well, while you're at it, right where it meets the rim. Then spin the wheel a minute; the oil should work its way down the threads, much as with a centrifuge.

This remedy may not work as well for aluminum nipples, because they suck. They seize to the nipples all too easily, sometimes; the spokes may just wind up and snap. But my colleague Dan Ditty suggests a solution, which may resolve this miniature dilemma. Grip the spoke with your fourth hand tool. Set it up down low, just above the spoke wrench, at an angle such that only the tool's pinch is focused on the spoke.

I feel like I'm suddenly bursting with information, when I just said this was all so simple, so perhaps we'll take a second to regroup … . The actual truing process becomes easy enough, once you're ready to begin; we've only these few considerations before arriving upon our sunny plateau.

The adjustments are made in small increments, which grow smaller yet as the wheel becomes more true. A nipple may begin with a full rotation or two. Healthy and wise wheels may start off with half- and quarter-turns; their less fortunate kin may need a good deal more. So find what seems to be the most grievous problem, and make your adjustment. Then check your work: spin past the calipers again to see how you did. You want to get down to the point of making adjustments in half- or quarter- or even eighth-turns, before spiraling in to oblivion and riding away from it all. But the only way you'll be getting there is by checking your work—consistently, methodically, every time you make adjustments. I don't want to sound like math class or anything, but that's just how it is. I've been truing wheels since 1993, and I still expect to do it this way, until the day I can true no more. You set and reset the caliper; you spin the wheel against it; you make your adjustment and you do it again, until the wheel is either made good or exposed as some kind of fraud.

And again, keep in mind that the truing process ideally coincides with the advancement of equitable spoke tensions. Discrepancies in this regard help us know which spokes to turn, in other words. If the tension is supposed to be fairly even the whole way around—keeping in mind, as noted, that the drive side may be a bit higher—you just go around and deal

with the oddballs. One spoke may be so loose it rattles; another may be so tight you can barely turn it. And where the rim is still useful, tightening or loosening the one or the other will move the rim in such a way as to make it more true.

Other smaller distortions are often made manifest, in the process of truing and tensioning a wheel. You fix these, as they appear, but don't let them throw you: the progress is *forward*, rather than strictly linear. Adjustments on one spoke are translated out toward its peers, through their union at the hub; we expect to surf through a few ripples on the way down home.

The hops and flat spots, our peaks and valleys along the rim's topography, are somewhat less common than the lateral kinks. Making imprudent leaps can earn your wheel a flat spot, of course, but it's far easier to install them inadvertently, with the spoke wrenches. And the hops, by nature, are always artificial.

The flats may well trace to some legitimate roughhousing—there is already a famous story, perhaps—but any combination of the hops and flat spots together will be roundly suspicious. This indicates a lack of discretion, on the part of the wheel's builder. The hops develop when a sequence of spokes is too loose; the flat spots appear when they're too tight.

The rim may still appear true, from the lateral view, in either situation. The one measure is necessarily contingent upon the other. And a bad lateral bend can look like a flat spot. So you want to keep the lateral true in mind, when resolving any hops or flat spots.

Our cures for the hops and flat spots are the up-and-down escalators. You can add to the tension, or you can let some go. As ever, it is contingent upon your goals for the situation. All will be as it was before, with regards to the range of our adjustments—measured, patient, incremental—but the axis flips 90 degrees, from the horizontal to the vertical.

The stand's calipers allow some provision for measuring the wheel's overall roundness. We need to dispose of the tire to really check this out, if that hasn't happened already. The Park calipers are especially good at this; you can set things up such that you're finishing the wheel by checking the lateral true and roundness simultaneously. And Travis at Freewheel showed me another nice trick for this: the calipers may be positioned against the *top* of the rim, to better isolate the flat spots.

The last thing we need to consider is the **WHEEL DISH**. The wheel's final centering, as it fits in to the frame dropouts. This detail should have been resolved when first the wheel was born, but any serious truing regimen may raise the point anew.

Where wheel truing valorizes the efforts of individual spokes, the dish is a fluid expression of their collective will. Everybody works together, in equal measures, toward a common goal. This is more relevant out back, because the hub gears are generally wider than the spacers over on the neutral side. And so the rim is made to sit off center, in relation to the axle's end points. The two sides may be simply balanced against each other—the drive side spokes are made a few turns tighter than their neutral kin—but it is more common to simply begin with slightly shorter spokes on the drive side.

You can check for wheel dish in the truing stand, by flipping the wheel back and forth,

such that each side checks in with one arm of the caliper. But you may want to conduct the final exam in the frame itself. The wheel should appear correctly dished in either location, in theory, but it has been my experience that older and cheaper frames will too easily lose their alignment. And of course you want to get such frames properly realigned, in the ideal, but failing that you should at least make sure the brake pad is not dragging ass on the rim.

Besides, the frame test takes no effort at all. You sight down the top of the tire, and you compare what you see to the frame. You just eyeball it, using the hole in the frame's brake bridge as your reference point. Adjusting for wheel dish really is also simple enough: all the spokes on the one side get that very same tweak, be that with tightening or even a little loosening.

The **FINAL TENSION** is the wheel's proof of enlightenment. In scientific terms, the spokes are tightened up to an average of about 135-millimeter pressure. The best results require a tensiometer, in other words, or at least a fairly exacting comparison against a well-built wheel. And you did oil the nipples, right? Important, with any thorough retensioning.

As your wheel approaches its fruition, the very last thing you want to do is stress the spokes. Grab them in pairs and squeeze hard, all the way around the wheel. You may also use the more thorough method, as described on pages 195-196 of the wheelbuilding section, for especially ambitious truing or retensioning projects. And then you check the true, one last time.

The **SADDLE**, also known as the seat, has handily become the bicycle's most controversial component. It is the one everybody knows how to complain about!

We may reasonably expect the poor saddle to falter some, weathering the weight of this endless criticism. And this has happened, after a fashion. The seat has all but abandoned its original designs. Excluding a few gracious examples, it has fled in a few different directions at once. We're blessed with so many individual forms, to put this another way, and the flourishing of our democratic pluralism has at last filtered down to consider the saddles. A veritable avalanche has since become available, alternately promising speed or comfort or both, and the territory is yours to explore.

Many of our bike rental customers are first concerned with their comfort, above all else. Most are already on vacation, in America; what else is there to think about? The recumbent option—where we are able to consider it, at last—may well be the most "comfortable" of them all. But the flying lawn chairs cannot be retrofitted to regular upright bikes, of course. The closest half-measures we find in this *general* direction are wider, with more padding, and often springs as well. And they are tremendously popular, as upgrades.

The switch itself is easy enough. An ever-smaller fraction of truly ancient bikes use seats mounted on the old flat rails, and I've seen a goofy BMX saddle with only one big rail, but all the rest can be relied upon to sport ubiquitous pairs of round rails. Their width may vary, between 7 and 10 millimeters, but to the best of my knowledge they all subscribe to the usual sorts of seatpost clamps; all of which means that we're able to swap out just about any saddle for another.

The comfort sponges' ample padding soaks up a good measure of our pedaling energy; they're also a bit too wide to encourage any truly efficient transfer of power. The racing saddles are smaller and narrower, and usually quite a bit lighter as well.

But the boundaries may be challenged, dependent on the perspective; a really good seat may be fast and comfortable at the very same time—something to work a day on; to ride to the next town and back with. I favor Selle San Marco's Rolls and some by Wilderness Trail Bikes, myself.

We also spy various saddles with curious splits to them, right down the mid-section. These were inspired by some doctor, who developed a concern that regular bicycle seats are potentially harmful to the male reproductive system. Specialized duly hired a dude to refine his gimmick, and it became a runaway success. The theme was found to resonate broadly! But the good doctor's theories have since become more disputed. There never was any epidemic among cyclists. Some minute strata of hard-training racers may benefit from the innovation, perhaps, but there is no public health crisis.

A number of manufacturers make women's saddles as well, of course. The tail sections are wider, to better suit women's wider hips. Terry may have been the first to come out with one of these.

7: SEATS

*Bicycles support us by means of their seats, which rest
in turn atop seatposts.*

Seatposts

The **SEATPOSTS** are to frames as saddles are to riders, but even more so. Each frame has one particular preference, in terms of the post size, and there is no room for negotiation. None! Newer frames are increasingly learning to enjoy the same tastes in this regard, but the random postings of history have already left us with a minor forest.

I would like to tell you that the posts file themselves into a nearly reasonable range of straightforward metric gradients, but as yet we're not quite so fortunate. BMX 7/8-inch seatposts are still fairly common; the long-obsolete steel stumps used with ancient Peugeot bikes still find occasional uses as well. And then we have the folding bikes, which have taken to exceptionally tall and wide posts.

These disclaimers made, *nearly* all the other seatposts are found to coincide with a basic pattern. Beginning down at 25.0 and continuing up to at least 31.8, seatpost diameters are measured in .2 millimeter increments. The numbers are carved to the front of the posts, just below the maximum height line, which itself is another important feature we'll soon arrive upon.

Frame manufacturers have used countless different seat tubes through the years, and distinct seat posts have duly trailed after each of these.

But some sizes—the 25.0, 25.4, 25.8, 26.2, 26.4, 26.8, 27.0, and 27.2, for example—have really become more common. Their sustained popularity, in fact, renders the more obscure sizes fairly conspicuous. A 26.6-millimeter post may be the most useful thing ever, in Eastern Europe or Middle Earth or somewhere, but it's quite an odd creature to see around here. I wonder if the 26.8 millimeter makes for a better match. But I first want to gather the frame's firm and immutable thoughts on the subject, about which it's less than useful to make any scurrilous presumptions.

The very best scenario finds you pulling a properly sized post from its frame, noting the digits, and marching these down to your friendly locally owned independent bicycle distributor. But seats are stolen all the time, with the posts as well, and it's even possible they have been replaced with something the wrong size. If yours takes gorillas to tighten, this may well be you. But first try greasing the post's pinch bolt.

The fit should be just snug enough. You can adjust the post's position by hand, once its pinch bolt is released. A nearly seized post will move only grudgingly, until you get it out and throw some grease down in there—and you may run it by the shop and have them hone the seat tube, first—but in no case should there be lateral play, across the seat post and its frame.

Sizing the post may theoretically be done with calipers, but the gradients are dispersed 5-to-the-millimeter, so we use stepped metal gauges instead. The diminishing sizes are etched to the face of each successive step.

But these sticks are shop tools. So we root through the seatpost box, to see which comes the closest. You may find your precise match, when the stars are shining brightly upon you, but this will probably follow upon the tedious process-of-elimination thing.

Don't *even* be trying to force an outsized post down a narrower seat tube. It's most likely to get itself stuck down there, once you set the hammer down, and then you'll be all kinds of fucked. A post too loose, by contrast, will slide right down. But it won't be any good to tighten it like that, because you add an obtuse new crimp to the seat tube. Or, in the case of either the carbon or aluminum frames, you simply crack the thing.

Steel frames can swing it better; the problem rendered mere amateur slop, rather than imminent danger. But it's still four times as stupid, because the seat's pinch bolt will suddenly be charged with compressing a sturdy tube to dimensions smaller than it was born with.

The problem is obvious enough, if your frame is so afflicted. The gap behind the pinch bolt needs to be parallel, not angled in towards the top. You remove the bolt and carefully lever things straight with the screwdriver, if this is the problem. You don't want to flare the tube's ears out; they need to be made round again.

So get the right post. And—unless you find yourself riding a carbon fiber seatpost, for whatever reason—make sure you get grease inside the frame's seat tube before installation. *Never grease a carbon seat tube, or anything accepting a carbon seat post.* The

grease makes it slide down forever and ever, just like poor old Sisyphus. Any oversights in this regard may be resolved with a clean rag and lots of rubbing alcohol.

You want to paint some grease all down in the seat tube, with any of the metal frames. This is probably not going to be any detail you spontaneously remember years down the road; you really want to do this when you first put it in. The danger—especially if the bike gets parked outside a lot—is that it may just rust in place. Happens all the time! And resolving such a dilemma, as we'll see, is just a mess.

The more we delve in to the myriad variables of certain more complicated component features, the better we appreciate the raw candor of such straightforward pronouncements. There's no two ways about it; metal posts in metal frames should get greased. The point is fixed and eternal.

This is one particular thrill to draw from the great soupy ether of cycle mechanistry, these precious opportunities to draw lines in the sand. There really are that many variables, across divergent situations. It becomes fully refreshing to make definitive pronouncements. But so it goes, right? And since it feels like I'm on a roll, I should probably keep going. So I tell you what: let it now be declared that all persons everywhere are forever forbidden from sailing their seatposts at any points above the ever-present maximum height line. Because this, too, is foolish and obtuse.

The post and frame are not meant to fly the seat any taller than a certain height. Trespassing upon this simple truth is only asking for trouble. The greater the transgression, the more likely something is going to bend or break. So they make this hard to do, by tracing a line around the base of the post. It's most obvious, were you to attempt anything foolish; you're surely facing the scorn and ridicule of your closest friends. OK, people? Let's stick together.

But there is more! The keen eye, harvesting seat stalks from bicycles, will in time notice that their final length may vary. Seatposts will most often stretch a good 300 or 350 millimeters, but those culled from older bikes or road bikes are often considerably shorter. We call it Compact Frame Geometry or similar, these days, because that's just how we've learned to talk about things. But people have not become much shorter, in the intervening years, so the modern seatposts are asked to be somewhat taller.

Older bikes—to include a majority of the first generation mountain bikes—feature the flat, straight-across top tubes. We can still find new bikes bearing such designs, and shorter seatposts for that matter, because not everyone is sold on this compacting idea. The newer style, with the shorter frames and lengthened seatposts, is less concerned with the bottom bracket flex. Improvements in frame construction and materials allow for such leisure. The frames are also left with a considerably shorter standover height, which can be quite useful in its own right. And the design provides major bike manufacturers the means to eliminate a suddenly redundant frame size or two as well, in the final analysis, and of course this lowers production costs.

The original seat mounting hardware may be understood broadly enough to be considered intuitive. The seat rails are collected within the pieces of a simple clamping assembly, which slides down around the top of a seatpost. Nuts to either side tighten everything in to place. Any tinkerer probably knows just what I'm talking about.

Said nuts are most often 14 millimeters across, and it is important that they're kept supremely tight. The clamping assembly is built around a pair of facing adjustment surfaces, which can be expected to wear themselves down if they grind against each other. And this is precisely what happens, if you ride the seat with the hardware loose. The hardware is routinely replaced, for this very reason. It is (almost always!) universal; any worthwhile bike shop has a set for you.

The clamp's business parts are meant to fit to the rear of the seat post, not out front. And excluding the very occasional strange old bats, these clamp assemblies are expected to tighten around 7/8-inch poles. Older BMX bikes often use a straight 7/8-inch seatpost; others are drawn in to fit this dimension at the very top.

These original examples are known as the **STRAIGHT POSTS.** They are distinct from what we call the **LAPRADE POSTS,** which have no obtuse side-nuts to tighten. They need only one sturdy bolt, buried back between the rails. Laprades fulfill the basic mission, in terms of allowing the seat to be tightened securely in a range of angles, but without the earlier design's obtuse profile. Makes 'em seem smarter somehow, more refined, which is why we city folk fancy them so. Their splined adjustment faces are more precise in their decisions, in comparing with their sloppier predecessors. The splines are more pronounced; their position is far more secure. But still they suffer the same ignoble fate, if they are not fully tightened. The mounting hardware is integral to laprade posts; you have to replace the whole thing.

We also come across an odd beast calling itself "micro-adjust" or similar, which updates and complicates our laprade. A pair of nuts or bolts fore and aft together seesaw the saddle to more suitable situations, essentially.

Seatpost suspension can be retrofitted to most bikes. And the shock posts, conversely, may be replaced with solid ones. These rear-mounted pogo sticks are only available in a couple common sizes, the 25.4 or 27.2 millimeter for example. Their lazy manufacturers only provide us with dubious shims, with which to explain their general statements toward distinct applications. These bear fat lips up top, to keep the hungry seat tubes from swallowing them whole.

The great majority of shock posts are metal sticks as well, but they manage to hide springs beneath chintzy rubber boots. We can not adjust them, any more than we may hope to service them. The seat happily wobbles side-to-side, in fact, because such fast-food suspension mechanisms require a good degree of play. There may be a ridged ring around the base; hand-tightening this lessens but does not eliminate the problem. Said rings seem to loosen over time, so keep an eye out.

The **SHOCK POSTS** do kind of nudge people toward correctly sized frames. Not by suggestion, but by fiat. It's as if the manufacturer has assumed we shop rats are too wicked or uninspired to get people on the right-sized bikes, all of a sudden. Something like that. Rather than provide incentives to hang around and learn the trade, our industry now strives to eliminate the very *possibility* of a poorly fitted bike.

The shock post is too wide to slide down the seat tube, after a point, and so it happens to enforce a basic frame-sizing orthodoxy. The seat can no longer be jammed all the way down, and this simple consideration handily obliterates an entire spectrum of poorly fitted bikes. And the video monitor fills in for the instructor, again, because ultimately it's all so much tired old book-learning in the first place. We don't even have to deal with

the cumbersome old numbers anymore, for that matter. Our Specialized rentals did away with a couple frame sizes at least, by switching to the more general S, M, L, and XL markings you may recall from the outlet store. Good thing there's only four sizes of people, huh? Boing-boing, boing-boing!

The heaving masses of shock posts have also been joined by a small elite of durable, more respectable suspension posts. Their materials and construction is better; the lateral slop is lessened to some degree. And we find at least some rudimentary means to adjust the suspension parameters. All of which means they are more expensive, and thus do the cheap-ass half-measures rule their cloying little world.

8: Handlebars

The handlebars extend out from the stem, gathering the bicycle's control levers beneath our personal command.

The **HANDLEBARS**, like the corner bars, are where everything comes together. Their platforms launch all manner of important decisions.

The wide and flat mountain bike handlebar sets the hands farther out and apart, which affords us more leverage, to better navigate the trails. They contrast sharply against the shapely drop bars, which favor aerodynamics and speed. But either of these, like the quaint old genre names they reference, is only a most general term.

Their border splits the romantics away from the intellectuals. Each invariably has its own things to say, of course, but polite society cautions us against making any salad dressing of these differences.

The **CLAMP DIAMETER**, measured across the handlebars' wider mid-sections, corresponds with distinct road and mountain stems. The clamps on older road stems also have half-moons carved from their sides, to allow the passage of the curvaceous dropstyle handlebars. (Newer road stems do not need to bother, of course, because they have the removable face plates.)

Really old bars were sometimes born with a 25.0-millimeter clamp diameter. Soon thereafter, 25.4 became the standard, but only the mountain bars have stayed with it. Well,

most. Someone recently introduced a bar and stem built around 28.6 millimeters.

Road bars moved on to 26.0 and 26.4 clamps some time ago, but just lately a few have joined with some of the snootier mountain bars to regroup around a new 31.7/31.8 standard. These new fat jobs are meant to diminish the minimal flex associated with our simpler handlebars. But this is only so much gold dust, sprinkled upon the precious fruits of Eden. The old bar protocols have already done us fine for decades.

If the handlebar clamp sections have learnt to expand and try different things, their outer lengths have adopted no such courage. These regions have traditionally been under the control of the road and mountain **BRAKE LEVER DIAMETERS**, neither of which will easily be trifled with. The protocols, centered around 24 and 22.2 millimeters respectively, have each enjoyed an impressive mandate. Nearly all the hand control levers ever made have been meant to work with the one or the other; there is no incentive to change a damned thing.

It's usually obvious enough if a given control lever is meant for the flat mountain or curved road bars, based on its profile. The curious new cross levers are more ambiguous in this respect, but we always have our simple litmus test: where it's not possible to fully tighten road levers around mountain bars, the mountain controls do not even fit on to the road bars.

There is a loophole, actually. Mountain controls built around steel clamps enjoy the flexibility needed to hop back and forth. (The road levers usually have steel clamps as well, but each is too wide for the 22.2-millimeter mountain handlebars.) And so we can get the Poor Man's STI, to take one example. It approximates the ergonomic advantages offered by Shimano's famous STI dual control levers, but without their rare but seemingly random propensity toward cataclysmic mechanical failure, by mounting a shift lever just inside and beneath the drop handlebar's brake levers.

The old Shimano Deore thumbshifters are ideal for such purposes, but any levers based on steel clamps will work. The design follows on Suntour's brilliant **COMMAND LEVERS,** which were designed to be installed just inside the levers. STI merely stole and profaned their precious truth. Neither command levers nor thumbshifters worth anything at all have been made for more than a decade, because darkness has come to rule Earth, but they're by no means extinct.

The almighty Suntour Command shift levers

Mountain

The vast majority of handlebars we are likely to come across will subscribe to the narrower 22.2-millimeter mountain lever protocol. It follows that most control levers are also aligned with this clarion mountain standard.

The controls themselves have witnessed a number of breathtaking evolutionary trends, such that it becomes possible to guess if they're older or newer. The eldest among them features steel levers and clamp assemblies, but steel levers have really fallen out of fashion. They still show up on garbage wagons, hidden within chintzy black plastic packaging, but that's about it. Everybody else has long since moved on to aluminum.

The alloy really is our best option, for many of the components. It is light, rigid, and it won't rust out. The original aluminum brake levers were contemporary to the ancient three-speeds, actually. Their simple chromed clamps, expanded to 24 millimeters, later feature on similar drop bar levers.

The old-fashioned aluminum cruiser levers are nearly frail and wispy, comparing to the first generation mountain bike levers that followed. We also started to find barrel adjusters perched atop their snouts, which really simplified our brake adjustments. Developments since have revealed these first examples to be somewhat overbuilt; they may have been happier with the motorcycles.

Shimano and SRAM have both produced various integrated brake and shift lever sets, but it's at least as common that these are attached as individual components. And this is preferable, actually. You don't have to replace the both of them, if only one takes a shit. The real brilliance is that everything so far still manages to coincide with the same handlebar. Those flash old levers from your dusty 1995 Stumpjumper can make the leap to your brand new mountain bike, in other words, but they can just as easily hop back to fit the old steel cruiser.

That said, some of the individual brake and shift levers get along better than others. We see this most clearly with the **GRIP SHIFT LEVERS,** whose relative bulk can sometimes prevent older brake levers from being mounted flush next to them. But this has been getting sorted out as well; most new levers have made the requisite accommodations in their profiles. This detail becomes relevant to the extent that it may impact upon the length of real estate along the handlebars. The wrong combinations of levers, grips, and accessories can render this simple measure as some kind of precious resource.

The bars can only be so long to still be useful. We may even cut them shorter, actually. The aforementioned combo-meal units are one obvious solution to this silly little dilemma, but the control lever clamps themselves have also been becoming narrower. (This excludes the various twist shifters, of course, which in cases have actually grown wider.) The stock bikes have already sorted this out; you only need to recall the point when you're switching things around.

SRAM fixes their brake and shift levers in place with metric screws answering to diminutive 2.5 or 3 millimeter hex wrenches. The handlebar controls are vulnerable to over-tightening; their gesture reminds us to take it easy. Other lever fixing bolts feature sturdier 4- or 5-millimeter faces, but these usually thread in to the aluminum clamp bodies. It's none too difficult to strip these out, if you get all macho on it. You don't need to really reef on anything! Each piece only needs to be tight enough to stay put.

Some SRAM brake levers cannot be fully tightened to the bars. You tighten the screws all the way down; the clamp simply closes all the way around. Fuck. But don't freak out; it's not your fault. Neither is it likely this has been any oversight. The brake levers are fairly vulnerable in crashes; leaving them slightly loose

like this enables them to rotate out of the way of the solid object's impact. Clever, eh?

When mounted on the hybrids and mountain bikes and the like, our brake levers are traditionally set at about 45 degrees to level. Their plane shoots right out over the top of the front wheel, basically. You shouldn't have to bend the wrists up, to pull the brakes. The angle is somewhat steeper, on cruiser bars, to better accommodate their more lateral hand positions. Most of the brake levers also have small screws, mounted to their insides, with which to adjust the lever's reach. These are dialed in, to better fit smaller hands.

We need to dispose of any hand grips, prior to rearranging anything in front of them. Those poor bikes afflicted with foam grips are less of an issue for us here, because these can be slipped off fairly easily, if they haven't fallen apart already. You may have to pop off some plugs at their ends, depending.

The more plush and durable rubber grips are installed and removed in the very same way, at each bike shop I've ever worked at; we use air compressors. The air gun's nozzle is slipped under the grip; you squeeze the trigger and the grip pulls right off. Simple. We then spray the bar and the grip's interior with hairspray to put them back on, because it acts as both a lubricant and a mild adhesive. The grips slip right back up the bars; the air gun comes back in to dry them in place.

You probably don't want to use hairspray, if you don't have an air compressor, precisely because it is so slick. The grips keep wriggling around; they threaten to shoot right off the ends. Don't be using oil for this neither; your grips get loose and stay that way. The home mechanic is better served to use something less synthetic. See if you can't do this with straight water; mix in a bit of soap or degreaser if you need to.

The process becomes easier yet if you're able to deploy the liquid from a spray bottle. Pry up the end of the grip with your small screwdriver; shoot your spray down in to the opening; twist the grip off and away. Rotating them like this makes for little channels underneath, allowing your water to get everywhere it needs to. The process simply reverses itself, putting the grips back on. Again, see if you can get by with water for lubrication, unless you do have an air compressor.

The grips and control levers all move in just a bit, to make room for any **BAR-END EX-TENSIONS**. With the exception of the odd triathlon assemblage, the bar ends will be built around 22.2-millimeter mountain clamp diameters. Control Tech was swell enough to fit brass threadings in to the bases of their bar ends, but most others use mere aluminum throughout; they're also vulnerable to the same ill-considered union of torque and machismo. They only need to become tight enough to stay put, in other words. But it is possible to bring them back to life, once they do strip. Drill the bolt hole all the way through, before retapping its full length to 6 meters. Or, if you have no taps, make plans to mount a nut opposite the bolt head.

We typically leave them sitting just better than level—in line with the stem, perhaps—but it is almost as common to find these pointed straight up, reaching for the sky. Such may stand in for a high-rise stem, to a point, but it leaves the new hand positions further removed from the control levers. Which is too bad, if you have to grab the brakes in a hurry.

Whatever it is you do, you should try to avoid cutting the grips down. We never even think about doing it this way at the shop; every-

thing on the bars is simply edged in towards the stem. The bar ends are meant to provide us with more hand positions; slicing the grips down diminishes upon the very same value. The whole thing makes no sense at all, it's just ridiculous. Any decent mechanic will notice the problem in a heartbeat, as well, so it also diminishes your street cred.

That said, I have found reason to make the occasional cut. The last time may have been with this odd red Schwinn I set up for my friend, Brad, a few years ago. Its bars originally featured bar ends and fairly wide control lever clamps, but they'd also been trimmed down quite a bit; there was no other way around it. And I don't want to be a hypocrite or anything, so I suppose we may grant the occasional exception. But the red Schwinn in question, assuming it has any paint left, is kind of an odd duck.

Only the narrower handlebars may reliably guide you through the tight spots. Slice through the gridlock some night; you'll see what I mean. I'll chop 3 or 4 centimeters from each side, typically. This can be done with the hacksaw, or a pipecutter. The cuts will probably flare out the edges a bit; you may have to file down the results either way.

Road

Anything with a wider 24-millimeter lever diameter is described as a **ROAD BAR.** The traditional drop style bars are only the most obvious examples. The sympathetic and generous road standard is gracious enough to embrace the broad and ungainly spread of the triathlon bars, as well as timeless superstars like the sexy moustache handlebars.

The control levers on any handlebars need to

become just tight enough. Excluding the curious SRAM brake levers mentioned earlier, we tighten everything to the point that nothing is able to move around. The positioning is left to the reader's discretion, needless to say, but the standard arrangements do tend to work out pretty well. The brake levers prefer to sit in a special place, on the drop bars. Line a ruler against the drop bar's lower extension; the very tips of the brake levers should only be able to reach its very edge.

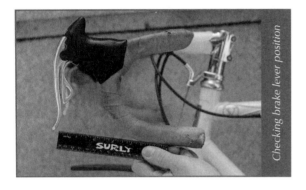
Checking brake lever position

Taping the handlebars can make or break a road bike, in terms of style points, but the act in itself is not so complicated. You only need to know how to do it right. The rolls we get are just barely long enough to tape the full handlebar, most of the time, and everything kind of falls apart if they're not wrapped tightly enough.

You may have already picked out the most righteous, spectacular **GRIP TAPE** to go with your bike. It is ever more the madhouse, with the cork alone. Adding to the swirl come several bright streams of padded vinyl grip tape. The cork is more comfortable, on the hot days especially, but the vinyl is a bit cheaper. Either will feature two additional smaller lengths, meant to wrap around that shadowy region just behind the brake levers, as well as a pair of plugs to fit into the handlebars.

The roads are quite a bit better, back home in Minneapolis—together with so much else,

really—and so I was more able to run with the classic cloth handlebar tape. It lasts for years, if you wrap right, and it also carries the unique tendency to look even cooler as it ages. The fade goes to natural and gets a bit shiny.

Whichever grip you choose, you first want to tie down any cables meant to burrow along underneath, using electrical tape. Those trailing from the bar-end shifters and the aero brake levers typically pass at least some distance beneath the grip tape.

Really old brake lever hoods sometimes dry up and adhere to their levers, but the better ones remain pliable and good. You simply fold their rear sections forward, to install the grip tape beneath them. Go ahead and wrap that small piece of grip tape behind the brake levers, and secure it with more electric tape if you need to, around the lever's body.

You're going to want to pull fairly tight as you wrap, to avoid wrinkles. But do not go excessively tight, because the grip can rip. (Unless, of course, it's the blessed cloth.) And do conserve your resources; overlap only as much as you need to. Women's handlebars are often a bit smaller; the overlap can be too generous.

For reasons of curious circumstance, I only learned to wrap correctly later in life, down at Freewheel in San Francisco. My friend Jon Londres hipped me to the righteous methods. You want to start by leaving a good centimeter of tape hanging all the way around the end of the bar, to start. This is bent forward and pushed in by the plugs, once you finish, to provide them the purchase they need to stay put.

The tape needs to wrap in a particular direction. It should loop from the outsides over to the insides of the bar, starting down at the base, such that the two sides' trailing edges form an arrow pointing forward. This affords us a solid foundation for the pattern up top, where the wrap's direction is more crucial.

Imagine the rolling motion the hands make on the bars, as you stand up and charge the hill: the grip tape can either be aligned with this force, or set against it. The hands either chafe against the grip tapes' edges, encouraging them to unravel, or they seamlessly traverse across its surface. Where you wrap towards the bike, across the lower reaches, you wrap back towards the rider along the top.

The brake levers are the drop bars' transfer stations, moving us from one plane to the next. These were traditionally wrapped in a figure-eight, to cover all the negative space, but advancements in lever hood design have really been rendering this obsolete.

This is especially true with Campagnolo's dual control levers, which need a little more breathing room than their peers. The hoods on their Ergopower levers feature small square hooks at their bases, which coincide with matching openings on the levers, and these need to be free to make a connection. Their union marks a small but meaningful frontier, beyond which the clumsy grip tape is not allowed to pass. The hood otherwise interferes with the shifting action, basically.

Control Cables

Having considered the handlebars, our next logical step is to discuss the cables. They are the faithful lieutenants, explaining our divergent whims to the disciplined parts array gathered hereafter. But they do hold something of a veto, in this respect. Not much of anything is going to happen, if they don't want it to.

Barring again the odd relic, the components will answer to one of three distinct sorts of cables. The shift levers go for one style, and the road and mountain brake levers each have their own.

The **DERAILLEUR CABLE**, being the thinnest, also shows up with the smallest head—little pinhead derailleur cable. But that's cool; its task is considerably less stressful than braking. The svelte dimensions also allow for greater imagination in the design of our shift levers. And these, like their cables, do not need to be overbuilt.

Italian component manufacturer Campagnolo decided the heads could be smaller yet, in fact, by .3 millimeters or thereabouts. And so while their cables work for anybody's shift levers, only their own work for their equipment. And the cables themselves are also some microns wider, at the very same time, so it's best to use some of their shift cable housing as well. Regular cable heads will get stuck in Campy parts, like boots in cement. You have to drill them out.

Famous Minneapolis wholesaler Quality Bicycle Products provides us with a decent but inexpensive Campagnolo-sized cable, fortunately, so you don't need to head to Italy or anywhere. Unless you want to, I guess. Q's version features two heads; Campagnolo's is stamped with a telling "C." You chop off the end you're not using, and just chuck it in the fire pit.

So long as we're on the point, it should be mentioned that SRAM shift cables are allegedly some microns thinner than their garden variety competitors. You notice that they're far more flexible, as well. But the cable heads are of their usual dimensions, so these can't fill in with the Campagnolo goods. I'm quite sure they're the best for SRAM shift levers, but in truth I've never had any troubles using those pulled from the garden. I hadn't even been hip to the distinction actually, until Travis pointed it out up at Freewheel.

The **ROAD BRAKE CABLES** bear heads roughly similar to those we find on the derailleur cables, but with a second wider section extending above the first. They may even be accepted in to some of the simpler shift levers, in a pinch, but they need to provide for their own housing as well. The modern shifter cable housing is too narrow to fit them. But we should stay focused, their central business is with the road brake levers.

Here again, Campagnolo has insisted on making brake cables just slightly too pretentious to coincide with the norms, only this time the dispute is with the cable housing. So they need their own, once again, all special. If the action on your modern Campagnolo brakes seems stiffer than perhaps it should be, make sure that Campagnolo cables and housing are used throughout.

We need to find a stout bar, pivoting across the typical road brake lever's interior, upon which to rest the cable's weary head. The pivoting is crucial; it allows the cable head to maintain a constant orientation as the lever is squeezed.

Those pivoting pillows featuring within Shimano STI dual control levers are slightly more complicated. Each end of the diminutive cable head rest is capped with a pair of even tinier plastic washers, to provide for a more fluid range of motion, and the cable head itself is trusted to hold all of this in place. And the plan works out well enough, on the road, but you want to keep an eye out during cable changes: the pivot assembly is only slotted into its position on the brake lever, and it jumps out of place pretty easily, once the cable's guidance is withdrawn.

Tracking down the four tiny washers is often

difficult enough, but convincing the pivot assembly to crawl back into its cave can be a royal pain in the ass. You're best to install it independently of the cable, in those circumstances, but it's even smoother to avoid all this hassle in the first place.

Nudge the cable's tail slightly forward in the housing, such that its head slips out of the pivot. You may need to get in there with a small pick or screwdriver, to lift the head clear of the STI shifting hardware, but as often as not it's done as much on its own. This done, put a finger atop the pivot assembly, and hold it right there as you pull the old cable free. And here again, we prove ourselves swifter than the blasted machines.

The floating bars found in various older road brake levers may have small slots for the cables, to simplify their installation. Only one side of the bar is drilled wide enough to accept the cable head; you may rotate it around with a small screwdriver to see this better. It may also be useful to put some light behind the lever, because the cable must shoot out through a tiny cable-sized hole in back. The hole needs to be small enough to prevent the cable's housing from charging back through; back-lighting the situation is often the easiest way to find it.

We will arrive upon the cable housing shortly, but circumstance advises a timely disclaimer! *It is important the cable housing entering an aero brake lever ends does not try to sneak in to this hole.* Its plastic sheathing will get hung up on the edge, while the more ambitious metal coil seeks to surge ahead, and the brakes will start feeling all spongy and crappy in consequence.

A majority of the more recent brake levers have considered this, keeping the hole small enough to fend off anything wider than the brake cable itself. And you don't want to sneak a cable-housing cap in to such situations, actually, because it may get stuck up in there, which sucks, if ever it is bent out of form. But the old Dia Compe Blaze levers, together with various others, are better served by using a wider brake-specific cable-housing ferrule. It's best to scope things out, before you make any decisions. Take one of the levers off for a second; see what it looks like in there.

The **MOUNTAIN BRAKE CABLES**, also found with many older cruisers and three-speeds, are different. Their heads lay flat, in plane with the cable, such that we see tiny metal lollipops. Their levers, of course, bear corresponding openings. And, if they're reasonably modern, they also feature small slots to simplify the cable's installation. Such channels tend to slice right through the barrel adjusters, as well; you line it up like a combination lock. But some of the oldest levers don't hear anything about this; you may have to go in and feed the cable through from behind.

We cut cables just a few centimeters past their attachment points, at work, but I tend to leave my own a bit longer. It encourages their reuse. Most of our cable cutters also make provisions to crimp **CABLE FERRULES** to their jagged new ends. The jaws do their slashing just outside the tool's pivot; you crimp where the arms cross just inside this point. Some cutters even have a pair of slight indents on the arms here, suggesting crimpage. But the armpit of some nice long pliers delivers an even better effect; the whole end section is pressed uniformly flat.

Some suggest you're also suppose to crimp the stainless steel caps meant for the wider-style 5-millimeter cable housing as well, but I don't bother. Crimping bends these all out of shape; they lose interest in rolling with our barrel adjusters. Cable housing by definition is plugged in to something or another, and not

likely to fray; the wee caps can easily be re-used if they're left unmolested. There's some tiny chance you can maybe damage the housing this way, if cables are somehow made completely slack and then suddenly jammed back together. But to my experience this is one of those situations where you really have to try to fuck it up. So relax, you'll do fine.

The cables are secured to their brakes and derailleurs by means of the **BINDER BOLTS**, which clamp fairly specific washers in specific positions to points along the component's hard metal exoskeleton. They're meant to work as a package with the part; the shapes fit to each other in particular.

You notice, peering into their embrace, that at least one side features a telling cable-sized groove. This is where you want to go. The cable may want to spring out of position; pull it taught to hold it in place. The detail takes all of a few seconds' concentration, but it's a judicious use of your time. We expect the cable's individual wire strands to gradually snap and begin to fray, in less exacting circumstances. The little grooves prevent our cables from being crushed flat, basically. But I will never be native to California, so I will refrain from describing their station as *groovy*.

The **CABLE-HOUSING** sections may bend or crack, over time, and so we often change them out with the cables. The bikes need distinct sorts of housing, for brake and shift cables. Make sure you grab the right stuff, especially with the brakes.

Cable binder bolt

Either sort proceeds from a roughly similar plan—some wire is encased in plastic; with a thinner plastic straw also running along the inside—but where the shift housing is comprised of long strands, the brake cable housing is wrapped as a coil. The one provides for a predictable, compression-less base for the increasingly strident indexed shifting systems; the other is able to manage the occasional panic-yank on the brake levers.

We expect a shift lever set up with brake housing to be marginally more fuzzy, with 9- or 10-speed systems in particular. And this is precisely the point of modern compression-less shifter cable housing; it is better able to hold a pose. You can often see the wrap of the wire, on brake housing, and the shift housing is also much stiffer.

You may suddenly be reminded of the distinction, if you are to pass over it here. The act of pulling the brake lever shoots a strident jolt of pressure down the line, which makes the shift housing literally *splinter*. The outer plastic cracks; the wires splay out in every direction. It's a spectacular little problem. You will be inspired to avoid it in the future.

The coolest cable housing of all time is the old-fashioned stainless steel. It is one simple coil, which is not sealed. We can oil it by osmosis, in fact. Run an oil dropper along the length; the juice soaks right in. A local wholesaler was once blowing out meter-long sections of this real cheap, made by Campagnolo no less, and I still have a couple lengths kicking around. But it compresses like an accordion box; the 9-speed drivetrains and mechanical disc brakes have long since stomped all over any such spontaneity.

The cables and their housing interact with the frame through the **CABLE-HOUSING STOPS**, which direct each along its own particular course. They let the housing in one end, and block it from exiting the other. Only the cable itself gets through.

Oiling by osmosis

A frame may also sport cable guides or cable-housing guides, which are fully wide enough to pass either the one or the other. We usually spy some cable guides under the bottom bracket shell, for example.

The plan seems to work out well enough, but I know of at least two recumbent manufacturers who have instead gone with the clumsy garbage wagon formula, using plastic ties to bind full lengths of cable housing to the frame. The effect is gracelessly efficient—as with the plastic pocket protectors—but it, too, has a logic all its own. The full-length cable housing is completely sealed; the corrosion and grit is considerably slower in arriving.

A good number of hybrids and mountain bikes are coming out of the void with their shifter cables in less than ideal routes. It's not so much whether they run across the top tube or under the down tube—cables stay cleaner up top, dragging through the dirt down below represents the romantic retro approach—because, in either case, the designers can be counted upon to favor straight lines over straighter routing.

Of the two or three cable-housing stops featuring toward the front of the frame, each shift cable traces reflexively to the one closest: right side to right, left to left. Which is fine, obviously, as it works. But it works better if you cross the right (rear) shifter's cable to the frame's left-side cable stop and vice versa. This means you make an "X" where the two cables cross on their paths to the rear. Looks nice and odd; makes not the slightest difference in performance.

"X" means this will not work on bikes with their cables zipped to the sides of the frame; you'll just scuff your paint all to hell. Sorry. It works well on many road bikes with downtube cable guides; less so with the first-generation mountain bikes. And you want to switch this, if you can, because the stock cable routing tends to put an extra bend in the housing. The section needs to be of a certain length, to allow a full rotation of the handlebars; the slack doubles up back by the frame.

Ride in the elements long enough, and you gather rust at the low point in this bend, which slows the cables in their important work. You can just oil the housing and be done with it. But if you're going that far you may as well cross your cables. You may need to replace the housing sections with something an inch longer. And, if you don't leave enough slack off the tail ends, their cables as well.

While we're on the topic of cable routing, Klein and a few other manufacturers have taken to tucking their shift cables up inside their frames' down tubes, as means to look cool perhaps, but the effort can too easily cause you some trouble.

If your bike presents some convoluted difficulty in displaying its control cables, you need to sit down and have a talk. Maybe it's time the bike just went fixed gear or something. In every other situation, the two of you should be able to just lay that business out in the sunshine.

We can forgive Klein and these other vain pretenders by thinking they were humbly taking our interests to heart, hiding the cables away from all the filth underfoot, but it actually may not be so simple. The campaign literature associated with Shimano shifting systems, for example, reliably warns against this type of subterfuge. Their concern, that the cables' reflexes may be slowed, is somewhat more incidental—any cabling system may slow, given the opportunity—but the real threat is more dramatic. If ever the cables are allowed to fully escape, they may never be convinced to return.

The sleek manufacturers drill pairs of pinholes in the outsized tube, and the blind cable does not easily find the second in their series. There is only one way around this tiresome dilemma, which is a length of thin plastic straw, known as cable liner, stretching from start to finish.

The more enterprising frames have already attended to this consideration, but not everyone is so cool. You need to make extra-special *certain* the liner is in place. You should be able to tug it up around the cable at one end, and watch its other end sneak up down below. It's like one long tube of spaghetti.

Shops can hook you up, if the frame is too square to think of it. Make sure you snag something long enough! It sneaks up from the cable from its back end, of course, because the cable head is buried up in the control lever.

Stainless cables can last for a really long time. The housing, which is usually mere galvanized steel, rusts sooner. When you do replace a cable, it's best to first make sure it doesn't have any sharp bends, especially those stretches where it passes through the housing. But this is an obvious point; it's like trying to force a triangle through a tube.

Cables do get roughhoused now and again; older and poorly routed cable housing tends to create such kinks over time. You just grab the cable with your pliers, right next to the problem, and bend it straight again. Not a big deal. Sharp kinks are often added to the cables just past the component binder bolts, as a matter of fact, to route their tails away from any dangerous moving parts.

The more you work on cables, the more you will pick up their other concerns. The linear wires inside the shifter housing, for example, seem to grow over time. The ends stick out, suggesting haircuts. But neither is this any big deal; you just snip the ends off. Reopen the plastic inner lining with your pick, and put things back together.

It is crucial that cable housing is long enough to do the job. It should not have to bind or stretch at any point in the handlebars' rotation. Things get fucked up, quickly. But neither does it need to be too long; this encourages a temptation to snag on railings and branches and the like. You're aiming for that mid point, within like a few centimeters, anyway. It is better if the housing is just a little too long; you should err on the side of caution.

Odds are best you can simply replicate the original length of housing on stock bikes. Failing that, you only need to figure out just where the control lever in question is going to end up, and you can measure from there. Stretch some housing from the mouth of its barrel adjuster to the first cable-housing stop it encounters on the frame, and make sure there is *just* enough slack to fully rotate the bars.

The cable housing length becomes an issue when we change out the handlebars or the stem. A switch to a high-rise stem, for example, renders them all just a bit short. You need to replace the cables themselves—the longer

ones, at least—but there may be things we can do for the housing situation. Do you see any loose brake noodles lying about? These trim metal straws are most often associated with the V brakes, as described on page 87, but they may fill in here as well. (These sorts of noodles are relatively spendy; it doesn't make sense to buy new ones for this.) The housing slides right down into the back, once you dispose of any cable-housing caps, and the noodle's pointy nose plugs right into the cable stop or barrel adjuster you're heading for. The fit becomes marginally more precise if you pull the press-fit nose off first, with your box pliers.

We may also noodle together two distinct pieces of cable housing, to make for one long piece. The industry provides us with cute little housing bridges, which look like two housing caps locked in an embrace, but discarded brake noodles grow from the corners of just about any bike shop. They may be made straighter, with a little effort, but their gracious curves will just as often coincide with their own cabling imperatives. Our extension merely removes the nose cone from a first noodle, to replace it with the tail section from a second. The cable simply jogs through the trim metal bridge, moving from one housing situation to another.

This particular wire transfer is not too interesting in modern America—we should always have enough cable housing and everything else—but it may be more useful, when and where this is not the case. It is the double-ended noodle cable housing extender (D. E. N. C. H. E.). Let's call them **CABLE DONKEYS**. They carry from one place to another.

SRAM brake noodles bury a small aluminum ring inside the chintzy plastic end caps they insist on using. I'm not sure why; the plastic end piece still breaks. (You have to pull this ring off to make a proper cable donkey. This happens the same way, with pliers.) The thing that can be said for SRAM's infernal plastic noodle noses is that they make releasing the cable somewhat easier. And I will assume this was their reasoning, because *nobody* wants to piss off the mechanics.

We have also been presented with various **SOOTHING CABLE PALLIATIVES**. Ride On and others have inserted a plastic liner between cable and housing; many more have been the various Teflon cables. Or, if you're feeling really odd—a little rich and eccentric, perhaps—you may invest in hydraulic brakes, or even electronic shifting.

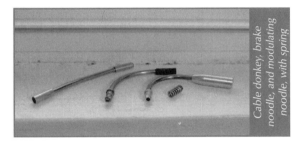

Cable donkey; brake noodle, and modulating noodle, with spring

I know absolutely nothing about electronic shifting systems. I would have to be thoroughly disinclined to explore the topic. But I have had to learn about hydraulics; we'll deal with those in a little while. The other specialty cable systems strike me as an economic phenomenon. *People will buy them!* But there is no need to powder the cables, let alone shrink-wrap them. Give 'em what they want, which is oil.

I am a big fan of reusing cables. I habitually spool up the useful remains of any stainless cables I am replacing, provided the time and opportunity. What can I tell you? It saves us some money. The shortened cables are probably still long enough for your front derailleurs or brakes. Not only that, but they're all done stretching out. Modern control cables tend to be prepared pretty thoroughly, but this was not always the case. Reuse simply removes the variable.

The only complication to this is putting the clipped cables back in. You need to make sure they don't fray. So you twist the hell out of them, continuously, in the direction they are wound. As with larger events, we hope that petty and self-indulgent drama may be avoided by referencing the larger and more immutable context. Can you feel me here? The fragile wires will not have any more time to become distracted, once they're spun fast enough.

I was somewhat disappointed with some of the newer SRAM shift levers, at first, because for once this trick did not seem to work. But I discovered that you really just need to twist the *hell* out of them. The cables are suddenly asked to bend through some pretty unlikely angles, in these ungainly new devices. And so we need to both increase the RPMs and ease off the pressure. The cable spins easily across your fingertips, but it also happens you're gradually nudging it forward as well.

Any sharper bends in components or housing can make cable reuse more difficult. Our best response is to redouble our efforts. I first want to see if any bends in the housing can be temporarily straightened, of course. (Some partial disassembly can quicken the cables into older SRAM shift levers, but this same task becomes far more arduous with some of the new jobs. The question is further explored on page 113.)

The short segment flattened by the cable's binder bolt should not end up inside any cable housing. There would be too much friction! Cables troubled by grit or corrosion can often be rescued with a bit of lightweight oil. Drip some on the rag; squeeze the cable through a few times. Check out the rag once you're done; the oil pulls that shit right off. Stainless steel cables are always likely candidates, but zinc cables sometimes become burdened with too much corrosion to deal with.

9: Brakes

The brakes step in to calm things down, when speed becomes an issue, by one means or another.

Everybody should have the options afforded by quality gear. Good bikes should not be any kind of privilege; it is antithetical to their very nature. But the point becomes a thorn in the industry's side, unfortunately, because it spawns many of our endless contradictions. Cheap bikes and parts are the easiest to sell, but in the end they're only a reactionary tendency, a function of cheap gasoline, which, of course, only makes them all the more fragile. Their bottom-feeder tendencies take a terminally short-sighted view of what we presume to call natural resources, and reinforces the same tired and wasted hierarchy.

Do yourself a favor, in the meantime, and see if you can pick up a good bike with good parts. *You're better to get a decent used bike instead of a cheaper new one.* The same point rings through all the more emphatically whenever suspension technology becomes involved. I must tell you, as your friendly mechanic, to either get the good stuff or get used to walking.

The precautionary principle advises us to begin with the **BRAKES.** There are a few distinct qualities that may fill out good braking performance. A worthy brake can be reasonably expected to stop quickly, effectively, silently, and with minimum effort. We may even ask them to be simple, durable, and relatively lightweight, as well. None of this makes for unreasonable requests, considering the available technology.

We like the brakes to jump back from the rims, just as soon as they're done, lest the pads become a drag. The brakes rely upon some springs for such purposes, whose tension soon emerges as a major theme. And it is further expected—by most performance riders, at least—that brakes do not feel too spongy. Brake cables are commonly found to be a bit looser than we may like them to be, for reasons we'll soon explore; any surplus in lever flex is simply asking for trouble. Our ground rule is that the lever should not be able to bottom out on the handlebar. Brake flex is largely a function of the materials used in construction, together with design imperatives, but cable lubrication can be just as important. Cables that stick along their housing encourage the brakes to flex.

The appearance of hydraulics, incidentally, has put the bike industry in the habit of saying "mechanical" when they mean "cable driven." That's all mechanical means, with bicycle brakes. Cables. The effort suggests we're due some discretion in selecting a nickname for the hydraulics. Fair is fair, right?

My principle concern, as the mechanic, is foremost with the brake's stopping power. It is the crucial, on-the-ground, real-time evidence of stunning success or abysmal failure. But it is another consideration, only casually related to this, that usually grabs the headlines. Let us all gather together and heap every curse and hex upon the real bitter-enders, the **SQUEAKY BRAKES.**

The infernal wail is our most flamboyant nemesis. We hear about brakes that squeak sooner than we hear about brakes that don't work, for the most part. Those braking systems that don't stop as well tend to be older. They may be suffering from one of a few basic problems. Every point at which metal crosses metal should enjoy both an absence of grit and just enough lube, for one thing; dropping a bit of oil in to the pivot points will often help things along. But this is only part of it. The brake squeak, like the frame creak, can too easily become a pointedly elusive prey.

The pads sweep the rims clean, in the course of their duties, and this eventually covers their faces with a layer of hard and shiny debris. It is pressed flat, and ground in to place. The sum of this works away between pad and rim, slowly and methodically wearing away at the both of them, and eventually the brakes wail out as the process continues. And when we hear the dreaded squeak, it means it's time to clean up.

To put it more precisely, both the accumulation of roadside debris and the structural vibrations inherent to some of the more wispy design prerogatives can cause the rapid chattering we hear as squealing brakes. We may even anticipate the foul influence either villain may impose, considering their leavings so far: the front brakes, less well-buttressed than their backward compatriots, have traditionally been somewhat noisier as well. The cleaner and more rigid a given brake is, in other words, the less you'll be likely to hear anything about it.

The horrible truth is that riding the bike makes the brakes squeak. Coaster brakes, drum brakes, and the fixes provide some alternatives, but a fair range of the elements make our rim-mounted brakes scream their heads off—rain, snow, mud, dirt, dust, etc. Even the famous trophy bike, precociously reserved for use on those absolutely perfect days, will in time surrender its nubile pads to the ravages of time. I've not made it through so many decades myself, but I notice those brake pads that have tend to be pretty well toast; hardened and dried-out into little rubber rocks.

Some pads and brake systems will whine less than others. But life is like that. The blessed silence may only arrive at the expense of braking power, in some cases at least. Road brake calipers squeak very rarely, for example, but they are not as powerful as V brakes, whose more ambitious designs leave them vulnerable to miniature vibrations. This steady current, also known as "chatter," can make for some noise. And the cantilevers, as well, are somewhat more exposed in this respect. With their power comes responsibility.

The pad's positions in relation to the rim they face are also important. Brakes will often feature some method for adjusting the pad angles, for precisely such reasons. I really wish I could spell out a simple, brilliant rule to explain away the squeaks and their solutions, but I'm not sure that's possible. The question is random, not linear.

The aforementioned road grit presents the most immediate concern. It is the first thing I look for. You want to clean up the rims and file down the pads.

This may be done with the wheels still on the bike, but I tend to drop them out and do it in a truing stand. The wheel's trueness inevitably confronts any rim-mounted brakes; you may as well check the true while you're at it. It's also best to avoid hitting the brake pads with liquid cleaner, as this will complicate their own treatment.

The rims are best cleaned with rubbing alcohol, because it tends to be very thorough. You can also use a citrus solvent or something similar, failing this. Anything short of oils! And of course it's always good to brush away any dried-up crap on the rims, in advance of spraying them. Just clear it out with a dry rag. The less crap that remains on the rims, the less likely the brakes are to squeak.

Every once in a great while we come across some serious hard case, where the brakes still squeak after both rim and pads have been thoroughly dealt with, and this is the only occasion when I've even considered **SANDING RIMS**. The task is kind of a pain in the ass; it's not something we just go and do for shits and giggles.

You need to take off the tire to sand down a rim. Sanding the tire down does not make a whole lot of sense. Steel rims are chromed or painted; it does no good to sand them either. It's just the aluminum we're talking about.

There was a time when I would habitually sand down a bike's rims if the horrible squeaking survived the most rudimentary pad-filing process, just as a means to shut it the hell up, but I've since learnt better. The fine aluminum dust released by sanding rims can itself make the brakes cry out in alarm. I sooner file the pads more completely, these days, because it is much easier. You take them off, clamp the post in a vise, and shave the faces smooth. Or, if you're lacking in vises, lay a file on your bench and run the pads across that.

You can just leave the pads mounted, of course, but it's better to drop them out for a minute. The lighting is much better; you

can do a more thorough job. And you can get away with using a coarser metal-working file, rather than the harsh wood-working file, which spares your pads some extra wear. You only scrape until the shiny buildup is gone. Whichever the case, this is no filing competition.

Wintertime is like a bike's final exams. Those that pull through earn our warmest thanks. Great volumes of snow mixed with equally ridiculous measures of salt and sand and their sum presents mighty challenges for the **BRAKE PADS.**

The pads work best when their surfaces and the rims they face are clean and dry, but these circumstances cannot be maintained through the salt and snow, and even during the melting of it all. The reality is that the time you spend one day is wasted with the next. The pads squeak, at the very least, and their power may fade at times.

Our frozen elements also encourage the pads to wear a lot faster. You can expect to replace them every spring, at the least, riding freewheeled bikes. I was inclined to stretch them as long as I could, back in the day, but you really don't want to push it. All the brake pads are grounded in metal, one way or another, so it does you no good at all to be carving up the rims.

The old Matthauser pads may have been the best, but they are getting hard to find. The Kool Stop pads will probably be the next most natural choice, in terms of stopping effectiveness, but as with the Matthausers, they're also more inclined to make some noise. I've worked the most with these and the Shimano brake pads, both of which have become fairly ubiquitous, and my experiences suggest an inverse relationship between the two. The harder pad compounds used by manufacturers like Shimano and Tektro tend to make less noise; the soft compounds associated with others from Kool Stop and Matthauser are often slightly more effective. This is especially true with linear pull brakes, and to a lesser extent with the cantilevers. But there are lots of pads on the market; your riding circumstances may indicate distinct suggestions.

If you are going through a lot of pads, you should be using the cartridges. Various cartridge brake pads are available from a number of manufacturers, for each of the braking systems. They're an elegant option in any application, and over the long haul they're good and cheap. The expired pads can be pulled out with pliers or pried away with screwdrivers. The new ones should slide most of the way in on their own. You press any remainder in place with some help from the surface of your bench or something like it, jamming the pad straight down in to it. Cartridge pads are directional; you want to make sure they're correctly oriented to the rim. There are right and left pads, in other words; they should be marked as such.

Modern rim-mounted brakes feature vertical windows for pad adjustments. The pad's rigid metal spine cautiously pokes its way through, whereby it is thrilled to discover it can fully slide up and down, to better meet the rim. All the excitement allows for a broader range of possible deployments, which eases things up in terms of our design specifications.

Each different braking system most often insists on using its own particular pads. Cantilever brakes want pads with smooth posts; V brakes ask for pads with threaded posts with stacks of washers; road calipers tend to favor either bolts or short threaded posts. We can usually convince the road brakes to accept V brake pads, if the washers get moved

around, but that's really about as crazy as we can get. Whichever sort of pad you're installing, you'll find its adjustments that much easier if you take a second to grease the hardware. Just dab a tiny drop into the tightening nuts on linear pull or road brake pads, or on the arm's tightening nut with cantilevers. Go easy though; it does you no good at all to get any grease on the braking surfaces.

The arrangements allow us to set the pads precisely in line with the rims, which is cool, because we don't want them charging up the tires or diving in to the spokes. Most systems also let us consider the pads' angles, in one way or another, and this becomes almost as useful. A good angle can eliminate squeaks by enlisting the wheel's very rotational force to drag the brake pad faces better in line with the rims. We call it the pad's **TOE-IN**. Imagine a dime wedged between the rim and the pad's tail; that's what you're shooting for.

A slight reverse toe may quiet things down, where a regular one failed to do so, but this is less than ideal, because the reversal will effectively work against the braking performance as well. Squeaks that survive the original cleaning and toe-in regimen may be better served by a more thorough pad-filing process, a more extreme toe angle, or even new brake pads, before we even get to talking about sanding down the damned rims.

Linear and cantilever braking systems enjoy the most elaborate toe-in hardware, as we'll see, because the issue is more critical with these systems. Some better road brake pads are now coming with similar kits, but the traditional method for road brake toe-in was to bend the arm a bit with a big wrench. I shit you not. Rough, in the old days.

Sidepulls

Our original screaming momentum first ended with the **SIDEPULLS**, also known as the caliper brakes. Other, more ambitious systems have since arrived on the scene, but none have yet become as svelte in their dimensions.

The name comes from the cable; from the way both arms reach over to meet it. The cable shoots down one side, dealing with each in turn, pulling them together in a tight smile. The arms pivot on a bolt above the tire; a spring of some sort holds them tensioned against each other.

Sidepulls have been with us for a very long time, and every opportunity has been taken to refine and profane each feature of their design. The arms have been both lengthened and shortened; brake-centering methods have been refined; the fixing bolt has ducked back into the frame. But their essential program remains blessedly straight forward; the biggest complication may only be in finding the right one for your bike.

The pinnacle in sidepull design has come with the dual pivots, as first popularized by Shimano. The name says exactly what it means; the pivot splits in two parts. And you can tell, looking down from above, because the brake suddenly features three distinct pieces. The dual pivots are the only sidepulls spec'd on new bikes, for the American market at least. They really are that cool; they offer so much more bang for the buck.

Anchoring a brake in one location directly above the tire is not the most impressive plan, considering what we've learned since, but the dual pivot sidepulls suck it in and make the most of things. Kind of heroic, really. They do tend to be both more burly and compact than earlier renditions; there comes less opportunity for flex and play. They just do the job, and that's it.

At the far, opposite end of this spectrum lurks the sidepull's worst case scenario, the oversized generic steel monstrosity. Years ago, before corrupting both cantilevers and V brakes, department store garbage wagons afflicted some "mountain" and "BMX" bikes with the most evil sidepulls in the history of the world. They are heavy and flexy as all hell, only grudgingly adjustable, and barely functional in the first place. Paired with junk steel rims, as was usually the case, they can only further suggest an especially shady cynicism on the part of the manufacturers. The distance between these and those brakes found on our modern road bikes is measured in all the things we have ever learned on the subject.

Sidepulls were previously asked to answer to a good range of wheels, including those found on wide-tired mountain bikes. This necessarily renders some of their lot both bow-legged and relatively delicate. But cantilever brakes soon entered the picture, sweeping away all the better mountain bikes, and the sidepulls were left with the luxury of focusing only on-the-road bikes. And so their arms grew shorter, to better grasp their newly refined responsibilities.

The distance from the rims to the frame or fork's brake mounting hole has varied considerably, over the years, and the sidepulls have accounted for this in a couple different ways. As with their peers, the sidepulls provide tall windows for the pads to settle in to, but the brakes themselves have also been made in different sizes.

The measurement is known as **BRAKE REACH.** It describes the distance from the mounting bolt to the spread of available pad positions down on the arms. Older frames tend to require longer sidepulls; more modern examples are clustered around the shorter versions. Most of Shimano's sidepulls claim a reach of 39 to 49 millimeters, but they have a couple longer ones. Tektro comes in with 47- to 57-millimeter reach brakes, as well as a 53- to 71-millimeter pair and even a 61- to 78-millimeter.

The newer sidepulls also have **RECESSED BRAKE NUTS**. The old centerpull brakes and the original sidepulls all shared an earlier standard; their 6-millimeter mounting bolts were capped with the expected 10-millimeter hex nuts.

But the new method shoots the fixing nut right down in the back of the fork crown instead. (The brake bolt's exit hole is drilled out just a bit wider, to let this happen.) Road frames and forks have been thusly drilled for a decade or two already, so this is one of those things we kind of have to get used to. As with the brake reach, a particular caliper's mounting protocol is only something you need to recall when switching parts around.

The older non-recessed brakes can still be made to work on the new frames, assuming the arms are of a correct length. They only stick out a bit. You can also bring an older frame or fork up to date, with a drill bit just a hair wider than the recessed nut. Leave the front hole alone! Drilling straight through will do no good at all.

Whatever it is you find yourself doing, the brake needs to be really tight against the frame. A loose brake will end up dragging one of its pads on the rim, as would one that's been tightened at an odd angle.

Do me a favor, though? *Double-check the wheel's centering, before the brake centering*

adjustment. I swear that maybe a fifth of all brake-centering scenarios are quickly resolved this way, by correctly aligning the wheels within its frame. And they should always line up, right down the center. Problems here indicate either incorrect wheel dish or a poorly aligned frame.

Old and cheap sidepulls lack any dedicated brake-centering technology. The best way I know to center these is to make sure the brake is mounted tightly; grip both fixtures topping the bolt and the fixing nut out back with the appropriate wrenches; and turn them simultaneously. Slowly, it doesn't take much.

Better sidepulls incorporate thin wrench flats, just before the bolt enters to the frame or fork. They measure 10, 11, 12, or 13 millimeters, depending upon manufacturer. Or maybe 14 millimeters, if they're old Modolo. And I think someone used 15 millimeters as well, now that I think about it. The thin hub cone wrenches appear to be ideal for their adjustments, but these flats will typically be cut straight vertical; the headset cups preclude their use. (We can use these by removing the wheel and entering from beneath, but this gets tedious.) The sidepull flats are best accessed with offset brake wrenches.

Mafac Racer centerpull brake

The original sidepulls were built in easily recognizable patterns. The bolt was fixed with a slotted round block, with which to support a stout wire wishbone, bearing sturdy curly-cues to either shoulder. The two arms laid themselves atop this, but with thin washers set between each piece, to reduce their friction. And topping the deck, of course, we found a pair of nuts. These were counter-tightened directly against each other, just before the arms began to bind. Popping one end of the spring out and stretching it some has the effect of putting more zap in your brakes.

The dual pivots use distinct brake-centering methods. A small bolt is set to the top of one shoulder, to better translate our aspirations down to the brake spring. These things tend to be stubborn, like most other brake-centering bolts, and therefore anxious to strip: press down hard, and work slowly. And do use the right tool; most likely a full-sized Phillips screwdriver. The brake will carefully, grudgingly shift this way and that as you go.

Campagnolo dual pivot calipers feature small bolts set in to either shoulder, each of which answers to a 2-millimeter Allen key. That appearing on the cable side governs the spring tension; its opposite concerns itself with the brake's centering. Or there may be slots for a 15-millimeter wrench, depending.

Again, it never hurts to drop a bit of oil in the mix, whichever of these you're using. When time permits, I take the whole thing apart and clean the pieces individually. A brake that's been through a winter or two likely yearns for such attention. There's probably grit way down in the seams; our solvent bath doesn't really get to it. Upon re-assembly, keep in mind that there should never be lateral play along the length of sidepull's pivot(s). The best adjustment would leave them with just enough freedom to smile and frown at their leisure.

Centerpulls

The **CENTERPULL BRAKES** epitomize the dusty old ten-speeds. They mount in the same holes we use for the sidepull calipers, but none of the centerpulls were ever spec'd with recessed mounting nuts. Hell, I've known some to lack even the nylock inserts. Centerpulls have fairly long arms as well; everything about them kind of dates to an earlier period.

Some of the very first mountain bikes used something similar, more properly described as the **U BRAKE.** These were mounted in back, under the chainstays. The U's arms crossed each other, to meet a cable hanger and its straddle cable in the middle. The action ended up becoming similar to what we'd seen with the old road centerpulls, which is to say that other braking systems would be lighter and more efficient. The U brakes kind of dropped off the face, many years ago.

GT was long alone among the major manufacturers, prior to their final debasement by Pacific Bicycles, in that they refused to give it up. As with the triple-triangle trip, the design was only more flash for the hard-rockers. But either of these features could have fulfilled the bike industry equivalent of "sportin' a mullet;" the display might have marked the outfit as more of a target.

The only advantage the U brakes ever had was in their svelte profile—for a boss-mounted system, at least—but the linear pull brakes have long since strolled away with even this minor glory. Mountain bike geometry no longer affords the longish chainstays the U's had originally clung to, but some of the BMX bikes do. The effort leaves the frame's upper platform free to support your foot, as you twirl around with awesome new tricks. It's about the only place we find them now.

The U brake's maintenance is fairly straight-forward. Those mounted down on the chain-stays get showered with a lot more mud; you want to keep a close eye on their sanitary needs. The pads borrow mounting ideas from other systems; the cabling method mimics a cantilever straddle.

The whole premise was fucked in the first place, unfortunately, because the original centerpull brakes were themselves not all they might have been. They can work, but the design absorbs and misplaces some of our energy. It allows for an unfortunate degree of flex.

A cable-housing stop of some kind suspends a straddle cable in a carrier, in the case of our originals; the brake arms cross each other to meet it. We're able to contrast against the smart dual pivot calipers, and the centerpull's humble arrangements come to seem necessarily convoluted. The pivots are spread out too far; the angles and distances involved allow for an excess of slop.

But they can work, in a pinch. Can you dig it? The coolest centerpulls were those made by Mafac. The design is a little better; they also look cool. A flat, curved arm with "Mafac" etched in to it arches across the front, like a fine old bridge.

Centerpulls have no means for independent cable adjustment, so you want to make sure there's a barrel adjuster at or before the housing stop. *The straddle hanger needs to be made really, really tight.* The straddle cable itself is of a fixed length, with buttons at either end; they pop in and out of the brake arms. These and their springs are bolted to a plate, which is fixed to the frame. The centerpulls are kind of a bitch to get back together; I do not recommend disassembly. You can pull the pads and drop the thing in your citrus for a day, if you need to.

The centerpulls are not equipped with any dedicated brake-centering hardware. They are just that old. But that's cool; it means you finally get to use the hammer. You want a punch as well, lest you fuck up the paint. A regular-sized flathead screwdriver is just about perfect, actually.

Tightening a cantilever brake pad

Center the brake as best you can by hand, first, and tighten its fixing bolt way the hell down. It is worthwhile to track down a nylock for this, if there's not one up there already. Line up the screwdriver on the side that needs to move in, and pop its tail with the hammer. Aim for the shoulders, right on top of the springs there. Tap, tap, tap … perfect.

Cantilevers

I would like to tell you that the cantilever has come full circle, because I want to be a writer, but I am in fact a mechanic and thereby am inclined toward patterns over progress. But also because, just lately, an update on the original old school cantilever design has again become fashionable. Paul Components' Neo Retro cantilevers have caught on well enough, actually.

The **CANTILEVER BRAKES** were well established and enjoying their zenith, when first I entered upon the zoo. They were soon eclipsed by the bright and righteous linear pull brakes, of course, but this did take a while.

I would guess that the originals were made by Dia Compe, with an infant Shimano following soon thereafter. I've worked on the progenitors from each company; the Dia Compe design looks to be a bit older. Both examples from each company were very stripped-down; more curious hot rod than established utility. Their designs are somewhat more graceful, but we find no specific brake-centering feature on either of them. And yet this was enough, because the frame-mounting protocol they began has prospered to this day.

The central advantage the cantis brought is in their leverage. The arms are able to lever against the frame, rather than simply pushing against themselves. If the sidepulls and centerpulls strain through their calisthenics in the airless void of outer space, the cantilevers are at least able to push off against the moon. This they accomplish by settling down atop the **BRAKE BOSSES**, which are installed to either side of the wheel. These are threaded metal stubs, 15 millimeters long by 8 millimeters wide, which act as pivots for the brake arms. They squat silent and motionless on the frame; the cantilevers pirouette above and around them. It works out pretty well.

Both linear pull and rim-mounted hydraulic brakes operate from the same bosses, in the same positions. It could be universal! But it's not, because BMX U brakes and their old GT admirers *and* the ancient roller-cam mountain brakes mount these very same posts in distinct positions. Don't sweat it, though; none of these look anything like the cantis. You would probably know about it, were your bike so troubled.

The various cantilever brakes each conform to a basic profile. The two arms are sprung out from the frame at appreciable angles; a straddle cable reaches down to each side from one central brake cable. The cantilever straddle ends up resembling an inverted "V," given its position, but it should not be confused with V brakes. This is the popular slang for linear pull brakes; they're up next.

A stout 6-millimeter bolt pierces each brake arm, securing it to threads inside the brake boss. These bolts need to be tight. Manufacturers generally treat them with thread-locking compound. The outsides of the bosses, by contrast, should be lubricated with grease. Any rust you find here can get scuffed away with a light emery cloth or sandpaper, with an oily rag flying in to clean the dust away.

Crouched down in the back rows, just before the brake arms meet the frame, you will usually find the end of a sturdy spring. This levers against the brake arm at one end, and a hole in the frame's brake boss with the other, to provide us the engine to generate the brake's spring tension. And this, shared equitably between the arms, also prevents the pads from dragging on the rim.

The Dia Compe 987 cantilevers, Suntour self-energizers, and even Paul's Neo Retros engage this dynamic with a slightly different approach, by anchoring the springs to a nut set around the brake boss, rather than to the brake boss itself. You loosen the brake arm's fixing bolt and turn this nut, to adjust the spring tension or brake centering.

These sorts of free-floating systems can become troublesome, if they're starved of lubrication, or not tightened with all due sincerity. The others are often simpler. Most brake bosses will offer the springs their choice of three holes, lined up vertically on the base, and almost everyone goes for the middle one. The upper and lower extremes are usually unworkable, actually. You sometimes use the top set, for older cantilevers, if the springs are all tired and worn out. Rarely, though. And so we see a second sort of brake boss, in which the three holes are clarified into the one.

The three-hole bosses do let you differentiate spring set-up between the two brake arms, if you really need to. If only the right side is dragging ass, for example, you may anchor its spring in that top hole. But this is ever more rare; all but the oldest and cheapest cantilevers have at least some kind of dedicated brake-centering technology. And so the springs' collective energy is redistributed, as means to create a more equitable society, and this allows for better forward movement.

The preferred method for this grand leveling finds a small screw threaded in to the base of one brake arm. The screw's tip bottoms out against one end of the brake spring; adjusting it will modify the spring's effective tension. Which, balanced against the opposite spring's fixed position, will make for a reasonably quick and accurate means to adjust brake centering. You turn the screw in to increase tension, or turn it on out to release some.

Increasing the tension on the one side, of course, eases it back away from the rim. You just pay attention to the process, and compensate as you go. Simple. But the springs sometime take a second to reposition themselves. Wiggle the arms back and forth across the bosses, to help this along.

The brake-centering procedure is a basic and common adjustment, but it's neither automatic nor mandatory. You only fix this if it's broken, like if only one brake pad is dragging.

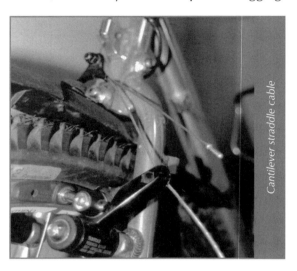

Cantilever straddle cable

We should also take a look at the **STRADDLE CABLES**, those wishbones charged with translating the brake cable's impulses to the two cantilever arms. A cable hanger may be bolted to the brake cable, with a separate straddle cable passing through it, or the brake cable itself will end up shooting down one side of a straddle assembly. (Shimano long ago experimented with an ungainly hybrid between these two—it required the cursed "pro-set tools," as described in *How to Rock and Roll*—but this crap is ever more rare. It may also be replaced, with more legitimate straddle wire solutions.)

The cable hanger is simple. It's fixed securely to an appropriate place along the brake cable; the straddle slips under the wire and reaches out. Where to hang? The angle formed by the two sides of this straddle cable should end up being around 90 degrees. Each side's angle against its brake arm should also be something similar. The general rule is that we like it to end up sitting just above the fender hole, such that anything mounted there may proceed unmolested.

It is certainly possible things were previously set up a little differently, if your existing arrangements depart from this. The brake pads may need to be readjusted, if they have been previously set to work with a slackened cable or something. But the oldsters (and their admirers) are designed to lean out farther from the bike, comparing with more modern examples. Their top edges become nearly horizontal, making for more acute angles against the straddle cable.

Old school is also more inclined toward distinct straddle cable hangers, rather than the streamlined straddle assemblies. And as with the dusty centerpulls, it is crucial that the cable hanger becomes super tight. It just slides down the cable the next time you jam on the brakes, otherwise, leaving you all the more powerless to stop anything at all. So make sure you test it, before you put the tools away. Squeeze as hard as you can; see what happens.

The end of the straddle cable itself gets fixed beneath a pinch bolt, on the top of one brake arm. The opposite brake arm features a kind of slotted round hollow, up top, which holds the straddle cable's round head in a tentative embrace. But this is only the quick release! You need to squeeze the brake arm up toward the straddle, creating some slack, to push the cable head out.

Tightening our straddle to a good position can be difficult, because the effort challenges the mighty brake springs, but fortunately the prescient fourth hand tool arrives to save us. This operation in particular totally justifies its place among its peers. The spring tension encourages the straddle to escape, from under the iron thumb of the brake's binder bolt, every chance it gets; this particular implement may be the only thing convincing it to just calm the hell down.

The straddle assemblies are simpler. There are no extra pieces; the brake cable itself is routed down to the brake arm. It passes through a burly straw on one side, while a matching length of cable fills in as the quick release on the other.

A flat interface, looking much like a squat fat coin, connects the two. Its backside features two grooves, separated by a tiny aluminum nub: one lines up at the end of the cable housing; the other is centered under the handlebar stem, right under where the brake cable comes down.

Shoot the brake cable down the housing section; the first groove falls in its natural course. This done, bend the cable just slightly to kick it over the nub, in to the more central groove. Use your fourth hand to soak up the brake cable's overflow outside the brake arm, getting it up to that optimal 90-degree angle before tightening it down.

Here as well, you should go ahead and squeeze the brake lever as hard as you can. The cable should stay put. These assembly things are not long enough to work with the retro cantilevers, but they do need to stretch out to their full extensions, so some especially tight set-ups are precluded as well. You want to substitute a hanger and straddle wire, in either scenario.

Your straddle assembly would like to look something like this

You also see a short diagonal line, running across the front of the interface. This is meant to line up with the assembly's quick-release cable, once everything is set up. Which, set against the housing on the opposite side, makes for our pleasant 90 degrees.

You threaded the barrel adjuster all the way down, right? Back it out again, just a bit, like a quarter of its length. This pulls the straddle cable up just slightly, to angles just less than our ideal. The pads are tightened in to position right up next to the rim; this lets us back them off to more useful positions.

Cantilever cartridge brake pads

The brake pad's post will slide right in to the top of a curious banjo-like bolt, which itself shoots through the cantilever's tall vertical window. A nut at the far end tightens their package in to place, together with a pair of concave and convex washers. These last coincide with features on the cantilevers themselves, allowing us to set the whole thing up at angles both more and less than perpendicular. The design was all the best of the 1980s. Bodacious; gnarly; totally awesome.

The bolt is usually handled with a 5-millimeter Allen wrench; the nut is most often for your 10-millimeter box wrench. Their particulars vary occasionally, within narrow and reasonable parameters. You want to enlist the appropriate wrench, whenever you're tweaking the nut. Things will go a bit quicker if you kind of roll the nut to a starting position with your fingers, first.

Veteran cantilever sets tend to earn a good deal of dried road debris. It creeps up in to the hardware and just sits there, forever. But you should take the assembly apart and clear this shit out, instead, because the effort greatly simplifies your adjustments. The gnarly old grit ultimately favors the pad's established status quo, in this respect; its layers discourage the arrangement of new positions.

Some of the brake pads have longer tails; the long end always points to the rear. The only exception I've been made aware of concerns some of Shimano's mountain cartridge pads, which flip the tails forward, up front. But these are spotted easily enough. The pads' ends may also be bent downwards, just slightly, to coincide with the round of the rim. And their hardware should become about as tight as you can make it. (Or just less than that, for really burly people.) But you get the idea. The whole project can be just that simple, but it's also possible you'll have to deal with some **AUTOMATIC TOE-IN** devices. These were horrible mistakes, snuck in by wretched losers back in the day. They've nothing to do with legitimate mechanistry. The guess was that adding springs in-line to the pad hardware could *automatically* set the toe-in. But it was only another presumptuous technophilic misconception; the effort in fact shunts the pads out well beyond any useful angle. The solution, fortunately, is simple! You unscrew the pad hardware for a second, just long enough to ditch anything therein that looks like it may be a spring.

Discarded automatic toe-in washers

Shimano may have been the original culprit. They relied upon these truly goofy spring-loaded plastic washers, at first, but they eventually replaced the goof-gaskets with more subtle flattened washers. But these bear slits, the sides of which are pressed in opposing directions; their function is essentially the same.

This last arrangement, unfortunately, crosses over to the early STX linear pull brakes. With cantilever-style pads, for some reason. And some of the more generic cantilever manufacturers have also buried the springs up inside the brake arms themselves, as well. So just you keep an eye out.

This matter settled, we're able to see to the more useful business about the **TOE-IN**. The front of the pad hits slightly before the back; that's all it means. Kool Stop sets this up for us; the tails of their pads are born with little lips that brace against the rim, which makes for a nice toe-in. The lips eventually wear down, as with the rest of the pads, but they do set up nicely.

Suntour Self-Energizing cantilever brakes

The Suntour self-energizing cantilevers were the coolest of them all. This was the name applied to WTB's roller-cam brakes, when Suntour licensed them in the mid-1980s. I think that's what happened; I would have been just entering high school at the time. I have also seen the names Scott and Pedersen associated with this most worthwhile cantilever design. But I will leave it to the historians.

Linear Pull

I was just cutting my teeth at Wheel and Sprocket in Milwaukee, back in 1994 or 1995, when the linear pull brakes started showing up. The originals were exclusively high-end, and also more complex. These sage progenitors installed minor parallelograms between brake arm and brake pad, which left the arms sitting a bit wider in the frame. The effort may have increased the leverage, in theory, but in fact the parallelograms became better known for loosening up over time. Their pivot points gain some slop, with extended use; the brakes start to chatter and squeak.

Most recent versions have since dispatched with the idea. The linears, more commonly known as **V BRAKES**, really do represent a meaningful improvement. The design takes maximum advantage of its situation, essentially; a fuller portion of your effort is applied to the braking process. Persons who have trouble with lesser braking systems will probably do somewhat better on the V brakes. A famous handful of the original test rides, in fact, are said to have finished with spontaneous endos. And ours has also, incidentally become a wantonly litigious society—denied real justice and security, it's assumed we should like to individualize such pursuits—so it should not surprise us that fears of the

V brakes' awesome power have actually encouraged some companies to engineer a degree of supplementary flex into the brakes.

This last is an attributed motive, but I do hope it's the right one. We otherwise need to find the manufacturers concerned either unconscionably cheap, or somehow stupid. The garbage wagon imitations also flex more than they should, for example, because the materials used are not legitimate.

This flex is known as modulation. It is only rarely associated with performance-grade bikes. But many manufacturers actually add a small spring to brake noodles, to modulate the brakes. We see this most often with the lower-end bikes, and usually just in front. The longer stretch and the flex associated with cheap parts basically accomplishes the same thing, out back. Brakes on better bikes, by contrast, are instead designed to swing in sharp and efficient arcs.

The SRAM Corporation was one of those that became interested in spreading the flex around. Their brakes were famous to me for an excess of modulation, the first couple years I worked with them. Little sponges, mounted to the handlebars. But you would notice an odd-looking finger screw piercing the levers' bodies on some of their newer units, which adjusted the lever modulation. I believe the funny screws' stated purpose may have focused on the cable pull differences between cantilever and linear pull brakes—a topic we will shortly explore—but it seems to fill in for these purposes as well.

You want to set up the pads before you arrange the cable, with the V brakes, lest you repeat your steps. Their relatively long threaded posts are adorned with several odd washers, which are meant to appear in pairs to either side of the brake arm. One washer

is concave, and the other convex; the pairs together allow for a range of dynamic adjustment. The brake pads can be asked to recline and rest at odd angles, basically.

One set of washers will be slightly thicker than its peers. Which pair goes where totally depends on the bike. You do want to make the most of your spring tension, so the brake arms should be drawn together as much as possible, but not so much that the brake noodle rams the opposite brake arm. The best arrangement finds the arms parallel to each other, in line with the wheel. And, depending on how the brake bosses were mounted, this will find the fatter set of concave/convex washers on the inside or the outside of the brake arms.

It is easiest to set up the pads with the springs disengaged. The spring's tail typically runs right up the side; you're able to pinch it out of the way with a screwdriver. But some handful of the Vs will pull the cantilever thing, hiding the springs inside the brake arms; you need to hold them to the rims as the pads are tightened in to position.

The V brake's cable housing ends in the curved metal straw we call the **BRAKE NOODLE**. The left brake arm is topped with a hinged carriage, the end of which is just big enough to accept the very tip of this noodle. The cable shoots out from the tip of this noodle, darts across the tire, and ducks under a binder bolt capping the other brake arm. And the noodle's graceful curve allows for the brake's quick-release feature as well, of course. You press the brake arms together with one hand, to slacken the cable, and pull the noodle back and free with the other.

Cables are sometimes flattened beneath the brakes' binder bolts, and this can complicate their interactions with the noodles. This is especially true of the chintzy plastic-tipped SRAM noodles, whose tiny nostrils are especially sensitive to such trouble. It's as if the thing tugs at your sleeve, urging you to just snip the old cable and buy a brand new one. But you don't need to. A fourth hand tool will pull that cable right on out and back through again. And next time, make sure the cable is clamped down squarely atop its groove, to keep it healthy.

Recall our chat on the brake modulation? *If the top of the noodle is noticeably taller and wider than its peers, it is probably concealing a small spring.* But it's easy enough to dig these things out with a pick, fortunately. These wider noodles, unlike their peers, will also swallow a cable-housing cap—the damned spring needs to push against something—but this simply bottoms out in the base, once you clean the spring out of the way.

The new bikes invariably plug their brake noodle's nose cones in to rubber boots, to cover the cable on its short trip across the tire to meet the pinch bolt. They're meant to keep the tire's spray of grit from backing up into the brake noodles, but it's more likely they'll simply complicate our cable adjustments, by getting in the way of the pinch bolt. I always get rid of the stupid rubber boots, when I'm able to do so, at least.

The cable should be tightened at least to such a point that the lever is not able to bottom out on the handlebar. This still allows for a pretty generous allowance, which can be useful, if the wheels aren't quite straight. I tend to run my own brake levers about as tight as they may become—I went to military school; it's just how I see things—but this does require a higher degree of truth, from the wheels. They need to maintain a good discipline, to acquire such a cadence.

The brake centering comes last, after the pads and cable are set up. There are small bolts

installed to the lower sides of each arm, in the case of the Vs, which control both brake centering and spring tension. Dialing the bolts in jacks up the tension, as with the cantilevers, turning them out lowers it. The bolts do become progressively harder to turn, as the spring tension increases. You will definitely want to be pushing down nice and hard on the screwdriver or Allen wrench, to avoid stripping the bolt. But of course the tension is our friend, in the case of the brakes. And so we rather turn the screws in than out; up to a point at least.

You should end up finalizing the centering adjustment in small measures; half-turns on the screws. As you finish up, follow each tweak by jiggling the brakes back and forth across their bosses. The adjustment screw's stark commands can take a few seconds to echo down the length of the spring; this helps the new truth sink in with the quickness.

V brakes and cantilevers are of the same family, but they are not cross compatible. *The V brake levers pull twice as much cable as the other mechanical braking systems.* The linear pull levers can command other sorts of brakes—the cables can be set to ridiculously tight tolerances, in fact—but the V brakes themselves refuse to listen to anybody else's levers. And they get away with it, because shit is just *like* that.

The brake cable's head comes to rest in slightly different positions, basically, and this changes the arc of its travel through the lever. There are some ambidextrous levers available, providing distinct openings for cantilever or linear pull cables, but most need to go one way or another.

We can still mix things around, to a point. They only need to happen in the correct sequence. I like to match linear levers with more pedestrian brakes, actually, precisely because it gives you this fantastic amount of breathing room.

It is curious to see how the industry deals with the great cable-travel dichotomy. Cantilevers are not quite extinct: the Avid and Paul Companies each still make a few nicer models; cheapos from Tektro and Shimano are also available. And the cantis have gone on a great many bikes already, as well. I expect to find replacements so long as the lights stay on.

They are still spec'd as original equipment on new bikes, in fact. There remain only a couple road brake levers that will work the V brakes; the cantis are still pretty mainstream on cyclocross and tour bikes. Most of these are also stuck with Shimano's STI dual control shift/brake levers—as ever, an unfortunate affliction—and, as yet, their highnesses have yet to set any of their silly joy-sticks on the V brake cable protocol.

Don't sweat it, though. There are other ways to cross drop bars with V brakes. I notice some of the new cross levers are linear-compatible, for one thing. Dia Compe offers the 287V, alternately, which is instead a classically styled aero lever. And of course we also see the Travel Agent pulleys, which by means of a special reduction convince the cables to do as we like them to.

Disc

There's nothing wrong with using a couple different brake systems on the same bike, so long as you honor the aforementioned details with regards to the cable travel. To the contrary, some bikes are interesting enough to require such arrangements. Ancient mountain bikes have cantilevers up front and roller-

cams in back, for example. And the tandems will commonly run a rear drum brake on top of their regular systems.

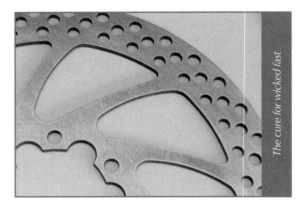

The cure for wicked fast

Such solidarity may or may not reach out to cover the disc brakes. I kind of doubt it. The discs are more iconoclastic. The mechanical models are run with regular linear pull brake levers, but it is kind of awkward to run one opposite a rim-mounted brake. A good disc will stop you like a heart attack; their effect is just that different.

Discs don't represent an ultimate solution so much as a different approach. Their central advantage—to stop a bike quickly, without heating the rims to dangerous levels—was first discovered with the much simpler and cheaper drum brakes. The discs are only more exotic, effective, and expensive.

Rim-mounted brakes create friction heat. They also collect mud pretty directly, and this encourages them to chew through their pads, and, eventually, the rims. **DISC BRAKES** sit right out in the wind, unlike the stoic old drum brakes, and this allows the friction heat to more easily evaporate. And so better, more effective brake pad compounds can be used. The calipers also sit high enough to collect a little less mud, and their arrangements allow both the brake pads and rotor to be replaced fairly easily.

Changing out a rotor is quicker, easier, and cheaper than rebuilding a wheel. It would be a circle of 6-5m torx bolts, or else cassette-style splines and a locking, various adapters let you switch back and forth between the two. But the forces associated with braking are focused toward the hub, where a good deal of stress was already concentrated. And so the disc hubs, together with the dropouts that accept them, need to be stronger. A Cincinnati company called Disc Brake Adapters has evidently found methods to retro-fit disc caliper mounts to some older frames; they also produce a range of mounting adapters.

The discs are also inclined to squeak, just like the Vs, but for slightly different reasons. *The oil in your fingertips is enough to make them squeal.* This last is revealed as the culprit often enough, actually. They're interesting; people want to grab at them. So they do, and the innocuous fingerprint oil gets all over the place, and we hear all about it.

This consideration seems to be intrinsic to those compounds used to make the brake pads. You are, quite literally, not supposed to touch the disc. And the fingers are not all that greasy to begin with, most of the time; you can imagine the cataclysmic impact a few drops of straight chain lube may have. As BikeE put it in their instructions for Avid mechanical discs, "Do not spray any solvents or lubricants in the vicinity of the rotors or brake pads." It makes me wonder about all the other grit that gets tossed its way, by road and trail. Sharp technology, but still young.

Our friend Travis T. offers further advisement, with regards to the disc brakes. You will want to avoid dry-firing them. When the rotor is removed from its caliper, do *not* squeeze the lever. I haven't yet seen this, in

my own travels, but he's had to rebuild calipers and even bleed hydraulic disc systems to resolve such situations.

The good news is that the discs can also escape the noise pretty quickly. It is easy come, easy go. You remove the wheel and clean the disc with rubbing alcohol, thoroughly. You can also slide a strip of emery cloth in between the caliper moons to sand down the pads themselves, if you really need to. But the juice usually does the trick, you know? I am not aware of anything else that may work here.

Rotor

Discs will not have the braking heat problems of rim-mounted brake systems—which are said to have very, *very* occasionally become hot enough to pop inner tubes—but this in itself does not leave them immortal. Discs don't bend easily, but it does happen. And, since the calipers invariably hang the pads incredibly close to the discs, the smallest deviation will either stop you cold or just rub, rub, rub until you really just wanna say fuck it.

The calipers will need to clamp down into an especially precise position, by one means or another. "Almost there" is woefully inadequate. The mounting tabs themselves occupy standardized positions on the fork and frame; we only need the wriggle-room to account for the mindlessly tight adjustment parameters. The calipers can too easily be tightened at slight angles to the disc; the wheel barely is able to move at all. And so we must draw inspiration from the microscopes and calipers; this really requires our close attention.

Disk brake rotors are usually installed with torx wrenches

Cable routing is also more important, with the disc brakes, for the same kinds of reasons. Something so simple as pulling across another cable's housing can cause a brake pad to drag on its rotor. Think it through; leave nothing to chance. The field of view is all things draconian, bleak, and extreme. There is not the slightest room for spontaneity.

You first want to make sure any bolts holding the caliper together are completely tight. They will come loose, occasionally. The brake cable connects to the caliper by means of a pivoting arm, which moves in an arc: see to it that the cable is fixed such that the arm rests at an approximate mid-point in its range of movement. We can fine-tune this later, to determine the lever pull, by reattaching the cable or fiddling with its barrel adjuster.

Loosen the caliper's fixing bolts. It needs to be able to float freely upon its base, to set things up right. You then tighten its fixed pad all the way in, until it presses against the rotor, which becomes clamped tightly between the two pads. The inboard side of the caliper will typically feature a broad flat dial of some kind; turning this in tight-

ens the fixed pad. Shimano Deore calipers enlist a 5-millimeter hex wrench for such purposes; Avid provides us a big red finger disc.

Tighten the fixing bolts all the way down, with the rotor clamped tightly between the pads. This done, loosen the cable pinch; the outboard pad should hop back from the rotor. And now back off that fixed pad, incrementally, *just* to the point where nothing is rubbing. This leaves it suspended as close to the disc as it may ever hope to be.

All that remains is to set the other pad, in accordance with your preferences. The central complication to setting up disc brakes, given their adjustment parameters, is in ensuring that the pads become precisely parallel with the rotors. This adjustment method brings the disc's idiosyncrasies to bear upon itself, basically.

It is engineers designing these things; I can only guess what they may be up to. My hunch is that they'd rather prevent the inevitable road grit from soiling the shiny new rotors, which to my mind trots right after the nefarious old windmills. All braking systems, excluding the drums and the fixed wheels, will inevitably confront the elements. The discs see much less, perched up by the hubs, but still the pads need to hug the rotors. What is it, a comfort blanket?

Leverage

We may contrast against the vast array of much simpler and more proven cycling technologies, many of which are understood upon the most cursory examination. The disc brake is emblematic of the wrong turn we've taken. It delivers far more power than most anyone could ever find useful, and as with certain other features prominent in our cycling economy, its presence among us relies upon a few too many presumptions. I move to banish the discs from our land, pending certain crucial improvements, but capital's saccharine pull has already led us well in to the dark forest of systemic mystification.

Having marshaled the working elements beneath us, we're at last in a position to better consider the more sublime roles pursued by the brake levers themselves. Their basic story is already known to us, having studied their charges; but as yet their essential role has not been closely considered. While developments in technology continue to rock the brakes' world, the levers themselves have not witnessed substantial changes. But the sexy new cross levers really broke the mold, in this respect. When mounted as they're meant to, at midpoints between the calipers and the staid old road brake levers, their action affects a unique result. The cable housing is made to move, rather than simply the cable itself. A fairly simple and intuitive trick, considering, but to my knowledge at least it has never been done before.

The cross levers' arrangements also allow for independent deployments, of course, as the solitary levers on our fixed gear bikes, for example. And they're just small enough to be gripped with a fuller portion of the hand, which provides us with improved leverage as well. I'd hoped to split a pair between a couple of my own bikes last summer, in fact, but things were such that I couldn't even put together the wholesale price. Kind of a rough season. But at least one bike still needed a brake lever, so I started fucking around, and eventually arrived upon something else entirely.

Recall that road brake cables can be made to fit with some shift levers? It happened that I

had various dusty old shifters scattered about the basement, broke as I was, and over time these provided materials for experiments. The early ones became more dubious—pushing down with the thumb is not a natural way to slow a bike down, as it turns out—but eventually the path forward became clear. The old aluminum thumb shifters can make for slick little brake levers, with a bit of work. More, their steel clamps can usually be expanded to fit most drop bars. So if ever you're wanting a solid but curious brake lever on your fix, you might check this out.

The shift levers themselves will generally be built around short 5-meter bolts, but these may be drilled out and replaced, with something long enough to pass right through and engage a washer and nylock nut. You do best with a flathead bolt—such as one of those left over from your Kryptonite lock's mounting bracket, for example—because its face can be made flush with the handlebar. You need to drill out the threads in the shifter's base to do this, of course. But the big hole is already up in there; you can just about finish it off free handed.

The new screw needs to be made just tight enough, beneath its washer and nut. You look for that fine balance, where the shifter's action is just loose enough to balance against the brake's spring tension. Overhauling the brake, in other words, probably allows the use of a less sloppy brake lever, which is somewhat safer. And that reminds me, one other thing? *Do not use plastic levers for this.*

The cable routing becomes our last outstanding variable. Anything may happen. Different shifters see their cables exiting into the void in slightly different directions, basically, and this makes for a range of possibilities. And if it feels good, go for it.

Those metal friction shifters suiting our purposes here only grow more rare, as the world turns to square; you may have to just kind of go with what you get.

The lever's pivot point is moved up in line with the handlebar, in the case of our old thumbshifters, and this affords a real improvement in the leverage. And the conventional brake levers may be setting their pivots too far from the bars, all of a sudden. It's the difference between grasping some relatively distant stick with the fingertips, and squeezing closed a smaller circuit with the full strength of your hand.

The important question was what to name this newest fruit. I consulted with my friend Xara, a local thinker of no small renown, but after endless brainstorming sessions we were still no closer to the light. It was only the next day, exhausted from all the mental gymnastics, that the answer landed before me. This high new device shall forever be known as the **SOUP SPOON**. It gets us a bigger bite. And so it is that I rock a soup spoon on my hooker bars.

soup spoon

Soup spoons can be made from the Falcon thumbshifters, which your friendly local bike shop could score from Q. These will likely be the least expensive new shift levers you will ever come across—in metal, at least—and they suit our purposes brilliantly. You even get a spare, to pass along to your friend.

The Falcons do provide for a minor ratcheting

mechanism, which is great for the shifting, but not for our braking. You need to get rid of this to bust out with the soup spoon. But it's only a tiny piece of plastic, balanced atop a diminutive spring, pressing on the shifter's splined ceiling. It all pops right out.

Hydraulic

Meanwhile, back in the enchanted forest, even stranger things continued to happen. The **HYDRAULIC BRAKES** have leapt from their motorcycles to land squarely upon the bikes, in both rim-mounted and disc variations.

Either will make any of those we've begun with look like a bunch of timid pedestrians. There really isn't any relation between lever force and braking force, with the hydros. This cuts both ways! If you're one to go really fast but not squeeze hard, hydros will stop you quickly, with only the slightest indication. You don't need to pull the lever, so much as move it. But if you're already accustomed to controlling speed more gradually, on the other hand, the sensation will be pretty abrupt. The awesome force delivered to the brakes corresponds best with sheer cliffs and sea changes; it is more closing down than slowing down.

Mechanically, hydros perch on their own distinct technical platform. Older, more common bicycle components watch bemusedly from the ground below. The hydraulics don't have to worry about rusted cables or anything boring like that, but this departure really launches them out into the void. They're picky, for one thing. Each company's systems operate on their own distinct hydraulic fluid. Some, such as Shimano's mineral oil, are fairly common and somewhat benign. Others are imported straight in from more toxic automobile protocols.

Using the wrong juice can destroy the hoses. The plastic literally seals itself up in protest! The calipers need to be soaked in rubbing alcohol, just to calm down. And where regular brake cables survive the occasional rough-housing, hydraulic lines quickly capsize upon the smallest pin prick. Stainless hydraulic hoses, available for many systems, can often survive better. Provided they're long enough and routed correctly.

If your hydros do take a hit on the fly, there's not shit you can do about it. You have no more brake, at all, wherever you happen to be. And unless you've got the full kit right there in your bag with you, it will take a good bike shop a piece of time and some relatively steep cash to make things right again, each and every time it happens. You didn't have any plans for touring, did you?

Other more reliable, tested, and serviceable braking technologies lurk in every corner, anxious to spring into action and take things over. Beyond the tiny cult of trials riders, perhaps, I've yet to see a hydraulic bike system that can not be replaced by a mechanical one.

Different hydraulic systems feature various means with which to adjust lever reach and brake pad positions. It's usually just the two features; the controls' particulars will vary.

Rim-mounted hydraulics, such as Magura, incorporate a quick-release lever behind one caliper. You pull the one side off to remove a wheel. But still we're left with certain more pressing questions. If the more common rim-mounted mechanical brakes are producing enough friction heat to substantially encourage the disc brake alternative, what may we make of hydraulically boosted rim brakes? Hot, hot, hot … .

Rim-mounted hydraulic brakes really don't squeak at all, but the disc varieties will quite happily make just as much noise as their mechanical kin. And as with their peers, caliper positioning will again become positively crucial. Squeakage is resolved in the same way, by cleaning the discs with rubbing alcohol, or flossing the pads with an emery cloth.

Broken lines are dealt with by replacing the fluid and the line itself. You drain everything, measure out an accurate replacement length of new hydraulic line, and then pump in the correct hydraulic fluid, until any air bubbles are gone. The planet's gravity becomes helpful with this last point, of course, but it's worth noting these hydros are incompatible with the very air we *breathe*. Like the vampires, with the sunlight.

We might consider the Maguras, one of the more common systems, to better understand the exacting scope of their ceaseless demands. We need to begin with the full servicing kit, of course. This includes a hose with a threaded fitting to drain the old fluid, a big plastic syringe for installing the new juice, and also a number of small metal rings. These last, which Magura calls "olives," need to be replaced each time you take things apart. The very act of tightening them into place changes their profile.

The hoses detach from their levers and calipers by unscrewing the compression nut, which turns out by way of an 8-millimeter wrench. Said nut usually hides under a rubber sleeve, as it enters the lever. The short stretch of line connecting rim-mounted brakes together over the wheel is neither removed nor replaced, unless it's also damaged.

Removing a damaged hydraulic line will empty any remaining fluid trapped therein, so don't be doing this over the Persian rug.

Your friendly local bike shop should be able to set you up with a correct length of the appropriate hydraulic line. It's proprietary, just like the fluid; you can't just go scrounge something out of the utility drawer.

The particular length may be based on the original, provided it wasn't binding anywhere in the bars' rotation. Cut the new line to length with a razor. Or, if you have an advanced degree, maybe you can try Jagwire's special new hydro cable cutters. *Not regular cable cutters, in any case.* Lay the line flat on a sturdy surface and slice, aiming for a perfect 90-degree cut.

Slide the old compression nut onto the new line, and then the new olive. Plug the line all the way down into the caliper: it needs to be tight in place for the seal to hold. Slide the olive and compression nut down, holding the line firmly into its hole as you tighten the nut all the way back down. The other end plugs into the lever in much the same way.

Maguras run on Magura Blood. Clever, isn't it? You unscrew a fill hole on the caliper, and a similar drain hole up on top of the lever. Fill the syringe, squeeze out any air, and thread its end piece into the fill hole.

Now go find the single most righteous can of beer you can. This sure as hell will not be a Coors product, needless to say; your local micro-breweries will probably be the first place to check.

Got it? Pop the cap and slam it. This is important, because the empty can will become the reservoir for the hydraulic fluids' overflow. Just tie the can's pop tab to a cable somewhere, up there on the handlebars, and the drain hose, which you plug into that spare opening on the lever, empties in to this handy container. As with the

syringe, this last should also feature a fitting to thread into place.

You fill from down low to drain up high. Gravity sorts out any air that gets in the way. Slowly pump the new fluid in, until such a time when no dreaded air bubbles are seen in the drain hose. You cap this top end first, securely. Unscrew the syringe fitting down below as well, once this is done, and put the screw back in there.

Other hydraulic systems will be purged and renewed along a similar pattern. The details will vary. Work slowly and deliberately, checking the effects of each adjustment as you make it. Any of these require your particular system's specific servicing parts and replacement fluid; do not experiment or guess or anything like that. And I wish you all the best with any quick, on-the-road hydraulic repairs.

10: DRIVETRAINS

The drivetrain coordinates our movement forward. It comprises the chain and all of its cogs, together with any derailleurs and shift levers.

The **DERAILLEURS** are those things kicking your chain from one gear to the next. It's the device with the two pulleys in back, usually paired with the fin-looking contraption above the chainrings up front. How smoothly the chain makes its little jumps—a constant source of consternation, within the cycling world—depends on a wide range of factors. The quality of your parts, the state of their health, your skill in using them, and even the weather itself can inform the situation.

It is difficult to describe the root of most shifting problems, simply because the discussion may well branch in several directions at once. The more specific you can describe a given problem, the sooner you'll be able to isolate its particular solution. So does shit go haywire when you're upshifting or downshifting? In some gears or all of them? Do the gears only shift with some discernable hesitation or do they come and go more randomly? Are things always failing or is it only when you pedal hard?

Our solutions, in addition, are contingent on our circumstances. To put this another way, some things are easier to fix than others. Those making our bicycle componentry know quite well how to make a righteous drivetrain—one snapping smoothly from gear to gear, weighing next to nothing and lasting for a good long time—but most bikes are not so lucky.

Department store garbage wagons, for example, are reliably stuck with the worst parts available. They weigh too much, bend too easily, and break far too quickly. And the cheapest independent bike dealer bikes will often do little better, unfortunately. We find some relief among older components of quality—they're often considered devalued well before they actually wear out, essentially—but even here there is the hierarchy.

It is easier and less expensive to produce the cheap crap, needless to say. The troubles only arise when they're compared against their more sophisticated kin. The simple riveted pivot points found on the cheapo derailleurs' parallelograms, for example, will allow the cages to sashay about of their own volition more freely—as you're trying to shift, for example, or charge up the busy hill. Know what I mean? Grab the bottom of the rear derailleur's cage and see how much it can be swayed side to side. It's much easier to shove the cheaper ones around; older, cheaper ones, all the more so. Smaller discrepancies in the rear derailleur's adjustment parameters can make for bigger problems than may otherwise be expected.

Friction

But we should return to the focus, lest I lose myself in cursing. The **FRICTION DERAILLERS** were first to convince the chains to hop around. Their name references the classical shift levers, of course, which at their best are stoic enough to hold a given position with nothing more than simple friction. You may remember this from when you were a kid; changing the gears just by their feel?

Friction is jazz. You need to come in with a little finesse. The experience does require a basic understanding—something on par with cooking breakfast, perhaps—and this evidently approaches the modern definition of tyranny, together with the gas tax, because great efforts have been expended to discover some more suitable replacement.

If nicer old parts interest you at all, it's worth recalling the friction shifting. The different component manufacturers' indexed rear derailleur systems, as we'll see, were never meant to be cross-compatible. So the friction levers are the only things saving some of the nicest old parts from ornamental obscurity. Because there was an enormous freedom, back then, the derailleurs did not really have to care about any rigid instructions, shouted down from on high. There was just this flow; it was rad. The more modern indexed shifting systems are pretty well obsessed with the shift cable's tension, but the friction units are still only passively aware of this detail. They just don't care that much. They try to work with what they have. It is mellow and good.

The only adjustments to concern us with friction derailleurs are a few basic ground rules, which are held in common with their indexed peers. All the pivot points should be oiled just enough, but not excessively, with some kind of lightweight penetrating oil. I like the T9 dropper bottle for such purposes. Those few bolts involved should all be tight, and the shift lever and cable should also be in good working condition.

You may also attend to the drivetrain cleaning, as described on pages 122-123.

Traditional gear reduction

Their setting leaves the rear derailleurs pretty well exposed to the wicked ways of the world. The rear derailleurs end up getting knocked around quite a bit, actually. You want to keep an eye out for damages.

The two pulleys are meant to be completely in line with each other, for one thing. Anything else indicates the derailleur cage has been bent. These can *generally* be straightened, if you take your time with it. You probably need a vise. The pulleys are removed; each side is leveled individually. Modern front derailleurs often share odd lateral contours, between their two cage plates, but those on all rear derailleurs are meant to be parallel with each other.

The derailleur cage should also be parallel with the back wheel. And the dropouts, and the bottom bracket, and the chainrings as well. Something will be bent, otherwise. If the whole piece appears to be out of alignment, this suggests that the frame's hanger is bent. Solutions for this common problem are described back with the other frame damage scenarios, on page 25. The derailleurs themselves are also sometimes bent, but a hit that hard will probably fuck up the derailleur hanger as well.

But the derailleur attempts to persist, regardless. It is a stoic little machine. Its boundless energy begins from a sturdy spring, which plays a constant tug-of-war with the stern yet whimsical shift lever. And so the gears shift beneath us, echoing the fortunes of their struggle.

The springs wear out eventually, after a good long life, and this marks the end of the derailleur's useful story as well. We sometimes see replacement springs, meant for some mid-90s Shimano derailleurs, but these are not meant to breathe new life in to any decrepit old machines. The pivot points have loosened up, together with the spring; such a project wanders off towards consumer fraud. The replacement springs are only mediators, by design, intending to resolve an old dispute between rival component manufacturers. But this last we'll consider in due course, see page 103.

In any case, the derailleur itself is all of an articulated parallelogram, suspended between two pivot points; there is precious little sorcery involved. We only need some method for preventing the bike's chain from diving into the spokes, or jumping off the edge of the cogs, and this comes with the **LIMIT SCREWS**. Derailleurs of any useful sort will have a pair of these threaded in somewhere, in such ways that they're pointed in to the parallelogram. Each screw bottoms out on a different edge, inside, and so do they come to govern the derailleur's range of motion.

The screws are supposed to be labeled L and H, for low and high, and they usually are. Older friction rear derailleurs often set the limit screws in line across the parallelogram's face, but at some point it became more fashionable to drill them instead into the derailleur's top section, and this pattern has held. *The low and high screws have been traditionally set in a reversed sequence, such that the L screw features toward the high end of the derailleur's range.* I can't imagine any

clear purpose for this; it may have been some inside joke offered in support of the general mystification of things. But SRAM has since come along to sort out this detail, reversing the poles, such that the limit screws governing each end of the derailleur's range feature where we might more expect them. The basic map is always the same, but its orientation will sometimes change.

If the markings are not clear, or if you do get the L and H screws confused, there is a sure-fire way to determine which is which. Upon releasing the shift cable from its derailleur, loosening one of the two screws allows the spring inside the parallelogram to contract, and the derailleur cage moves down towards its hanger. And this marks its "high" screw, of course. But here, too, there are exceptions. We sometimes come across derailleurs too rusted or grimy to really give a shit either way, for one thing. And we also have Shimano's ridiculous Rapid Rise derailleurs, which rearrange things such that the derailleur expands as its spring contracts.

For the truly scientific experience, it is easiest to see the limit screws in action if you first removed both the cable and the chain. Each of these impact upon the derailleur's range of movement; setting them aside leaves it free to hang out and do as it likes. The derailleur will instantly fold down to show you its high gear position, if it is healthy and good; if it is not there already. You'll also be able to push the parallelogram all the way up to the low end of the range, alternately, to see how the L screw operates. But here again, the Rapid Rise will reverse each of these equations, because it secretly holds all of us in contempt.

Any skeptical grass is quickly bent low, of course, before the gathering winds of innovation. Rapid Rise, rechristened as the Low-Normal return spring, has in fact become the only option for Shimano's top-flight XTR mountain derailleurs. It sounds as if the LX and XT ranges are headed in the same direction as well.

Low-Normal retains XTR's refined and classical stylings, save for the barrel adjuster: as with SRAM drivetrain products, we only find one aboard the shift lever. And lo, dependent on their age and pedigree, some number of Shimano mountain rear derailleurs have learnt to dance backwards.

You can also check on the limit screws' adjustments with the chain still mounted, of course, by suspending the rear wheel and turning the pedals. This is how we tend to do it at the shop, actually. The derailleur is then pushed all the way in toward the spokes, to make sure it can stop in time. The L screw is meant to keep the chain from flying over the biggest cog, on all rear derailleurs, and the H keeps it from falling past the smallest one. You need to turn them in, to limit the range of motion. They are turned out only if the derailleur will not reach the cogs in question.

Travis showed me a brilliant way to test the limit screws, up at Hayes Street Freewheel. You turn the cranks, and you yank on the cables. It sounds rough, I know, but it really works; unless you're working on a high-end carbon fiber bike, in which case you want to be far more delicate. The frame cable stops can be pulled right off with a little force.

You grab the cable(s) as they pass along the down or top tube, in the more usual circumstances, and pull. This tells you everything you need to know about the far limit screws' adjustments. Does the derailleur secretly want to get up there and throw the chain at the spokes, or is it restrained enough to be chill? Now's the time to find out! This cable-shifting business also has

the effect of seating the cables and housing more thoroughly in their stops, which is arguably the largest part of the "cable stretch" we worry about.

You want to loosen the derailleur cable, before you adjust the H screw. Their relationship balances atop a seesaw, essentially; adjustments to the one become contingent upon the other. The limit screw's particular adjustment sets the starting point for the derailleur cable to work from; turning it will necessarily modify the cable's tension. But the cable just goes tense and stays that way, if you keep turning it out, nullifying anything else that the limit screw may have to say.

The limit screws are meant to be adjusted just the once, when the derailleur is first being set up. You put them where they're supposed to be, and you go ride the bike. And that's it; you should not even have to worry about them. Their threads are tiny, and often treated with some thread-locking compound; they don't rattle loose or anything.

I find myself adjusting the limit screws on tune-ups very occasionally. (Following on the sheepish grin of an ill-advised home tinkerer, for example.) But I first want to make sure the frame's derailleur hanger has not bent. This problem is more common than maladjusted limit screws; either can just as easily toss your chain into the spokes.

Each of the limit screws are dialed in to the point where the derailleur's pulleys can just *barely*, very slightly move past the top and bottom cogs. The textbook methodology has us stopping the pulleys directly above the high and low cogs, but it has been my experience this can be improved upon. Imagine you're noble enough to become just barely generous, in sizing the derailleur's lot, and it will likely reciprocate the gesture.

Stand directly behind the bike and imagine lines radiating out in plane with the cogs' teeth; we compare against those spun from the derailleur pulleys. The pulleys should be able to get just barely, barely past the last cogs.

We need to get the rear derailleur dialed in first, in order to set up its mate. And our work up front, in turn, first makes sure the front derailleur itself is properly installed. The specifics will vary, but the lowest point on its cage always needs to clear the top chainring by 2 millimeters. You simply pull it forward with the fingers to check. And one aspect of the cage also needs to become precisely parallel with the chainrings, beyond this point, and this is generally the longest section of the cage's outer plate. The topic is further explored shortly on page 108.

In any case, once the front derailleur is positioned correctly, go ahead and shift the rear derailleur all the way up in to its largest cog. While in this position, the inside plate of the cage needs to clear the side of the chain by a very slight space as well. And we do need to leave it so vague, because this tiny distance has actually been shrinking with time. The more advanced front shifting systems do best with all of a millimeter's breathing room; older examples may require twice that. Any of which presumes a good chainline, as well as healthy components and a well-oiled cable set to a useful tension. The sum of variables confronting front derailleur adjustments discourages the quick-fix approach. But this only means it is important to check your work. So you tweak one of the limit screws and then see about shifting through the gears, to make sure the chain is doing the right thing.

And this is where the limit screws come back in. We dial the "L" screw to set the initial

adjustment, and finish with the "H" screw. Spin the cranks and pull on the cable. This too is the best way to scope things out. And if the chain does hop off the ring, you need to go back and check on that high screw.

The limit screws are the principle characters in our story, but we may also come upon a **B-TENSION SCREW**. It has become a ubiquitous feature on the rear derailleurs, but it is often overlooked, because it claims no major role for itself. It doesn't even show up on many older friction derailleurs, actually. It just hangs in the background, when it does make an appearance, right up next to the hanger, kind of behind and below the mounting bolt.

The B tensions started coming in when manufacturers began putting springs in the top pivots on derailleurs. The two elements kind of face off against each other, such that the B-tension screw determines the derailleur's resting angle in relation to the cogs. The derailleur's mounting bolt becomes the pivot point; adjusting the B tension rotates it back and forth across this axis.

The belly of the beast

The intention is to better accommodate different ranges of cogs. Top cogs are generally pretty small across the board; we're speaking more of those ranges spreading out behind them. You thread the B tension out to better reach smaller cog sets, or turn it all the way in to fit larger ones. Just about everyone has settled upon the bigger mountain-range cog sets, so in practice this means we generally want the B-tension screw dialed in.

The only time you actually need to adjust the B tension is when the derailleur pulley rides up against the largest cog; you go ahead and dial it all the way in. And you need a derailleur with a longer cage, if this does not solve the problem. No B-tension screw can provide the wee road derailleur the courage to conquer a huge mountain gear range.

The oldest Campagnolo derailleurs simply omitted the B-tension screws as well, of course. They eventually began showing up around the derailleur's mounting bolt, as we may expect them to, but around 1999 they snuck down under the derailleur's knuckle. Their effective function remains the same; they've only moved to a more happening location.

Excluding SRAM's MRX and Shimano's Alivio, both of which top off around 30 teeth, new mountain rear derailleurs are expected to handle cogs up to 34 teeth. But this in itself is nothing so special; a lot of the oldsters do as well. We had this ancient Osell recumbent in for some parts the other day; the first-generation Deore LX rear derailleur it wore was all over the big 34-teeth cog. The longer the cage, the more teeth it can happily deal with. It is with the road derailleurs that things really shrink. Campagnolo's derailleurs finish off on cogs between 26 and 29 teeth; Shimano's road range accommodates cogs up to 27 teeth.

And the whole damned looking glass may well shatter, beyond this point, so don't say I didn't warn you.

Indexing

The **INDEXED DERAILLEURS** sought to improve upon their forebears, by snapping sharply from gear to gear, or at least striving earnestly to do so. Their dream was first realized with the chromed, though comparatively ancient Shimano Indexing System (SIS), which comprised all of six gears. Numerous others have followed, most of them seeking to do things just slightly differently. Distinct indexing protocols declared by Suntour, SRAM, and Campagnolo, set against the additional requirements of 8-, 9-, and 10-speed shifting systems have since formed a kind of multi-directional tug-of-war. Their net in itself does not mean to trap you; it only supports the original premise in novel ways. And you only need to recognize your particular strand, to navigate its contours.

Jtek Engeneering of Minnesota has more recently introduced its Shift Mate adapter pulleys, which modulate the control cables to carefully translate betwixt Shimano and Campagnolo indexing protocols, allowing us to more or less mix and match as we please. (Four distinct models accommodate current and earlier products from either manufacturer.) Suntour was the first to depart from the safety of Shimano's original orthodoxy, by incorporating two slightly different cog spacing measurements into their freewheels. (And, later, their cassettes.) Thus cogs appearing across the lower half of the range were spaced slightly farther apart than their smaller siblings, as means to coincide with a distinct Suntour rear derailleur, which was no longer compatible with the Shimano products.

Suntour XC Pro rear derailleur

This seems like it was an odd thing to do, in retrospect, but such is the wisdom of our age. Shimano was several times their size; the curious designs pursued by a number of Suntour's innovations suggests nothing so much as a manic and fateful desperation. Picture the *Millennium Falcon,* fleeing a *Star Destroyer.* Suntour closed U. S. operations in 1994. They're still with us, having joined with another entity known only as SR, but for the moment at least they've lost a good deal of ground.

Suntour eventually acquiesced, producing a series of cogsets meant to work within Shimano's proper imperial context, which were marked as "Powerflo." And the question of their original parts compatibility has become somewhat less relevant with the passage of time, but the simple fact is a number of their better components were certainly built to last.

The cog-spacing distinction corresponds with adjustments to both the shift lever and its derailleur. The shifter is made to pull just slightly more cable with each click; the derailleur's parallelogram is modified just enough to alter the speed of its arc.

Of the two, the cable pull details are far and away the easier to mess with: they end up becoming quite similar to the Shimano protocols. I've been running Suntour shift levers on Shimano-compatible derailleurs and cas-

settes for most of a decade, actually. I find the old Suntour Command Levers to be particularly worthwhile.

The union of Suntour derailleurs with Shimano-compatible cogsets has always been more controversial. It's not likely we find ourselves attempting the inverse—cogsets matching Suntour's original indexing patterns have not been made since the early 90s; they can only grow less common—and so you do best to enlist some good friction shift levers, when mounting Suntour derailleurs upon Shimano-compatible cogsets. But it happens that things line up slightly better, when moving to an 8 speed. Were you able to find an indexed Suntour 8-speed shift lever, its matching Suntour rear derailleur may be made to roughly index atop an 8-speed Shimano-compatible cogset. But it's still controversial, in that the cable tension parameters are exceedingly narrow. A bad sneeze may throw them off. And so I can't recommend this approach, as such, unless it really has to happen. You're more likely to just drive yourself nuts, trying to get this right. Shimano's own 7- and 8-speed parts are not even cross-compatible, strictly speaking—the cogs end up spaced just slightly differently, across each range—but among these at least we've often been able to establish a workable peace.

Rear Derailleurs

Derailleurs are essentially parallelograms, which are normally pulled to more extreme angles by their springs. It becomes possible to see an even rectangle, shifting through the mid-range: the dimensions of these boxes define the rules of indexing compatibility. Where Campagnolo's is tall and thin, SRAM's is short and squat. The Suntour, Shimano, and Sachs boxes fall between these.

Campagnolo still does lead the race, in terms of the particular quality and integrity of their designs, but our graceless and disposable sensibilities have succeeded in rationing them away to a fortunate minority amongst the road bikes. Their indexing systems were not designed to work with those from other manufacturers, and—as with their rivals—some of the newer products simply don't work with their older peers. But there do come special opportunities with Campagnolo, in this regard, as with updating the Ergopower levers to 9- and 10-speed for example. Updates on their indexing compatibility protocols are best pursued through the company's website.

SRAM is the fruit of a union between Sachs and Grip Shift, both of which have previously produced Shimano-compatible parts. Once together, they soon decided to present a wholly new indexing standard. The SRAM cogsets are still spaced to the expected Shimano distances, but modifications to the derailleur design have succeeded in doubling the cable travel associated with each shift. An absolutely brilliant improvement! It is amazing nobody did it before. The precision of a healthy indexed drivetrain is largely governed by the tension on its shift cable; doubling the interval involved allows for a much more generous range of useful adjustment.

SRAM derailleurs will eschew the barrel adjuster traditionally threaded in to the rear derailleur, because the shift levers already have them, upstairs. A groove simply flows the cable down to its binder bolt. It is redundant to have barrel adjusters in both places, of course. And those threading into derailleurs are always more vulnerable to rust and the elements.

My shelf once featured an ancient Huret Allvit derailleur, which bore some of the world's very first **DERAILLEUR PULLEYS**, which, in its case, were simply round biscuits. But someone eventually noticed that these poker chips weren't necessarily required to roll with the chain at all—they could just sit the damned game out, if they wanted to—and so teeth were duly carved to the wee scones. The interior was made to feature a bushing, held in place by a screw, shot through a pair of protective washers. And so began their mission, to guide the chain through the forest of gears.

A fine example indeed

The pulleys have grown successively narrower, scaling up to meet the 8th, 9th, and 10th cogs used in the modern age; the wide old relics could not be asked to fill in for their svelte progeny. And Shimano has brought us the curious floating pulley, which leaves the pulley's bushing just slightly wider than the pulley itself, allowing it to slide back and forth on its axis. And this affords the earnest indexing derailleurs a most useful discretion, rendering their jumps from gear to gear more free-flowing and natural.

These last are stamped as "Centeron," before emerging from Shimano's bustling boom towns, but other manufacturers have picked up on the idea as well. They couldn't steal the name, of course, so we just look for the essential feature instead; the pulley is able to slide just a bit along its axis. Any of these floaters need to be mounted in the positions nearest the cogs, to do any good at all.

More exotic yet is the sealed bearing pulley. The bearings are supposed to be perpetually smooth; it provides for a pretty straightforward advantage. They're often fairly obvious, as well. Many are machined from aluminum, nakedly displaying the cute little sealed bearings at the cores. The pulley bodies are sometimes thinner than bike chains; we set a washer or two to each side to make things work.

Shimano has elected to obscure this useful distinction, rendering its sealed bearing pulleys in materials other than aluminum. But the uppers in such pairs still retain the useful floating feature, which has not always been the case with the others. Shimano sealed pulleys are also more modest, covering the bearings with dust caps, such that they look a lot like regular pulleys. So just you keep that in mind, when next you get around to soaking the high-end derailleurs in any kind of solvent, which of course will lick all the grease right out of the bearing cartridges.

Shimano has more recently taken to putting larger-than-usual lower pulleys on many of their rear derailleurs. I'm not sure just why—I suspect marketing, frankly—but I don't think it's a bad idea. It may succeed in spite of itself. We expect these big 13-teeth derailleur pulleys to last a little longer than the usual 10 teeth ones; their extra teeth spread the chain's ravages across a slightly wider range of teeth.

The SRAM pulleys are off in a different place entirely, in that they're much more integral to their cages. The SRAM X.O and 9.0 use sealed bearing pulleys; 7.0 and 5.0 use replaceable bushing-style pulleys. But the 3.0 won't give the pulleys up at all; the cage is all one piece. Cheesy.

The single most important thing to remember about any of these other derailleur pulleys? Always, always, always make sure their mounting bolts are tightened securely. And dab a mild thread-locking compound on the threads, if ever you do take things apart.

Front Derailleurs

The **INDEXING FRONT DERAILLEURS** can become alarmingly complicated, given the evident simplicity of their responsibilities. I'm not trying to be a smartass; this is just how it breaks down.

The front derailleur cages have become increasingly specialized, bending and expanding to focus upon various different gearing ranges. Mountain and road parts are most usually wholly distinct, in cage shape and profile and perhaps the frame mounting particulars as well. And the fresh schisms dividing 7/8-, 9-, and 10-speed component groups factor in as well, needless to say.

And the rules of their compatibility are still kind of Wild West, to some extent at least. Manufacturers present their inevitable dictums on what is right and proper, but the fact is certain other endeavors seem to work out as well. But not all; you really need to test things out to know something for sure. I was charged with upgrading an 8-speed Sora-equipped Peugeot the other day, to take one recent example; while the chintzy steel rings stamped as "8 speed" made the jump just fine, the clumsy Sora derailleurs did not. What were those books called? Choose-Your-Own-Adventure?

The new compact road cranks may or may not require special derailleurs of their own, to take another example. Campagnolo provides such kits to accompany their new compact cranks; Shimano's 2006 R600 compact is said to work with a regular Ultegra 10 speed derailleur. The cables also travel to meet the derailleurs from either on high or down below; each requires some distinct accommodation. Their instructions in turn inform one of two common derailleur styles, and this in itself will reflect upon the unit's position on the frame. You may not be able to switch from a "top-swing" unit to an otherwise-identical "traditional" model, in other words, because the new clamp may fall across the frame's water bottle screw. I last saw this with a 2003 Specialized Sirrus, back with the old rental fleet. The bike wasn't spec'd wrong or anything; people simply hadn't communicated enough through the design process, which doesn't much surprise, I suppose.

Were this not yet enough, the front derailleur's mounting parameters have been broadened to include at least five distinct methods. I know of five in present use, which are arguably more than enough already, but our world remains vulnerable to the blandly egocentric and pretentious whims of those who presume to further the confusion. The sum of things already leaves us exposed, in that we need to secure a fairly specific replacement, from amongst dozens of quite similar pretenders. The wrong example either works very poorly, or doesn't work at all. Hope you saved your receipt! We need to install a moratorium.

Shimano is the only company able to provide a full range of front derailleurs, for the moment at least. But considering their famous supply problems of recent times, I'm not sure we can expect the blast doors to hold. Suntour did make a superb showing in their time; I still rely on their finer drivetrain parts extensively. And Sachs made a few as well, and of course Campagnolo still produces a fine road range. We can discover a few more

precedents, plumbing the time line, but these will have fallen before all the big changes began happening.

The dreary limits imposed by the mindless new cacophony of front derailleur choices, reflects in miniature the new global trade rules, in that they each can only encourage monopolistic practices. Shimano would surely hasten to obscure and rationalize the question, just as any other transnational would, but the simple fact is that their strenuous efforts have brought to being an entirely new classification of extra confusion.

We can surely find some handful of myopic enthusiasts to eagerly endorse the new ways, but the simple fact is that those not sufficiently technically sophisticated are again left mystified and alienated. And a popular technology is further relegated to the whims of a select few specialists. But it is not in the ownership's interest to democratize anything. We have no real alternatives, until we find or make them.

A majority of the front derailleur's recent design changes serve aesthetics or novelty, which is to say they fail to counterbalance the original and more fundamental liabilities. The spread of our gearing preferences can accommodate somewhat simpler means; the imperatives proffered alongside these other "improvements" are not worthy of serious discussion.

The fit is the most substantial consideration before us, in that it's least able to compromise, unless you're able to find or make a metal shim of complementary dimensions or something. I've had to do it that way a couple times, actually. It can be done. And in all fairness, it should be noted that Shimano has more recently produced a set of fairly ubiquitous front derailleur shims, allowing a single compact mountain front derailleur to transcend our three tube sizes. And some of these work extended cable grooves in to their pivots, allowing the cable to run from either on high or down below.

The front derailleurs have traditionally and quite happily clamped themselves around the frames' seat tubes, but these very pipes have been expanded not once but twice. Newer materials and understandings have emerged within framebuilding; there remains a diversity of thoughts about the seat tube dimensions. And so we have our three clamp sizes.

The fifth of our derailleur mounting protocols is an ungainly creature of Shimano's creation. It, too, was yet a further redundancy. But some of the nicer road bikes had previously decided they didn't want to bother with the cumbersome old clamps at all. Such shackles could only interfere with the artful trace of a fine paint job! They also burden the poor bikes with entire *grams* of excessive weight. And so the sympathetic engineers devised a conciliatory remedy, which the whole world would soon know as the **BRAZE-ON FRONT DERAILLEUR**. Its universal charms have been able to stand in for every front derailleur mounting protocol the world has yet to see.

Braze-on front derailleurs can be knocked out of alignment, if you're roughhousing, so it is a good idea to secure their bolts with a mild thread-locker. Some clamp-style front derailleurs tend to rotate slightly out of place on the seat tubes, as they're tightened in to position; hold things down with your free hand to prevent this. The final position is best realized with the clamping bolt just slightly loose, in any case, such that the derailleur can be usefully nudged toward improved positions. Just make sure the bolt gets nice and tight, once you do settle the derailleur on a good position.

Shimano's indexing front derailleurs rely upon slightly more spectacular cage profiles. Their long boxes just begin to experiment with becoming wedge-like when viewed from above, and it is the longest edge featuring therein that we like to line up precisely parallel to the chainrings; usually, but not always, the front corner of the cage's outer plate. As with the front derailleur's other adjustments, this is only determined by testing out the shifting.

The end result usually leaves one or both edges of its tail splayed out to either direction, but this is fine. It appeals to the chains or something.

Campagnolo figures things somewhat differently, suggesting that the inner plates on their products are meant to become parallel with the chainrings. But their serene road drivetrains allow for more natural cage profiles than their competitors' jumpy mountain cranks; they're easier to manage with simple rules.

The cages are sometimes bent farther still, by later events, but this is fairly unusual. It's fairly obvious as well, when comparing to a similar but unmolested example. And there is not much we can do, in such circumstances. It's difficult to replicate the cage's original profile; the damaged front derailleurs are usually shitcanned. But the fearsome cranks and the frame itself will likely step in and take the hit, before forsaking the neurotic front derailleurs; it's quite rare that we actually get to this point.

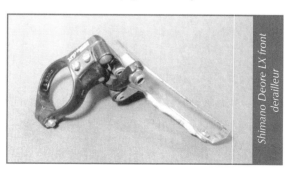

Shimano Deore LX front derailleur

A given example is more inclined toward double- or triple-chainring cranksets. The doubles are thinner and more fin-like; the triples demonstrate more of a stepped effect.

The inner plates on triple-ring front derailleurs extend considerably lower than their outer halves, which in turn is taller and more pronounced than their double-ring peers. The effort allows for more productive exchanges with the smallest chainrings. This is something you notice, trying to run a triple crank with a double-ring derailleur; it really makes a difference.

We also want the front derailleur cages to faithfully match the contours of the chainrings they're focusing upon. This is another place where things could have been simpler. We're again forced to pick through an excess of nearly identical options. A good fit will find the cage's outer plate maintaining the 2-millimeter gap against the top ring, across the full length of its leading edge. The frame's seat tube usually rests at a fixed angle; this provides us with a reference point. (Some of the recumbents do their own things in this respect, with their diminutive front derailleur stalks. These are often kicked back to more rakish angles, to better support the larger chainrings commonly associated with the smaller 'bent drive wheels.)

So we're looking for either a road or a mountain front derailleur. The double-ring cranks are set aside for the road bikes, in usual circumstances, so we don't find double-ring derailleurs in the mountain ranges. Road cranks typically top off with chainrings of 52 teeth; the double-ring derailleurs expect to see something like this. The mountain standard has recently centered around 42 or 44 teeth, but the top rings on such cranks have ranged from 38 to 48 teeth.

However, the mountain front derailleurs can be *further* configured as top-swing top pull, traditional top pull, top-swing bottom pull, and the old favorite, traditional bottom pull. A further number of the top-swings in either top- or bottom-pull appear as E type units, which attach around the bottom bracket.

This E type mountain bike fitting is quite distinct, comparing against our jolly old braze-on buddies. Different mount; different height. The engineers seem to have assumed we shop rats can't manage to remember which derailleurs go where or something. Fuck. Excluding the E type thing and the braze-on units, each of the four styles are built around a clamp designed to fit a seat tube of 28.6, 31.8, or 35.0 millimeters. (Note that this measure is distinct from the seat post up top; it is the seat tube's outside diameter.)

Shimano Deore front derailleurs have been arriving with shims to fit each of the three main tube sizes, and this allows their hosts to more or less come and go as they please. The cable routing has always been the more challenging consideration. SRAM and Shimano have both tackled the question, in recent years—for the aforementioned compact mountain gear ranges, at least—and of the two, SRAM's solution is more righteous. Where Shimano's approach runs the poor cable through an unlikely roller coaster of obtuse bends to accommodate both top- and bottom-pull cable routings, SRAM simply fixes two cable binder positions to opposing sides of the same pivot point. The SRAM design also plucks the derailleur spring from its dusty old dungeon behind the cage, relocating it to within the pivot assembly, where it is likely do somewhat better.

Crossing these distinct mounting options against the range of choices in gearing and quality levels, we find a vast army of different possibilities. This does allow for more pluralism in our frame designs, but it also means a given bicycle will work best—or only—with one of several potential configurations.

The widest clamps sometimes stumble absently upon their own low limit screw adjustments—you turn that puppy out past a certain point, its cage simply runs in to the seat tube—but this may be our only qualitative concern. The distinctions relate primarily to the bike's tubing and cable routing specifications. (And, likely enough, to various goofy ideas on aesthetics.) The salient choices come in the different price points, carefully aligned along each of our configurations. It is generally possible to get anything from cheap shit to bad-ass for your replacement, but you probably need to special order any truly exacting requests. There's just too many; it is the nature of the beast.

An indexed derailleur's precision is governed by the tension of its control cable. Adjustments to the barrel adjuster—found on the derailleur itself, at the frame's cable stop, at the shift lever or in-line on the cable housing—should provide us all the help we need, provided the aforementioned details regarding set-up have been attended to.

If the cable is entirely slack, you'll first want to dial the barrel adjuster all the way down, before re-tightening it at the binder bolt. You'd then increase cable tension by turning the barrel out—nudging the derailleur away from its starting position—and the reverse is also true. Work in small adjustments, checking your work at each turn: when the shift lever is notched up a gear, the chain should move up by the same measure.

Shift Levers

Guiding all of this along are the bike's **SHIFT LEVERS**. Their most rudimentary examples first clustered around the down tube, of course. A few of the more adventurous sorts soon ventured up toward the handlebar stem, while others eventually developed their own basic ratcheting mechanisms. There were even some that did the two things at once!

A further minority, led by the inspired pioneers over at Suntour, had already begun the determined trek out to the ends of the handlebars. A few of their numbers then doubled back again, to rest at midship points on the happening new bull-moose mountain bike handlebars. These roughly mimicked their progenitors on the old three-speed handlebars, of course, just sitting out in the open like that. And it was there, clamped front and center beneath the hands, that the experiments began in earnest.

A protracted conflict has since opened, up on the handlebars, and the old guard has not fared well at all. Excluding a few especially gifted creatures, the new bikes have all been made to shun and fear the original shift levers. All manner of obtuse plasticized complications have been allowed to manipulate the clarion purity of their purposes.

Bar-end shifters have been relegated to an ever-smaller portion of road bikes. The noble thumbshifters have witnessed their own tragedies as well; those few remaining have largely been reduced to plastic. Down-tube levers have been all but wiped from the showroom floor! I don't know what to tell you; that's just how it is.

The replacements, generally speaking, have sought to remove anything remotely emotive from the shifting process, much like the Daleks, on *Doctor Who*. The first grip shifters were pleasantly simple, if less than durable, but their children have become increasingly confused. And the ever-more ubiquitous shifter pods, needless to say, represent the very crucibles of imperial presumption. They never negotiate with or argue against, let alone refine or repair. It is time we move the battle forward.

Righteousness shines its sweet light across the vast sweep of our line, pressing us firmly to the front. Where the new pretenders are *necessarily* vulnerable to all manner of dread mechanical ailments, a fair number of their progenitors may well live forever.

The worldview presented by transnational conglomerates suggest that the new shifters humbly make things easier for us, by at last removing the tedious imperatives of subtlety and intuition, not to mention their wealth of related skills. Sympathetic voices within and around the industry expect to endorse the project, for various reasons, and so it comes to seem nearly natural and inevitable. But the impulse speaks for itself.

As a mechanic, my concerns must be with the myriad new complications sheltering within our modern shift levers. We're able to repair some of the more basic SRAM rotary levers, and even some of Campagnolo's brilliant Ergopower levers, but the balance of their peers is all but hopeless. You need to keep them going, however this may happen, because never in our lives will their madness be repaired.

Our friend Travis T. showed me a useful method for regenerating some of Shimano's rapid-fire pods, up at Freewheel. The pod's graceless jolts are traced to a pair of delicate palls, ratcheting away beneath the cover, and the lubricant these rely upon seems to dry out after a while. So you remove the lid, dose a bit of T9 or similar around the palls, and very carefully work this in with your small screwdriver. Sway the palls lightly back and forth, until their tired wire springs are convinced to return the things on their own.

Pods are only the obvious example. The relentless novelty drapes our village like a leaden blanket, blocking out the sun. And the pods themselves have become sealed, in fact. The originals featured useful escape hatches for cable replacement, but these were eventually sealed with clumsy plastic plugs, which have more recently been paved over with unlikely contoured plates. And these last, while distinct to each of the shift levers they afflict, are invariably held in place by pairs of especially tiny screws.

You need a smaller Phillips screwdriver to attack these. The itsy-bitsy screws are so small and light, in fact, that most only briefly stay on the screwdriver tip. And be careful when pulling away, lest the tiny spike tumble forever into the abyss. You'll never find it again; you can only wail and remember and write poetry. Cup your hand under the screw, pulling away until you're able to stash both it and its damned plate in a jar lid while you work.

The carbon steel featuring around SRAM's new X.0 shifter, by contrast, is more easily removed for servicing. Shimano had previously relied upon a much simpler approach to this goal—the aforementioned threaded plastic plug, removed with the regular Phillips screwdriver, which did the job fine—but it was not so long ago that even the fancy shifters didn't plug up their cable holes.

It has been in my livelihood to service these, since that time, and I cannot imagine a valid reason for the change. This new hermetic-sealing fascination would only *possibly* be useful if you were out trolling the handlebars through mud puddles or something, and it's still not clear how this imposing darkness represents any meaningful improvement. We would want to strip the shifters down and clean them up, after a night like that. The sealing impulse works quite well in other applications—some bearing cartridges, for example—but it comes off a little ridiculous, perched up on the handlebars there. Come on. The mud is all the way downstairs, on the ground.

All the shift cables are removed by the same basic method, clumsy plates or not. Shift all the way down, such that the cable is as slack as it ever may be, and release its tail from beneath the derailleur's pinch bolt. You would need to snip off any ferrule or frays, to pull it back through the housing. There may even be a kink or two to bend out with the box pliers, as well. The binder bolt will have flattened a small stretch of the cable, unless you're able to press it round again; you may have to yank it out with the fourth hand tool.

The cable's head should back out of the shifter. *It must be in the slackest gear for this to work, on the Rapidfire pods, or STI, or Ergopower.* The cable's head is sandwiched in to things in such a way that it comes around a bend as you downshift; it will not be able to move freely until the very end.

BAR-END SHIFTERS are all we have left for beautiful shift levers. They still recall the best decisions: they're made well, with appropriate materials, in accordance with a blessedly simple plan. There's no goofy indicator windows or creepy modulation. Many are still able to run well on the otherwise-extinct friction model, and this makes them quite universal.

Campagnolo still makes these, but I've come across all of a few pairs in my life. The last time was on an M5 I saw in 2002, if mem-

ory serves: nice crisp action, smooth design; artisan, but also obscure. The only bar-end shifters we really see new are Shimano's top-end Ultegra or Dura Ace. They're spendy, 8-, 9-, or 10-speed either way, but they will last. You would need some kind of active conspiracy to destroy such equipment. Were I needing to buy new shift levers for something, I would naturally call upon some of these.

Bar-end shifters have been with us for a long time. The originals, made by Suntour, had friction on both sides. The mounting hardware slips in to the handlebar; the shifter hooks to its face. Said base is built around a bolt; turning it counter-clockwise expands its tail inside the handlebar.

This particular set-up plays out as a kind of mechanical mirror. Letting this bolt tighten clockwise, as the world hopes and expects, finds the manufacturers investing in all kinds of goofy reverse-thread machine toolage. But nobody is supposed to be getting in to see this bolt, except us bike jockeys. We're none too particular.

Bar-end shifters

With the modern Shimano bar ends, easily the most common now, the shift lever itself is essentially a down-tube shifter. The profile is only a bit different to better suit its new station. The world has eventually agreed upon a set of standardized bosses upon which to mount the down-tube levers; the bar-end hardware simply brings the pair upstairs to the balcony. Your old Shimano down-tube shifters can serve for spare parts, in other words.

The Shimano bar-end mounts are installed first; the shifter bosses are pushed through their sides. As with other worthy bike parts, there's precious little to complicate here. Bar-end shifters do not fit in the ends of flat ATB-style handlebars. They are not meant to. You have a tough time sneaking them past any serious curves in road handlebars: plugging flipped-and-clipped drop bars, for example. All they need is a bit of straight pipe, in the road dimensions.

The twist shifters have become pretty famous. The dusty old 3 speeds began borrowing them from motorcycles quite some time ago, but the idea did not really take hold until Grip Shift arrived on the scene. And their original shift levers really were blessedly simple, accomplishing their business with only pairs of moving elements. A linear spring set between the body and its shell allowed the pair to ratchet away contentedly, all but oblivious to the clamor all around.

Grip shift disassembly

The original plastic springs did not hold up so well; we're still able to replace these with the more useful metal ones. And the hard plastic casings would not weather any rain of hammers, needless to say, but this leaves them light and inexpensive enough as well.

But the new SRAM conglomeration is evidently afflicted with some excess of presumptions, as things pan out, because this original harmony is quickly forsaken before the looming altar of novelty. An unlikely and entirely redundant spring is jammed in to some of the newer high-end levers, such as the 9.0, as means to obscure the reliable sensations associated with an otherwise reliable indexed gear reduction system.

The effort recalls Suntour's short-lived F7 and F8 lever settings, which also sought to blur the borders betwixt friction and indexing: now as before, the product development teams ask performance riders to patiently sit on their hands.

These smooth new fruits may well appeal to some especially nervous sect of leisure cyclists, but this only transpires at the clear expense of worthier design imperatives.

It has become much more difficult to change the cables, for one thing. SRAM typically sets a sharp 90-degree bend in the cable's path, just before it exits to cable housing, but those featuring on these cheerful new cans secret this channel away in darkness, which effectively discourages us from reusing cables. You can still manage, but only if you really twist the *hell* out of them. This is always useful in preventing frays, of course, but right now we need to kind of go crazy with it. You're rolling the cable in your fingers, just kind of absently nudging it forward into the shifter.

The only other alternative is to pull the lever apart. It snaps together, lengthwise. But this becomes five times as stupid, because the new design is also rather complicated. Remember the spring, forced in by the marketing department? This strange new serpent is situated directly opposite the shifter's working mechanical spring, and both will struggle forcefully, as you try to press their cage back together. You may be camped out for a while, actually. Does this really need to happen?

Secure the handlebar in a vise, or see to it that the bike remains quite still, and get in there with your smallest screwdriver. Try to jam the new spring back in place, while carefully easing the lever closed. As this happens, you also want to make sure the gear indicator's wispy neon straw is correctly aligned in the appropriate position. Have fun!

Grip Shift and its SRAM progeny have parked the cable head in different places, over the years. Old-fashioned examples will sometimes bury it up inside the shifter itself. A cable head may be just visible, up a shallow hole on the lever's innermost side. Such can likely be replaced with a new, uncut cable, but you need to take the lever apart to reuse cables. Lots of bends inside; cut ends fray all to hell.

You may just have to take the thing apart anyway, if you don't see a cable head somewhere on the stem side of the lever's base, because some older levers actually hide the cable heads up inside. The body and its shell may be held together by a curious U-shaped clamp; an opening at its base lets us slide the thing aside with a flathead screwdriver. Other models rely upon reasonably sized release screws here, featuring as the noses on curved triangular faces, and yet others are simply pulled apart. But do look for a release screw or the carefully disguised clamping piece, before yanking on things.

And the humble MRX levers show up with a better plan, actually, which the others have since picked up as well. The MRX grip sections each feature exactly one rubber corner, which is pushed aside to see the cable head's escape hole. (This becomes a conspicuous rubber flap, with other SRAM levers.) You need to shift the lever to its slackest position, to spy our elusive opening. And yet it may not be so simple, because SRAM is also interested to make sure the cable heads are not able to back out of position, and thereby develop various methods to hold things down.

A trim plastic lip clips just over the top of the cable heads, in the case of SRAM 7.0 and similar levers; this is pried aside with the same small screwdriver. The 9.0 levers, on the other hand, thread a tiny cable-set screw down atop the cable head itself. It's the very one we're using with some of their planetary hub cables, actually; it turns out atop your 2.5-millimeter Allen key.

I'm not able to describe any specific map, with regards to the routing of cables within SRAM/Grip Shift levers, simply because they've tried a number of things over the years. But things should really be obvious enough; a telling cable-sized groove will likely illuminate the way forward. If there's a carved-out, cable-sized valley around part of the shifter, you want to take advantage of it. This will sometimes find you forming a loop with the cable, before reassembling the lever.

Before going much further, we should clarify SRAM's relationship to the patterns of Shimano's mainstream indexing protocols. The SRAM flagships—those bearing the revolutionary 2 to 1 cable actuation ratio—are identified by odd numbers. The 3.0, 5.0, 7.0, and 9.0 each have twice what it takes. All other SRAM levers feature names like MRX or Rocket or Attack, or perhaps an even number; these are destined for the Shimano derailleurs. These are wholly distinct from the others; there is little confusion about what, went, and where. Either something will index or it quite simply will not.

SRAM and Shimano have at last made a kind of fragile peace, for the advancement of certain common interests, but things are not always so peachy. Shimano's derailleur springs are meant to work with smaller, counterbalancing springs set up in the shift levers; the early Grip Shifters lacked any such thing. Their timid linear springs were no match for the bold and furious Shimano derailleur springs; the result was an unfortunate propensity to drop out of gear, especially over time. And so the retro-fit derailleur springs were made available, to balance things out, but these were always kind of a half-measure. SRAM has since learned to modify some of their levers just enough, needless to say, and by all accounts these have learned to play nicely with the Shimano derailleurs.

SRAM's original MRX shifters, unfortunately, have another distinct concern. Some of their number grow tired after a while, and come apart … all the time. The wrap of the cable has a tendency to push the shifter apart, and this they do, all day long. The plastic bit that accomplishes the snapping wears down; the levers end up being held in place by the stationary portions of the grip.

At the very same time, a good number of the handlebar grips supplied with inexpensive new bikes have developed a conspicuous tendency to loosen up over time. And we're blithely assured this is merely an incidental function of their exciting new comfort ratios or some shit, but frankly it strikes me as a way to sell more grips. Your hands end up rolling them away from the stem; they also wear out more quickly. And, since these things are too often charged with holding the chintzy MRX shift levers snapped together, the troubles spring easily upon the drivetrain as well. The shift levers come apart, as the grips loosen, and after a point we can no longer shift the gears.

You might have better luck with some of the more durable after-market grips, but SRAM still pumps out plenty of their fragile MRX flowers, to suit triple-chainring systems employing five through eight cogs no less. And rest assured the longer half pipe MRX models available for 7- and 8-speed drivetrains have

at least as many problems in this regard; their shorter grips loosen sooner. (The MRX name is also applied to a small number of sharper-looking levers, which don't fail as easily.)

And so you need to convince these confused comfort grips to stay in place, in order to use them with the original MRX levers. I've never had much luck with the grip glue products, and it's not like grips don't wear out. The summer of 2002, when first I focused on this stupid little dilemma, my fix-it-for-free rental bike approach was zip ties. The grips on all the MRX-afflicted rental horses were duly strapped in place, with a little help from the mighty fourth hand tool. But some of the renters began complaining of the (relatively) sharp zip tie ends, almost immediately. I'd set things up with the zip tie heads down by the fingers—not pressed under the palms—but all the input led me to follow a suggestion Caitlin had, to leave an inch of zip tie hanging off the end. And lo, it soon emerged that this too was incompatible with summer vacation plans.

A month or two after we'd shuttered the rental shop for the season I finally realized the best solution to the dreaded MRX dynamic … bar-end extensions, a useful upgrade in the first place. You get some extra hand positions; your crappy little shifters get some solid guidance on keeping it together.

Later still, putzing in the basement on a crisp winter afternoon, I began to wonder how setting up every last MRX-afflicted rental unit with its own bar ends may square with the famously slim margins associated with bike rental. And I realized the cheapest (and best) MRX solution yet … BMX handlebar plugs.

BMXers are known to get all rugged with their bikes, and among other things they've called into being various sturdy bar plugs, to guard the grips from life's potential abrasions. But this very logic can be flipped around, to prevent the grips from escaping, which in turn keeps the shoddy MRX devices from becoming unsure and unraveling themselves. Their tendency to come apart is my principle complaint. They work well enough, otherwise.

One thing that can certainly be said for SRAM is that they will roundly whomp their closest competitors. Shimano's Revo-Shift is still a pointless joke, especially when joined to one of their C. I. Decks. And such is their natural state, unfortunately, on the low-end comfort bikes they settle upon. The fairly straightforward rotor-shifting platform is harnessed to an unlikely new complexity, as means to run the damned indicator window. The Happy Meal now requires a second cable, in fact, just to run the display.

The C. I. Deck sits there on top of the stem, smirking up at us, proudly insulting our collected intelligence. *The Central Information Deck, together with its stupid purse strings, is entirely superfluous to the shifting process.* And it's just as well; the thing is fragile as eggs.

We're able to remove the decks easily enough, but their wires are dug in a bit deeper. You have to pop of a couple more of Shimano's odd plates, which are attached with the same ridiculously tiny screws. The whole edifice will some day crash to the ground.

Worse yet is the horrible SEC Shift. But this may be obvious enough on the face of things, actually. The shifting action just sucks. The shift up is like climbing a dangerous hill; the return action feels perpetually on-the-way-out.

"SEC Shift, U. S. Patent" is all we can read on these new pretenders: no model name, no manufacturer, no nothing. Just the patent number, scratched in far too small to the underside of an unlikely spot, to claim the title … *bullshit.* Grip Shift did the most to match the rotor-shifting concept to modern bicycles, before joining Sachs to form SRAM. The glory is theirs, if it belongs to anyone. And here comes this SEC slime, claiming the project as their own, some incidental abstraction to casually imprison within the money zoo? No, fuck these losers. The gesture speaks for itself.

This background, together with the fact that the SEC piles tend to work only marginally in the first place, suggests they were probably hashed together on the whims of nameless investor scum, which indicates all you need to know about warranty service and replacement parts and the like. These things arrived on our 4 KHS Tandemania rental tandems early in May: of the eight SEC levers involved, five broke down and stopped working before July was through. So I went ahead and replaced the remainder, lest their failure rate strive on toward completion.

The bikes in question sell for $700 or $1,100, new. What the royal fuck? Those enlisted as rentals are abused more often, perhaps, but so is everything else in our fleet: in my four years as the rental mechanic, I cannot recall any bicycle component with so atrocious a record. SRAM's poor little MRX lever, once improved, quite handily flattens the miserable SEC to the ground.

Planetary Gearing

Expired SEC unit

The derailleurs are forthright, in that everything is out where you can see it, but this does leave them more exposed to the elements. This may or may not become an issue for you.

The alternative is to move the shifting indoors to the hubs. Or, in the case of Schlumpf's heel-activated Speed and Mountain Drives, to the bottom bracket. This aesthetic and inward tendency is most properly known as **PLANETARY GEARING**.

You can probably imagine the original planets. They are the curiously thick chromed canisters that move the old 3-speeds. A closer inspection often reveals the manufacturer as Sturmey Archer. We know they were made well, by virtue of the fact that so many are still on the road. The production year is often stamped on the hub body, actually. It is not uncommon that we find examples three or four decades old, still tooling about.

These originals provide for an oil port, right there on the hub body. It sticks out, with the little plastic cap. You want to drop some motor oil (something of that consistency, between thick and thin) into this now and then, like a couple times a year maybe. Phil's Tenacious Oil may be the best option here.

Planetary hubs needing more oil often make more noise because they want you to feed them. Most hubs do fine with regular bearing grease, but the hub gears are more demanding. There's a lot more going on inside; grease kind of gums up the works.

A rod running through the axle is charged with dragging a Drive gear past different orbiting gears in the hub shell. Our original examples put diminutive indicator chains in charge of the planets, but some modern versions have managed to usefully update this interface.

A number of parties have marched the planets in distinct directions, actually; the classic steel model has been edged toward the museums. Its shiny steel body is a bit heavy and no longer quite fashionable; the 120-millimeter axle spacing is fully quaint in its antiquity; a paltry 3 speeds is simply no longer enough for some folks to get excited about.

The proprietary Sturmey cables are also curious, in that they're already sized to length. They have two heads, in fact, distinct to each end. A prescribed length of cable housing spans a portion of their middle distance; moving its stop up and down the frame tube sets the ground floor for the cable tensioning. We also find a barrel adjuster down by the hub, for purposes of fine-tuning the same measure. You attach the cable at both points, then slide the housing clamp up the down tube until the slack disappears. Pretty unique. If you do have troubles with a Sturmey, you want to check the cable line first. Make sure the housing is anchored securely where it needs to be, and that the cable itself is not hung up on anything.

Adam Cornell went into some detail on these in *How to Rock and Roll*. As he suggested there, you really don't want to take a planetary hub apart just for the hell of it. It's not any quick-thrills kind of thing. You want to hunt down a schematic drawing particular to your specific project, prior to beginning excavations.

The rod at the end of the indicator chain threads into the hub's innards, shooting straight out through an elongated axle nut. Its top is beveled inward, like a mouth opened in surprise; our indicator chain snakes off the lip and quickly hooks up with the cable. But the thing is an absolute dwarf, comparing to the regular bike chain; strong enough to transfer a shift into the hub, but not nearly rugged enough to handle much for impact. They die all the time, actually, like when the bike rolls in to the barn after a night of heavy drinking. Some more happening bike shops may yet have a few odd indicators kicking around somewhere; at other places they may just glare at you for asking such a thing. Kind of a city-mouse, country-mouse thing maybe.

The hub interfaces aboard newer Shimano planetary hubs make provisions for more judicious outcomes. Everything transpires beneath a sturdy metal shelter. Brilliant. It means nothing gets broken, next time somebody's drunk.

Better still, the shelter's interior is not crammed with any excess of rocket science. Its lower section comes off with a small screw—one far too small, once again—and the shelter is revealed to hold only a binder bolt mounted on a pivot point. This is pressed against a blessedly simple one-piece push rod, which disappears into the hub. And there is no tiny indicator chain for you to accidentally destroy. The rear of the metal shelter even features a small window, to help with calibrating the adjustments. Well done, Shimano.

Hub gears, like the external drivetrains, are governed by the shift cable's tension. Planetary hubs tend to rely upon barrel adjusters, set somewhere along the cable run: at the shifter; on the indicator rod; outside the hub. But at least one more basic system, the SRAM Monsoon TS200, seems to manage without. Those examples I've worked on, at least. Planetary hubs are more generous with the cable tension parameters than some derailleurs we see around; the Monsoon gets away with it.

But SRAM was thinking ahead. Their Monsoon system, together with the original 3 x 7 and various others, links the indicator chain to shift cable by means of an adjustment sleeve. There's a small plastic box, wedged in front,

bearing the tip of a linear brass spring on one side. The opposing end of this very spring is pressed against the indicator chain's threaded end piece, inside the adjustment sleeve, such that we can press the exposed tip to release the chain. Or the chain's end piece is simply pressed forward in the sleeve, alternately, to increase the cable tension. The shift cable's tail passes through one nostril set in the sleeve's narrower end, where it is clamped by a cable-set screw and sent out another. Our Monsoon's cable tension parameters are generous enough to subsist on the sleeve's ratcheting ministrations; other systems will slip in a barrel adjuster at the shift lever.

The airy sleeved approach is lilting and melodic, comparing with the original planetary hubs, which presumed a more exacting approach. A small hole drilled to the side of the hub's elongated locknut provided a glimpse of the indicator chain; marks on its end piece and the hole itself means to line up when the hub was shifted to second gear. This was accomplished by tweaking on a tiny barrel adjuster, linking cable to chain.

This premise is carried forward by some of the newer planets, such as SRAM's Dual Drive or the Shimano Inter 3, but either provide for a more useful interpretation. The cable interface features a small window; your cable tension adjustments only need to align a couple brightly colored lines. But you can actually see if things are out of adjustment, with the adjustment sleeves. The sleeve itself balks and jumps around, as you try to park it in second. Or, if the cable's too tight, the hub simply does not go into its last gear.

Each of these hub gears is best matched to its own specific lever. You can't just grab one from the sock drawer! The different intervals of cable travel will not reliably overlap with those offered by regular derailleur shifters, as far as I know at least. You may accidentally get away with this, sometimes, but I think you will have a hell of a time trying to manage hub gears with friction levers.

DUAL DRIVE is SRAM's 3-speed planetary hub, paired with an 8/9-speed freehub body, allowing 27 speeds with a single front chainring. It updates the 3 x 7 hub, which featured a 7-speed freehub body. Everything is run by a solitary lever over on the right side, which becomes reasonably intuitive when you see the thing. The lever's design is very space age; totally Buck Rogers. And it does leave the left hand free, so you can run a standard triple-ring crank as well, for a total of 81 gears. Blast right the hell out into the void.

The Dual Drive incorporates the ingenious Clickbox downstairs, which basically shoots the cable right down to the end of the axle. The top side of the Clickbox features a simple button that functions as a quick release, as well as a small plastic adjustment window. The cable pinches down to a pivot with a sharp yellow line drawn across its top, which is what you look for to check on the adjustment. The barrel adjuster is right there on the Clickbox; it's all very straightforward. (The one up on the Dual Drive shift lever itself is for the rear derailleur.) It's all very tight; we get the sense they passed a few late nights with this one. As SRAM's literature puts it, "a big team of twenty-five engineers from all around the world worked for two years on this project."

It is not complicated to remove the Clickbox, when you need to drop the wheel out, but putting things back together may take a little work. The Dual Drive's particularly tiny push rod just barely peeks out of the hub, before ending with a little cap; this is meant to slip under a catch on the Clickbox. It comes off easily enough, but you may have to kind of wiggle things around to get it back.

The Dual Drive's cable is also asked to end quite abruptly, just past the binder bolt. The walls close in around it, basically. Pinching a cable so close to a fresh cut invariably results in a spiky bouquet of frayed wire, which is less than ideal. You forget it's there; you rush in and jab a finger, blood everywhere, it's crazy. Lucky for us, SRAM was nice enough to provide for an out. The rear of the Dual Drive's interface features a small plastic plate that snaps into place; the bottom of which features a nice big hole a proper cable tail may pass through.

The bike's original handlers may not have been hip to this—their supervisors would likely have hosted the efficient management-style assessments of aesthetics, whereby the loose ends are summarily tucked away—but that's their problem; there's no stopping you. Just let the cable flow out a short distance, next time you change it, so you can clip and cap its end properly. You will have to put a couple small bends in the cable to get this going, but it will work.

Rohloff has also enjoyed some success, with its legendary 14-speed internal hub. No cassette is able to fit on top of this one, but the 14's range works out to be wide enough already. It provides a reasonable approximation of those gears we may otherwise call upon. We also have the Speed and Mountain Drive planetary bottom brackets from Schlumpf. The Speed adds an extra accelerator range on top of an existing drivetrain; the Mountain provides for more generous climbing gears at the bottom. Your number of gears is essentially doubled, in either case. These I have played with some, and they also seem quite worthwhile. The spindle bolts are hollow; the heel kicks a rod back and forth to change gears. Said rod wears decent-sized caps on its ends, which may be further shielded by crisp wings coming down along the crank arms.

Chains

The planets are none too common, stateside. They're most often associated with dedicated city bikes and folders, neither of which has yet to become all that big here. But the chains provide us with a grand unifying theme.

Some freak busts out with a shaft-driven bicycle transmission system every few years or so, but as yet I'm not sure why. The famous and inevitable drivetrain wear, which reliably results from the transfer of our energies? Any shaft-drive system concentrates all of this upon a pair of nervous transition points, rather than displacing it along the full length of a chain. And if the chains are replaced every 3,000 miles or so—on derailleur-equipped bikes, at least—how long can we expect any shaft teeth to last?

With **BIKE CHAINS,** our widest model, commonly called the 1/8-inch chain, is meant for 1 speeds—BMX, cruisers, some of the more doctrinaire track bikes. And various older 3 speeds as well, actually. The next size, 3/32 inch, carries over from the original derailleur bikes. Our new 3/32-inch chains are meant to work with 5-, 6-, 7-, or 8-speed gear clusters. Ancient 5- or 6-speed equipment may sometimes balk, but more usually the cogs are *generally* of similar widths.

The world has only narrowed, with the arrival of 9- and 10-speed gear clusters. The chain, the cogs, and their spacers are fractions thinner than all else before, with each successive step. And this is the way things have to be, really; the clunky old 8-speed cogsets had previously reached what may be described as a useful limit to our shifting parameters. Widening the hubs to accept more cogs would have been tremendously difficult to sell, given the growing cohesion of the industry's standards, and squeezing more cogs

in back against the spokes would have made the wheel exponentially weaker. Eight speeds had already tacked a spare cog to the back side of 7 speeds, essentially, and it transpired that the resultant width was about all we may reasonably ask the bespoken wheels to deal with. This is a function of the wheel dish, of course, as described on pages 194-195.

And so the gear clusters, together with their indexed shifters, are meant to translate 5, 6, 7, 8, 9, or 10 speeds. Really old chains—from 3 speeds, dusty Schwinn Collegiates and the like—were already well established by the time 3/32-inch chains even appeared. The plates are a bit wider; their pins extend out a bit farther. You can totally tell the difference, laying a 1-speed chain next to a 7/8-speed. And, with a little practice, you can spot the 9- and 10-speeds away from the 7/8.

New chains arrive to our world coated with an especially thick and luscious lubricant, incidentally, but it is only the packing grease. I previously had been told this stuff was some kind of awesome factory super-lubricant, which the service crew up at Freewheel found reasonably amusing. But we should actually be oiling the new chains, including those on new bikes, using a top-quality chain lubricant such as the Rock and Roll, for example. This will likely quiet things down, and can certainly help new chains retain their youthful vigor.

7/8 sp top; 1 sp below

The adjustments you make on the chain are absolutely crucial. It is very much worth your time to do the math, when **INSTALLING AND REMOVING CHAINS.**

The chains need to be uniform throughout. You cannot safely assume distinct manufacturers' links are compatible with each other. This is especially true across the different chain widths, from 7/8 to 9 speed for example.

Shimano chains are assembled with their proprietary Hyperglide chain pins, which are twice the length of their fellows. They have pointed front sections, which are meant to smooth the way for the wider tails. They snap right off with pliers, once the rear is in place. Distinct Hyperglide pins are used with 7/8-, 9-, and 10-speed chains. Each is a bit shorter, of course, and their steel enjoys three different hues as well.

The pins are one-shot deals; you use them once and they're done. Nor do we want to break a chain upon the Hyperglide pin's nose; their tail sections widen out the chain plate holes just enough to preclude this. A new Hyperglide pin can only replace a regular chain pin, in other words, lest things threaten to fall apart. And you most likely need to loosen the new pin in the chain tool's upper saddle, as described shortly on page 124.

Campagnolo wants us to install and remove their 10-speed chains with their own UT-CN200 chain breaker, so I do not advise you to use the regular old Park tool for this, with which I've also had some luck. The chains themselves have interior and exterior sides; only the latter is stamped with a production batch number. And the chain pins are designed to always press from the inside to the outside, whether cutting a chain to size or installing a new master pin.

Campagnolo 10-speed master pins are also unique, in that they're fronted with big plastic noses. These dummies slide in to place between the plates, but only to stake a claim for their more precious cargo. They simply pull

out and get disposed of, once this is in place. And the ensuing tolerances, needless to say, are quite exacting: the 10-speed master pin means to protrude an even .1 millimeter from the inside chain plate, when you finish.

The information Campagnolo has made available for its C10 chains is contradictory in one respect. Where the booklet accompanying the C10 HD-L chain advises us to resolve tight links, "with delicate lateral bending," the company's website warns us, "after closure, do not laterally bend the chain." Based on its currency, we have to assume the latter represents their true and correct viewpoint.

Campagnolo's chain pins can only be fired the once, just like their Shimano peers, and they actually cost a few bucks apiece. But it happens that Wippermann's conneX master links work just as well, over and over again, for a fraction of the price. I do not recommend their use with Campagnolo or Shimano chains, as this contradicts technical materials available from either party, but I can tell you people have had some luck with such methods. It is a bit dicier with Campagnolo; their chain pins and plates are narrower. The 8-, 9-, and 10-speed conneX links are sold individually or with the full conneX chains.

The Shimano and Campagnolo pins—together with the master links, as supplied by other more happening manufacturers—are meant to guide the outcomes, whenever it is you must break a chain. The precision is just that important. It is thought that any less structured incisions will reduce the chain's overall strength.

Lacking such conveniences—or to shorten a chain—we need to go to work with the chain tool. Its handle ends in a fairly sturdy pin, which bears down upon one of the slightly more transient chain pins, shoving it out of the way. Center the tool's pin right atop one of the chain pins, to begin. Recall that the tool's pin is only fairly sturdy; it will probably snap if you are trying to jam it down off center. And listen, use the tool's lower saddle to install and remove the chain. The upper position is only used to fine-tune a link's tightness. It is *fragile*, comparing to the downstairs.

You push the chain pin all the way through and out, to install one of the Shimano pins, but in every other circumstance you only push it about 4/5 of the way through. You want the pin's tail to retain an edge, just inside the chain's outer plate. You bend the chain sideways a bit, to break it: they snap apart, and later snap together. The pin's inner lip acts as kind of a placeholder.

Chains are best broken and reassembled on the lower lengths of their runs, with the chain all the way slack. So shift it down to the smallest gear combinations, at the least; or set it down on the bottom bracket shell for a minute.

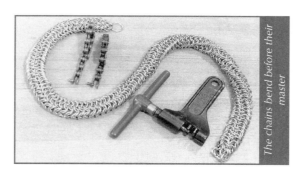

The chains bend before their master

We do not expect the chains to break of their own volition. I first suspect some confusion in the chain's installation, when they do fail. The chains are replaced periodically—we'll look in to that in a minute here—but we more commonly break them for purposes of **CLEANING THE DRIVETRAIN**.

This is a glorious spring ritual, equally messy and joyful, meant to celebrate the arrival of

better seasons. Bikes in regular use earnestly look forward to this, especially if they've been piloted through the elements. But drivetrains are not cleaned nearly enough, as far as I can tell. The lucky summer bike's chain may even go a couple years without being cleaned, provided it is fed the best sorts of dry lube—those from Rock and Roll, for example—but not everybody knows about this stuff.

Besides, there's still all these shitloads of obsolete wet chain lubricants to sell. These make some sense in the winter—just before we take the drivetrain down for its cleaning, that is—but the chains they settle upon draw in all kinds of gunk, like obsessive magnets. And we're left with the dreaded liquid black snake, which leaves its mark upon your good pants every last time you go for a little spin. Sucks, don't it?

The elixir required to tame the serpent is a bicycle-specific citrus degreaser, such as Finish Line or Zep Orange. I have experimented with some of the more common general degreasers; they don't seem to work as well. Pour an undiluted amount of the good stuff in a big old Tupperware container, something with a tight lid that can be shaken a bit. The dish becomes your parts washer, now. It quickly becomes pretty disgusting. No more cold spaghetti for you.

Any of these degreasers can be diluted with water, but they become that much weaker. It makes more sense to do this right the first time. The good news is that you can keep using the same batch over and over again. All the parts-washing machines at the shops are already doing this, actually. (The rare sonic machines are the exceptions. They bombard with sound waves or something. It's very new wave.) Your soft broth will turn to coffee after a while, but it still works just fine. I did a good bit of work out of my basement shop on

Oakland Avenue; I think I may have changed out the Finish Line all of once while I lived there. And I can't even tell you how many parts that batch cleaned! Do make sure you keep the lid in place, to prevent evaporation.

So the chain comes off, as described, and you toss it in the soup. You want to let it sit for a night or two, ideally. Make sure you stop by and shake it up a few times, to help loosen the gunk. The chain's grimy companions also need to take the plunge.

The hub gears and the cranks are both more properly introduced later on, up on pages 150 and 137 respectively; suffice it here to say you can remove them for cleaning. The derailleurs also need to take a bath, provided any sealed bearing pulleys are first removed.

Your spider crank is not going to fit in the Tupperware dish. Come on; it's huge. You may remove and clean the individual chainrings, if they look really bad. But the cheap cranks won't let you do this, because they suck.

Gear cassettes can get dunked, but this is not a good idea for freewheels. Soaking them in solvent wicks away any lubricant they manage to squirrel away. We can feed them some more, by dripping a good bit of light oil around the seams in their backsides, but this can be done regardless. So spare the bath, OK? Just leave it on the wheel there, and douse the cogs with lightweight oil—something useless and disposable, WD-40 for example, and floss them clean with a rag.

The freewheels each contain a good number of moving parts, but we don't take them apart. It's like cold fusion or something; theoretically possible but entirely uncommon. You want to let the parts dry thoroughly, whatever it is you're working on. We enlist an air gun for such purposes, at work. You

may set yours by the window for a day, instead. Let 'em take a breather for once; check out the scenery and stuff.

There is no point at all to spray the freshly cleaned parts array with oil, once things are dry, because this invites the gunk right back on board. The spray cans only waste our time. Grab your trusty oil dropper; drip a bit in the pivots. Work it in a little; wipe away the excess. That's all you have to do.

Everything goes right back where you found it. Procedures for mounting the derailleurs, cranks, and hub gears are each described in their relevant sections.

And it is with the chain's reassembly that we really understand the brilliance of the new SRAM-style master links. You set them in place, and you pull the chain taught. They lock right in to place.

With the derailleur-equipped bikes, our work becomes somewhat easier with the creation of another basic tool. Run out back and find a spare spoke somewhere, and crimp a 90-degree bend to its mid-section. And bend the ends again, by similar measures: you now have a **CHAIN HOOK**, with which to hold the disparate chain sections in union. You slip each end of this device in to chain links a few back from the break; it sits just like that while you work. The rear derailleurs' spring tension tends to pull the chains apart, left to itself, but the chain hook slides in to relieve the pressure.

We are looking for two things, with the chain's final adjustment. Each end of the chain pin must pass *precisely* the same distance through the outer chain plates, and the link itself must also be just loose enough to pivot freely. The chain tool presses the links together, across the one pin; this intersection needs to be spread out again.

So go ahead and set things up in the chain tool's lower saddle, with its pin coming down to face off against that protruding from the broken chain. You first press the chain pin back in place, until its length is almost but not quite centered between the outer plates. The adjustment for tightness to follow must also be considered. You get things almost perfect, with one end of the pin extending just a hair farther out than the other end—this is the "fine" in our fine adjustment—and then you level things out, by pressing it another quarter-turn in the chain tool's upper saddle. This should loosen the chain link, just enough. And again, the heavy lifting is all done downstairs! It is only when adjusting the link's tightness that we shift up to the top deck. The chain's farther plate is not braced against the tool's body, in the upper saddle, and this lets the chain expand just as much as it needs to.

Neglecting this last step will usually leave you with a **TIGHT LINK**. These are easy enough to spot, on derailleur bikes; we only have to spin the pedals backwards. Does the chain bump around, passing between the pulleys? Your suspicions about a particular link can be confirmed by bending it between your fingers, of course. So get in there with the chain tool; let the upper saddle work its special magic.

You **REPLACE YOUR CHAIN** when it starts to skip. All bicycle chains loosen up and stretch out over time, just as their cogs more gradually begin to wear down. Neither condition is necessarily obvious to the eye, but with the derailleur-equipped bikes they will together cause the chain to skip out of gear, under pressure. You may know just what I'm talking about, from that last time you tried to charge up that bad-ass hill!

You want to make sure the shifting systems are healthy and well adjusted, as described on page 110, before concluding any drive-train parts are worn out. A maladjusted derailleur can affect a skipping chain, as can the rusty cables; you want to check everything out before replacing anything.

The chains may be replaced independently of their cogs, for that matter. It is always safer to replace the two simultaneously—they do wear together—but changing out the chain alone may stop the skipping, if you catch it in time. Nothing is immortal, but we may stretch a single cogset to cover the lifespans of three chains, using this method.

Park Tool's Chain Checker describes a chain's wear on a scale between 0.0 and 1.0. We're told to replace chains registering above 1.0, but in practice you can *generally* avoid replacing their cogs as well if you catch them at .75. Try it, at least; see if the bike still skips. ("Chain stretch" is the phrase we all use, but it's not strictly accurate. The rollers wear down, straining against the rows of sharp teeth; their diminished mass effectively approximates a stretch.)

A worn-out cogset quickly reduces a new chain to its own level. That's just how it works; you can think of it as corruption or something. The smaller cogs are usually devoured sooner than their larger kin; the mechanical torque is more concentrated. But the only way to really know for sure is to get on and go, using an uphill test ride as our proof.

The chainrings up front do still wear, incidentally; a toasted chainring feels all grainy when pedaling. And its teeth look all spiky, in comparing with a fresh example.

The fixed wheels are more adept at handling this dynamic, as are the planetary hubs and the basic 1 speeds. The chain, simply put, has nowhere to skip off to. You only pull the wheel back in the frame dropouts, to increase its tension. But the tension is only enforced by tiny springs, with the derailleur bikes; a toasted drivetrain essentially pits these crickets against the strength of our legs. They will lose, every time, unless you develop the discipline to always, always pedal softly. But that would be like playing dumb or something; it's just not much fun after a while.

I have heard different things about the particulars—these vary, to degrees, in accordance with a rider's imperatives and the drivetrain's quality—but you'll likely be changing out the chain and cogset every 3,000 miles or so. You just try and do it when you need to; parts in advance of some grand tour for example.

You can also check the length, if you forget your chain checker at the bus stop. The distance from the center of one chain pin to the next is precisely 1 inch, when the chain is new, but they stretch as they wear. So find a 12-inch ruler; see how the pins line up against it. The difference from good to toast need not be much; a worn-out chain will have stretched fractions of an inch over the course of the foot.

Using chain checker to determine chain wear

We also need to make sure the new chain is of the correct size. Not too long; not too short. A chain too long droops down, especially when shifting to the smallest gear combinations. (That's often what this is, at least: worn-out derailleur springs can manifest roughly similar effects. But we are able

to spot these easily enough: their cages will no longer be parallel to the ground, when shifted to the smallest gear combinations.) A chain too long has more slop to it; the shifting may not be quite so precise.

Chains too short are not able to wrap around the largest gear combinations. The rear derailleur finds the effort terminally exhausting, regardless; riding the bike like this fucks it up proper. This very thing happened to a pair of our Specialized FSR rental bikes a couple seasons back, actually. The bikes' stock Shimano chains had evidently failed, at some point; enterprising renters had reassembled them minus the broken links. And rather than simply fail again—as we may have expected, in the absence of proper Hyperglide chain assembly pins—both shortened chains managed to reduce the bikes' firm Shimano LX rear derailleurs to spaghetti, by the time they came through for service.

I have no idea what could have caused the original breakage—busy fleets of rental bikes become necessarily enigmatic, in this sense—but we strive to learn from their examples, lest more innocent derailleurs perish in vain. Our pedaling force is transferred straight down to their pivot points, in such situations; they carve themselves to bits.

You can get away with running a short chain, if you really need to, but this requires some commensurate adjustment with the derailleurs' limit screws. You want to turn in the low screw out back, to close off the larger cogs or chainring. And you may dial in the front derailleur's high screw as well, in the case of especially drastic emergencies. But the chain most likely has failed across a solitary link; you only need to shut down the biggest cog in back to account for the one link. But it's not a bad idea to pack a few spare links in your tool kit.

Chain links very occasionally bend out of line, if you're especially forceful with their shift levers. These may be straightened, with two pairs of your sturdiest pliers, but in the ideal we like to replace them.

We may check on the **CHAIN LENGTH** by a few different methods. The simplest of these is to first shift down to the smallest two gears, in order to check out the rear derailleur cage's position in this setting. If the two pulley bolts form a neat parallel line directly above the lower chain run, the chain is presumed just long enough to finish its work. This quick guess is almost always accurate, to my experience, but it's not the ultimate science. Bikes pairing super-small granny gears to the huge 34-teeth mega-range-style cassettes, for example, likely fall outside its grasp.

The better way to check chain length is to measure things out in the largest gear combinations. You don't want to be riding around cross-geared like this, needless to say, but as stationary objects the derailleurs should be able to show you what they can do.

Checking chain length in the big-big gear combination

The manufacturers' official chain length formula generally adds two pins' worth of chain, after its length has been stretched across the biggest gears, irrespective of anything the derailleurs may have to say.

Pedals

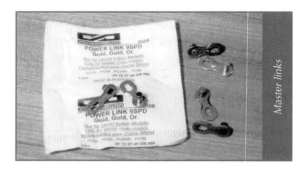
Master links

The **PEDALS**, I must tell you, are thoroughly downtrodden. Their very station betrays no mystery—they support all the weight; they're always getting stomped on—but we see this as well, too often, in their very composition.

We may hope the pedals are sturdy and good, given the scope of their responsibilities, but the sad fact is that most are not. The major transnational bicycle manufacturers have long assumed the portly old habit of cutting corners—under your feet, for example—because the scope of their research suggests you're either too disinterested or distracted to pick up on the distinction. Isn't that grand?

Most bikes ship with plastic pedals, nylon pedals; whatever the hell they want to call them. They're fucking plastic. These have always sucked, and they always will. What happens, when you stomp on the diminutive plastic box over and over again? *It will crack.* And you will hear an annoying creak, every time you ride the bike.

But it may also persist, because the plastic may be somewhat resilient as well. And so maybe the pedal won't up and fall off the bike—it just may, you never really know—but its crack will conspire to fester and grow, until such a time when the pedal is able to drop away and be done.

This full scenario, all the way through to its end, has *always* been immediately obvious to the "engineers" who have taken to design the plastic pedals. This is no accident, in other words, let alone oversight. These sorry pimps only want your cash; they could really give a fuck if the bike works or not.

This same basic farce has persisted for decades. But people started to pick up on the con—this was always a matter of time—and so the grand transnational bike industry responded with a further duplicity, by smuggling the same defective plastic pedal bodies within chintzy steel cages.

Our basic Specialized Crossroads rental bikes came with these, my first three years at that shop. Left to their own devices, the steel pedal cages simply unscrew and fall off. But we couldn't let that happen, so I got in the habit of checking them out, every time I did put a Crossroads up in the stand. I needed to make sure the damned pedals were not falling apart, of all the useless things! I've never had to do this anywhere else, before or since.

Better pedals have been available all the while, but it was earlier decided to set these aside for those with the means. Thus we still find brand new bicycles, costing several hundred dollars in cases, arriving with the nylon pedals. The dominant course in bicycle marketing has long resigned itself toward its idealized "recreational" rider, whose imperatives and expectations are both presumed low enough already, and so we find ourselves standing on plastic. The effect can only be sold as some obscure function of value—as if there were no other considerations—but the plan, once again, fails in even this narrow purpose.

The greed-addled insomniacs pushing this crap upon the world know damned well their shoddy wares will not make it through the fucking summer. They were not designed to do so. They only need to hold their precious original pose, out there on the showroom floor, until your money has been taken. But a number of these simple devices are inevitably pressed to hard service regardless, over the miles and through the elements, and it falls to us in the service department to explain why the ensuing repair bills get to be so steep.

This, too, is part of the job. But let's look at that: what if I don't want to sell the bike the alloy pedals it needs, because I can already tell both the rear derailleur and the tires are not going to make it through the season? Should I "Go on, take the money and run?" That shit's so *fucking* cheesy. But maybe I can't encourage the rider to save and buy a real bike, as I would like to do, because this person works a shit job and makes even less than I do!

The bike is a fucking disaster. But it really needs to ride tomorrow, because there's no bus out to the job. How is all this suddenly my problem? It's not, but it is, because I live here, too.

The good news is that pedal axle threadings are broadly universal, across a simple pair of modern sizes, such that any plastic pedals you may come across are replaceable. I'm not aware of plastic pedals cut in the old French threading, though. The size itself is long obsolete, and frankly I am not sure the French have stooped so low.

This leaves us with the two common sizes, which are usually referred to as 1/2 inch and 9/16 inch. The former is for most kids' bikes; the latter will go with everyone else. The two sizes are easily distinct from each other; there should be no confusion in this respect. The confusion arrives with the threads' directions.

The one on the neutral side is always reverse threaded. The implacable dictates of physics may have encouraged the neutral pedal to back out and away from the crank, were it to enjoy the standard threading. But the drive side enjoys the conventional threading we're familiar with; righty-tighty and lefty-loosey. Many pedals have "R" or "L" stamped to the ends of their axles, for just such reasons. The threads themselves are fairly pronounced. They're under a good deal of stress; they need to be.

One step from momentum

Imagine lines tracing out in plane with these threads, extending out to the front and the rear of the bike. They angle in to form a triangle in front of the bike, when it is right side up. But it is much easier to install and remove the pedals with the bike upside down, if you don't have a repair stand, and this finds the same lines crossing to the rear. Get in the habit of visualizing such lines, and you will know which pedal goes where.

Many of the newer high-end pedals are installed and removed with 6- or 8-millimeter Allen keys. They slot right in to the backsides of the axles; the wrench ends up kind of under the bike. But more usually we're using a pedal wrench for this. Its handle is long enough to provide for some torque, and the jaws are just narrow enough to fit the trim wrench flats we find with various sorts of pedals. The regular old box wrench often is too wide to fit; the cone wrench is too narrow to deal with the torque. Its edges start to wear down.

And here rises the mighty Park pedal wrench, serenely surveying the vast forests of hardened steel pedal axles, to present jaws of precisely the best dimensions—none too hot, nor even too cold; just perfect. And we're lucky the tool is so dedicated, because it doesn't have too many other uses in other settings. It makes for a passable war-club, once civilization collapses. But I bet you'll want something bigger, unless you are fighting it out in tunnels or something.

But let's first **INSTALL THE PEDALS**, shall we? This is another stereotypical bicycle task, in that it soon becomes very natural, but it's also very easy to fuck things up. You do not want to mis-thread the pedal, but you do want to make sure it's able to come back out again.

You should *never* feel as if you're forcing the point, threading the pedals in, and every last one should be greased. We leave tubs of grease sitting around, at work, for just such purposes. But you don't need to be a slob about it, OK? Just dip the axle up to its knees or something; the grease will spread everywhere it needs to.

You first clean up the pedal threads, if they're all gritty or something. And the poor old oily rag again volunteers its services, because it has long ceased to expect much for fulfillment in the first place, which in turn allows the pedal axle and the crank fitting to slide together like butter. See how that works?

The pedal should go in perfectly straight—the wrench flats bottom out, to become flush with the crank arm—and this journey home is none too difficult. Anything less would make me wonder if I was stripping out the crank's pedal threads! I would want to back it out and start over. You might also stop by the bike shop and ask after a pedal tap set, if the crank threads are all ugly and shit.

Nice old pedal

Most crank arms are aluminum, these days. Were there some dispute with the steel or titanium pedal axles, the crank threads would always lose. The dead crank threads may be removed and replaced, by means of an old and fading technology known as the Helicoil, but you can expect to search for this. Helicoils take a bit of time and work; many shops presently find it more cost effective to simply sell you a whole new crank arm, whatever that happens to cost, in terms of resources and energy.

You'll be able to thread the pedal most of the way in to place with your fingers, if things are nice and clean. There is no pressure; you are not risking a mis-threaded crank. But you switch up to the wrench toward the end, with which you want to press pretty hard. You want to get it on there about as solid as you can. Tight, tight, tight.

REMOVING THE PEDALS calls on equal measures of strength and insight. You can't just go in and be a hard ass; you have to be somewhat clever about it.

You could indeed stand there and flex to your heart's content, if that's your trip, but you also need to figure out how to enlist the best leverage for the project. And, if the pedals are really seized in place, you want to know how best to get some more.

Park offsets the jaws on its newest war club to opposing angles, and this does seem to

help, but the handle is also a little longer. Our leverage relates more directly to the lever's length. Nothing should distract from the press of its force. Make sure both the bike and its stubborn arms are braced firmly, before you get all serious. The lever's energies, left to their own devices, would much rather ask the bottom bracket to roll the crank toward a more neutral position. So flip the bike upside down, if you don't have a good repair stand, and hold the one crank firmly as you bear down upon its mate.

Is that going to do it? Maybe not. Our odds are improved easily enough, with the power of the Jesus bar. It slides right over the end, all the way down, like the best condom ever. The damned pedal keeps you from doing something similar for the crank, but you probably don't need to.

Is the opposing arm still in place? Again, things will be best if you just push off against this. The alternative is to use the same crank you're working on. Many pedals shine their wrench flats in a few distinct orientations; this can work to your advantage here. You acquire the most leverage by squeezing the wrench and crank arm together, clasped tightly beneath your hands.

The pedals are supposed to be on there pretty good, even if they're not seized, so we can expect them to release rather suddenly. You will want to anticipate this: make sure your hand is not positioned to slam in to the chainring, once it gives. This seems to happen to everyone at least once, but I'm not sure it needs to. The bikes provide for more happening rites of passage.

The Jesus bar will accomplish its singular mission, in most circumstances, but some hardened and especially unrepentant pedals may still refuse to believe. But that's fine, because our crusade begins with the supreme advantage. We have the means to fuck with their reality. Pull the crank arm from its spindle—this procedure is described with the cranks, pages 137-138—and clamp it lengthwise and level in a good vise. Get in there with the wrench and the bar again; I expect you'll have some better luck.

You can literally put your whole body in to the effort, this way. The sum of your being, focused on simply loosening a 15-millimeter pedal axle? The fucker never has a chance. I have taken seized crank arms to just such points many times myself; this final option has yet to fail me. I cannot even remember the last time I required heat to remove a pedal, in fact. So you just put the torch away, OK? We have no need to burn the heretics.

The rust is blessedly ambivalent, in selecting its targets. Shit just does not seem to matter all that much. Whole pedals were once made of steel, back in the day, before the cursed plastic pedals came along to mock us. Most all of these oldsters have at least started to rust out by now. Some have neat rows of small teeth; others incorporate long rubber blocks. You may know just what I'm talking about. These are always a good deal heavier than they ever need to be—it's only their axles that need to be so burly—so nobody has made them for some time now. As with the steel crank arms—or the sweatshops, for that matter—we'll only greet the sun with pride when we're no longer relying upon them.

There are all kinds of possibilities to explore, moving past these earlier mistakes. It really depends what you're looking to do. The poor road pedals may be the least popular, because they lack the crenellations associated with the more gnarly mountain pedals, but this only means they're more specific. The road pedals do just fine on the

perfect summer days; they're less ideal if it's slippery out. But the world has seen some truly fantastic examples. They came together back before we found the woods trails; there was more time to consider aesthetics and the like.

The mountain pedals, known in the Midwest as the **RAT-TRAPS**, face their cages with rows of pronounced teeth. It makes a difference. Simpler rat-traps couple steel cages to aluminum bodies; better varieties use the alloy throughout.

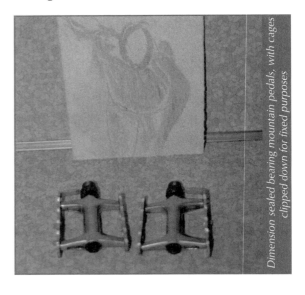

Dimension sealed bearing mountain pedals, with cages clipped down for fixed purposes

The best among these, which I rely upon extensively, are built around pairs of sealed cartridge bearings. Nearly all of my horses wear just such kit, in fact. They're just that cool. The detail jacks up the price a bit, in the short term, but I've burned through far too many lesser pedals—their dust caps fall off; the grease wicks out; the bearing adjustments become loose. And the pedal develops its persistent creaking; you lose the element of surprise.

The basic pedals are more finite in this sense, like the chains or the brake pads. We are not able to improve their condition, because we lack the means to mess with their bearings.

We need to move a socket within a socket, essentially. This is possible, theoretically—I bet this has happened often enough with the nicer old pedals, many of which were built to last—but the effort is more trouble than it's worth, in other scenarios. Especially if there's any plastic involved. The dust cap seals may be kind of fragile; the adjustment is truly awkward.

The platform pedals are similar to our rat-traps, but the cages are wider, thicker, and likely anodized all to hell. I've never even known any of the macho platforms to sport the **TOE CLIPS**, in fact, which require a couple minor refinements. But the clips are only practical utilities; it seems like the platform pedals just go rock out.

The clip is attached to the front of the cage with a pair of screws, given the chance, while its strap sneaks through flat openings to the rear of the pedal's body. Most road and mountain pedal cages have a front and back—or an upside and a downside, dependent upon the perspective—and we see this most clearly when we're mounting the toe clips. The two holes needed to attach the clip may only feature on the front of the cage. Its rear features a large tooth, midway along its bottom edge: we press this down with the toes, to flip the toe clip up in to position. And just like that we go faster, easier. Everybody is always saying that about everything, I realize, but this time it's real. Less energy is wasted; our efficiency is measurably improved.

A smaller number of the older road-going toe clips are made of stainless steel—and rightly cherished, as such—but the great majorities have always been plastic, which is usually fine, in this application. We're not supposed to be stomping on the toe clips; they only happen to fit around our boots. But some fixed gear riders really take the toe clips

through their paces, skidding and so on; steel clips with two leather straps apiece are more reliable in such situations.

You may even find the clips in a distinct size or two, looking around. And Wellgo produces their stubby Mini Clips, which have no straps. But the Power Grips may be the coolest yet, because they do away with the clips themselves. They're only double-wide straps, cutting at diagonals across the pedals, attaching at angles to the front and rear. Pretty sharp. I have not really tried these out myself, but I can tell you they're quite popular with some in my know.

Our most boisterous bells and whistles, of course, are set aside for the **CLIPLESS PED-ALS**. If the toe clips are clever, the clipless pedals are genius. They take care of all the same business, but with half the trouble. Is that swell or what?

Shimano released the first of these in the early 1990s, if memory serves. A cleat is fixed to the sole of a cycling shoe; a corresponding face on the pedal catches and holds it. Most systems to follow have aligned with Shimano's original two-bolt cleat mounting pattern, which cuts a pair of long slits to each sole, just beneath the balls of our feet. The cleats themselves also provide smaller degrees of side-to-side adjustment; allowing us to refine the position farther still. The endless clipping and unclipping perpetually threatens to shake them loose; you want to make sure their bolts get nice and tight. And these cleat bolts should always be greased, lest their charges rust in place.

Those cleats following Shimano's lead are fairly well recessed in to the shoes; it's much easier to walk around in them. The road versions offered by Time, Campagnolo, Look, and others instead use much larger plastic cleats, built around a distinct three-bolt pattern. Walking is more duck-like, but you totally soar on the bike. But many curious cleats have flown from the forest, these last few years; the ensuing chatter becomes distracting. And you'll want to recall your shoes' bolt pattern, of course, before getting carried away.

Different pedal systems offer varying ranges of movement, while clipped-in. This measure, known as "float," is a selling point. As with the discretion afforded in the cleats' positioning, our knees will likely appreciate the elbow room. But we can't assume that different pedals and cleats will work together!

They were not meant to. You may come across lucky coincidences, among those systems that closely mimic Shimano's cleat pattern in any case, but you want to test any of these thoroughly. A poor match does not catch or release as well as we like it to. This can become supremely important, riding along next to the cliff.

We typically jab forward and down with the foot, to clip in to the pedals. The tip of the cleat catches on the pedal; you push the heel down; it clicks in to place. And the brave springs executing these transactions can usually be coaxed toward more and less severe adjustments, by means of small tensioning screws. But make sure the both sides are adjusted to similar positions, with the double-sided pedals.

Releasing from the clipless pedals is also simple enough. We rotate the heel out to the side, maybe 30 degrees or so. And that's it; you're up and away. Clipless pedals release with less effort than that required by the toe clips, actually. You don't have to kick the foot back; you only rotate to the side just a bit. Just know that the cleats do wear over time. Worn cleats are often more difficult to release with.

Some friends in Minneapolis pair clipless pedals to fixed gears, in place of any hand brake. I'm more inclined to use them on a tour bike, personally. I find myself clipped in only half the time, riding in city traffic. But my fixes run hand brakes; clipless pedals seem kind of superfluous. I'm stuck in the odd clickety-click shoes, but without fully realizing their advantages. Thus my Blundstones push the rat-traps. But this is a function of my routes, and the traffic. You may have better luck.

Cranks

Glancing to the insides of the pedals, our gaze falls upon the **CRANK ARMS**. There are exactly two of them. Their pair is known as the crankset.

The most basic example, the **ONE-PIECE CRANKSET**, is found aboard cheaper kids' bikes and various oldsters as well. It is one long metal stick, bent to straight angles passing through the frame, drilled and tapped for pedals at each end. Their frames' bottom bracket shells have to be quite a bit wider, to accommodate this passing business. These American-style bottom bracket shells are smooth and featureless; the smaller European BB shells we more commonly see will have threads. The difference is quite obvious to the eye; you can't miss it.

The one-piece bottom bracket cups are press-fit into their American shells. And as with the headset cups upstairs, we like to do this with a special press up at the shop. The neutral side pedal needs to be removed, to pass the crank out the drive side of the shell. But the one-piece cranks are usually just not that complicated, their bottom brackets are described on page 142.

We also see high-end BMX renditions, in which distinct spindles are suspended between nicer sealed cartridge bearing cups. Two crank arms are tightened down to either end, by means of a threadless headset-style preload bolt, which passes through the bottom bracket spindle. A few manufacturers have already offered proprietary splined spindle and cup arrangements; each tighten with pinch bolts set perpendicular to the spindle.

This last detail brings to mind another older system, the **COTTERED CRANKS**. These are identified by their cotter pins, which are also laid across the spindle ends. But their relation to the better one-piece style cranks is like that of cat litter to the beach; there's nothing to talk about.

Every set of cottered cranks I've ever seen has been made of solid steel, which is ridiculous, but a lot of people just didn't know any better back then. Garbage wagons and a scattering of unfortunate IBD bikes forced this discredited solid-steel plan on to modern cotterless cranks a few years back, but these were layered with plastic, to hide the truth. Steel cranks become lead weights, upon the wings of our destinies; they're as obsolete as coal. Just recycle them, together with their lame-ass spindle. The balls and cups you can maybe reuse; any other cranks you find to fit will be smarter and lighter both.

The cotter pins have an obvious slant to one side, which corresponds to a matching angle cut in to the spindle. The short, threaded end section of the pin slips out on the other side of the crankarm, where a nut tightens everything into place.

Whenever we come across such a system, the natural temptation is to whip that nut off and pound the hell out of the pin with a hammer. This has been known to work, but

you should know that cotter pins are made of softer metal. They're supposed to reform a bit as they go down, to conform a bit more tightly against those surfaces they come to interact with. So you may just smash the head flat, and leave its wider body in place.

Park Tool makes the CR-2, whose only purpose is to loosen these cotter pins. It looks like an oversized chain breaker tool, and works in much the same way. Turning a handle threads an extractor down, to push the cotter pin out. The CR-2 is relatively expensive, considering how rarely it is called upon. You may just track down a shop that still has one.

The world has long since moved toward the **THREE-PIECE CRANKS**. Their same label describes the cottered cranks, technically speaking—or even the high-end, one-piece sets mentioned earlier, for that matter—but in common speech at least we're discussing the majority option here, which is both cotterless and European-sized. The bottom bracket shell is smaller and threaded, as with the old cotters, but the crank arms attach themselves in a much better way. The spindle ends are either splined or tapered, and bolts threading in to their very tips end up holding things down. And perhaps you need to be a calloused and grimy mechanic to fully realize how wonderful this leap forward has been; I can only tell you it is a beautiful thing.

Bottom brackets appear in force somewhat later in our story, but I must tell you a few other things about them right now, as means to draw out and develop the major cranks. The spindles' aforementioned factions, the tapers and the splines, are distinct and non-compatible crank mounting platforms. Each also shelters a number of more subtle variations, which together serve to direct particular cranksets to the most appropriate bottom brackets.

We need to use Campagnolo cranks with Campagnolo bottom brackets, for example, because the angles and lengths to their tapers are just slightly different than those used by Shimano.

These taper disputes are not easily seen, unassisted—we look for stickers or engravings on the bottom bracket's mid-section, to navigate ambiguous situations—but the splits between the splined pipes are often more obvious. They are also considerably wider, because they are hollow.

The new pipes have settled upon but a pair of overall lengths, for the most part—for use with double- or triple-ring cranksets—but the old tapered spindles display more of an imagination, in this sense. We find them in a half-dozen lengths from 107 to 127 millimeters, to correspond with the numerous crank profiles favored over the years. Older cranks sit farther out, on longer spindles. Newer styles are considerably more svelte; it's not uncommon that they completely obscure their spindles.

I am only telling you this because the cranks are going to ask. But we also have to think about the crank length, the pedal threading, and what we call the bolt circle diameter, if ever you're replacing things or swapping parts around.

Pedal threading, really, we can almost dispose of. Just about every last three-piece crank we find is threaded to the same dimensions—English thread. Something well less than 1 percent—those associated with some ancient Gitanes, for example—are cursed with obsolete French-threaded pedals. You'll be scouring the planet for replacements. Good luck!

There are only two common pedal threads that we come across. The smaller size, 1/2

inch, is used for one-piece cranks. The larger 9/16-inch pedals go with the three-piecers. And you see the difference, comparing the one to the other; they're totally different sizes. *It is much more important to recall that the neutral side pedals are reverse threaded, in either case.*

We come across three-piece cranks in kids' sizes every once in a great while, but the shortest common crank length is 165 millimeter. They are measured center-to-center, from pedal threads to spindle hole. The two more usual ones are 170 and 175 millimeters; 172.5 and 180 make more occasional appearances. Shorter cranks are more suitable for shorter people; longer arms better match the taller sorts. There is some marginal loss of efficiency associated with the shorter cranks—5 millimeters less leverage and so on—but you really have to strain to see it. Kind of hazy.

The length is almost always stamped somewhere along the crank arm's inside surface, in tiny little numbers. You can also simply measure a crank arm against one of its peers, of course, and it is important that the two sides match. But you don't go mixing-and-matching with your boots, do you? The one knee starts complaining.

The chainrings appear on what we call the spider crank, and they may or may not be integral. The cheaper and less interesting spiders simply rivet everything in place, to form a super-cheesy chainring combo meal. Such rings are steel, rather than aluminum; the bike earns precious little in nutritional value.

Chainrings really living the life eventually wear themselves down, of course, and the more useful spiders strive to anticipate this. And the rings may even be exchanged, depending, for bigger or smaller examples.

They link to their spiders through measured hoops of mechanical verse, known more commonly as the **BOLT CIRCLE DIAME-TERS**. Which, like the crankarms themselves, are measured center-to-center. You imagine midpoints in the holes, and count off the distance between them. But this not as complicated as it sounds; numerous references are available. Manufacturers tend to stick with the safest and most fashionable BCDs, while they're still current at least; many chainrings also bear these details etched to their faces.

The grand old favorite is 110 millimeters, once used for road and mountain bikes both. Its rings have been available in sizes from 34 to 62 teeth, which pleases anything from older mountain bikes to the small-wheeled recumbents. Most 110 cranks also have a second set of holes drilled on the inside, for a 74-millimeter BCD granny gear.

For road bike cranksets, the world standard is the 130 millimeter. I've seen 130 rings in sizes from 39 to 63 teeth; triple-ring road cranks pair the 130 with a 74-millimeter inner ring. Campagnolo set their standard at 135 millimeters, which is a bit awkward and obtuse, if not entirely unreasonable. The chainrings have long been available in a wide range of quality levels, in terms of design and materials and craftsmanship, and this exclusivity has allowed them more control over which ones are fixed to those arms bearing their name. But Campy did see fit to go for a standard 74-millimeter inner ring, on their triple cranksets.

Newest of all are the **COMPACT ROAD CRANKS**, which have really come on strong in the last few years. They pick up on the classic old 110 BCD pattern, to sport chainrings in the range of 34 to 50 teeth. Our svelte double-ring road gearing range becomes less macho and more generous. Which, given

that spinning faster is generally healthier and more efficient, actually makes a good deal of sense. Come on; who the hell spins out in a 53-11-teeth gear combination? Batman? Campagnolo and others are already providing compact road derailleurs to accompany these new members as well, to better navigate the sometimes meaningful changes in angles and dimensions.

The 144 BCD is kind of an odd track bike thing, as memory serves. More recent is Shimano's Compact 58/94 BCD crank protocol. The rings—together with the cogs, in back—are all a few teeth smaller than the existing 110 standards. The sizing went from 46, 48 teeth top rings to 42, 44.

Similar reductions occur out back, with the smallest cog shrinking from 13 to 11 teeth. Some enterprising soul pointed out that parallel reductions front and back make for a matching gear range, with a slight weight savings. Suntour began doing something similar but not quite compatible, with the Microdrive system, but then their spaceship exploded. This is all history, in any case; 58/94 is no longer spec'd for use with the new bikes. But as with 110, parts are still to be had. And so it is we spy dozens and dozens of fiercely territorial chainrings, nearly all sharply distinct from the others, collecting dust on the back shelves of bike shops all over the world. Their collective energy, properly harnessed, can surely spin a bike to the moon.

Everything mentioned so far features five-bolt holes, in the circles. Improvements in materials have more recently allowed the spiders to ditch an entire digit! And they had to, because the fucking gram-counters were watching.

The road cranksets are still on the five-bolt patterns—the wider rings seem to require it—but the smaller mountain cranks have regrouped around the new, pleasantly symmetrical four-bolt spiders. And so we're left with even more BCD patterns.

Little 58 millimeters are ambidextrous or androgynous or something—we find 58-millimeter circles with both four and five bolts—but these other new throwing stars are on their own. The 64, 68, 104, and 112 millimeters, at last count, each register as distinct four-bolt BCDs.

We can also find special intermediaries, known as gear adapters, that are meant to work with the **SPIDERLESS CRANKS**. This is an option for newer Shimano LX, XT, and XTR cranksets. The drive crank is set up with odd splines and a short stack of threads; a proprietary spider and lockring settle atop these.

We are afforded some discretion as to the BCD, using these things—gear adapters are available in a couple patterns—but their grander purpose is to allow the spider be replaced independently of the crankarm. But I can't say I'm sure why this is suddenly so important. Spiders get bent sometimes, but almost all can be straightened in a vise. You just can't be a spaz about it. Work slowly, or the alloy might snap.

Everything so far coincides with standardized **CHAINRING BOLTS**. Shorter and taller versions are available—to better pierce single, double, or triple chainring sandwiches—but each enjoys an established threading and width. There were a few misunderstandings about the chainring bolt size, before these glorious standards set in, but that was all the way back in the day. True heads don't even think about it anymore.

Spacers for either chainring bolts or their (wider) nuts are commonly inserted at points between the two, to compensate for slight differences in thicknesses amongst various chainrings and the spider crank bolt shelves. Steel rings are often a bit thinner than their aluminum superiors, for example. And it's your job to make sure all things are right and good, all the way around, because the chain and any indexed front shifters are both counting on this measurement.

The chainrings may also have different profiles. A given example may extend straight out in plane with the crankarm bolt shelves, or it may lean forward just a millimeter or so. You will want to consider this as well, prior to changing things around. Look straight down from the side, while comparing to a stock crank: are the rings *perfectly* spaced? Differences here can probably be resolved with one set of chainring spacers or another, to fit in front of or behind a particular ring.

Aluminum chainring bolts can also be found. They're quite light, and possibly even anodized all to hell. But it isn't a good idea to deploy such agents on your fixed gear simply because they aren't as strong as their steel kin. As with the SRAM-style master links, the fixed application in particular leaves us worrying about the implications of any sudden back-pedaling. Truvativ recommends using mild Loctite in place of grease on those aluminum chainring bolts supplied with their cranks, but I can't imagine why.

It is also useful to install the chainrings in their correct orientation, in terms of their timing on the spider. The individual rings generally feature small engravings, at some point in their circles—the number of teeth, generally—and a well-timed example finds each of these ducks lined up in a row.

Their starting point is determined by the outer chainring, which typically incorporates a small free-standing post at some point in its circle: this chain pin means to line up directly behind the crankarm itself, to keep the chain from jumping between the two. The big ring's chain pin most usually is accented by solitary in-bound teeth on the smaller rings, pointed toward the spindle. The inner and outer surfaces of the chainrings are distinct as well, in that they may or may not provide indentations to seat the top or bottom of the chainring bolts. And so we finally come full circle—to know these are lined up correctly—because the aforementioned numbers form a short staircase of their own. Pretty trick, hey?

The purpose of the exercise is to align the individual rings in accordance with the manufacturers' original plans. It is the very same imperative pursued with the carefully aligned cassette cogs, essentially; it serves to make the shifting easier. Fancier multi-speed chainrings commonly rely upon various pins and ramps to facilitate a smoother shifting process; any such presumptions become a function of the rings' relative timing.

Some Truvativ chainrings are even stamped with the year of manufacture, in fact. They're meant to be used with others of the same vintage, with their date stamps aligned, to lock in the timing.

110 BCD chainring, with bolts

The smallest rings on triple cranks wear out very rarely, because they are used less than their peers, but the middle rings are pretty well mortal. You start to feel a curious grinding sensation, whilst pedaling in a worn ring.

And its teeth, seen from the sides, earn a meaner shark-tooth profile.

The big rings displace the chain's business amongst greater numbers of teeth, and thereby wear at slower rates, but none contradict the accumulated ravages of time. Bikes that have earned a new cogset and chain may well be up for a new ring or two.

Chainring bolts are small and unobtrusive, comparing with the burly **CRANK BOLTS**, which pin the crank arms to their bottom bracket spindles. You can imagine how much force is channeled through this point.

At least one manufacturer produces aluminum crank bolts, but these are only half useful. The torque required to tighten a crank securely in position would rend their threads to shreds; they function more as placeholders. The bolts that mount the cranks are made of hardened steel, and they always need to become about as tight as you can make them. Manufacturers' instructions yield more precise readings for your torque wrench, but this is essentially what it comes down to.

You want to check in with the crank bolts periodically, in the course of your travels, because they will sometimes loosen up. And it is not smart to ride loose cranks, because after a point their soft aluminum underbellies are left rocking around on the hardened steel spindles, and soon enough they become too loose to tighten at all. You have earned more shiny new paperweights.

It is better to **REMOVE YOUR CRANKS**, with the socket or Allen wrenches. (And, in the case of our three-piecers, the appropriate crank extractor.) You spy the cranks' wispy extraction threads, once the bolts and their dust covers are removed. The extractor winds its body up into these, fully but also quite carefully, such that its spine threads down inside and pushes off against the spindle. But firm the body into the crank threads with a big wrench, before the spine comes down. You want to make sure the thing is all the way up in there.

The success of this mission is absolutely critical to the bike's future. Stripped extraction threads will effectively cement the cranks in place, trapping as well any demons lurking in the bottom bracket. You can only pull the bolts out and ride up the big hill, over and over again, until the cranks' dry husks finally clatter away to the pavement beneath, unless you're familiar with automotive gear pullers, which are also rumored to work here.

This is why the **SELF-EXTRACTING CRANK BOLTS** are so cool. They take full advantage of their situation. Their sharp aluminum dust caps squirrel down in the crank's extractor threads, to surround a distinct crank bolt and washer. But the dust caps are burly little fuckers; they hold their positions as the bolt is released. And so the crank bolt, in other words, is given the authority to actually attach and remove the whole crank—a rare and precious autonomy.

The SE bolts are becoming common enough; some nicer bikes are even born with them. It's easy enough to test for them, of course, but you also see two small spanner holes in the dust caps. These have been grappled upon, to install the device. At this point in time, SE crank bolts may be released with 5-, 6-, or 8-millimeter hex wrenches. Back in the day, Campagnolo may have made one with their old 7-millimeter crank bolts, but as yet I haven't seen it.

The cranks' threads are nearly universal. I know of only a pair of exceptions, in fact. I came across a pair of fairly modern Strong-

light cranks on a Quintana Roo tri bike the other day, the extraction threads of which were reversed. They also bore their own self-extracting bolts, fortunately. And I understand Campagnolo once pulled this as well, producing a corresponding extraction tool to match.

You only have to screw this up once, to learn things the hard way. I first blew my chances with a nice old Stronglight spider, several years back. And so it totally amazed me, a couple summers ago, when I managed to strip out an innocent STX spider crank. I had not realized that I'd grabbed the **WRONG CRANK TOOL**! This was Park's brand new unit, with the wider face, which I had never seen before.

This tool was meant to be used exclusively with the new-style splined "pipe" bottom brackets, as it turns out. And so its face is wider, to better greet the new pipes: it will bottom out inside the crank arm, instead, when faced against one of the thinner tapered spindles. Which, if pressed, strips you out the fucking crank. "Wow," I thought, "this sure is pretty tight." Then came the dreaded evil feeling, where the extractor pulls the crank's wispy aluminum threads out in to the daylight. Fuck.

I am not proud of that day's work! My purpose in telling the story is to caution you away from grabbing the wrong crank tool. Pedros has since produced a proper shop version of the same, and there will surely be others: make sure you have a match, before you do anything else. *A given crank extractor is meant for either pipe or tapered spindles.* New pipe bottom brackets are typically sold with a solid metal button, which allows for the use of a tapered-style extractor, but this horse pill provides for the only exception, OK?

The only thing that can be said for my sorely ignoble afternoon was that I failed to destroy anything really expensive. Things could have just as easily been far worse. Cranks can be ridiculously expensive! The truly fancy members, like FSA or Race Face or whatever, will use carbon fiber or CNC-machined aluminum to keep things light and strong. You can pay $600 for a crankset if you want to.

As exciting as the aluminum cranks can be, in comparing to their rusty steel ancestors, some are far more interesting than others. Where most aluminum cranks are formed in simple molds, with varying degrees of evident grace and sophistication, a lucky few are forged instead. Huge machines come along and stamp the hell out of refined aluminum blocks, impressing upon them the discipline required to maintain a superior performance for an impressive length of time.

We often spot the forgies easily enough, by the careful trace of their lines or the even tone of their luster. Lesser cranks have often been more sloppy, even murky. But some have been watching developments carefully, and a few have even taken on reasonable approximations of the better cranks' finishing details. This does not make them any stronger, needless to say—they still fail just as easily as their more honest classmates—it only means that some of our charges have learned to present us with a further duplicity. But you can still tell, if you know what to look for. The new pretenders are just not all that clever, basically.

Any of these gems are meant to run with a distinct bottom bracket. Shimano and Campy both make their parts available as matching sets, marching right up the income ladder; each successive layer has its own math in this respect. And the more exclusive strata, predictably enough, will only

deign to co-mingle with the commoners at their supreme leisure.

There is no "standard" spindle, in other words, outside the model year of a particular component group. But the particulars have evolved over time, with the goal of drawing the chainrings as close to the frame as they may become. This aligns them more precisely with the hub gears to their rear, which is to say it provides for a better **CHAINLINE**. A good chainline is more efficient; it also shifts better.

There have been a good number of crank manufacturers, but differences in spindle length relate much more to a crankset's placement on the time line. The **CRANK PROFILE**—the lateral positioning of the drive crank's spider, essentially—has moved in over the years. In general terms, older cranks are meant to run on wider spindles. But the young generation is already smarter. They go for the more efficient, less flexible, narrow spindles instead.

The spider crank is the great crouching tiger, amongst its kindred components—it defends itself well enough, with but the slightest prompting—and so the cranks' enemies are forced to attack from angles. And where the damaged pedal threads may be replaced with the brilliant Helicoil inserts, as mentioned earlier, the same can not be said for the crank extraction threads. Happening shops have the shallow and obscure tap used to clean up gritty extraction threads, but that's about all we may do. Stripped cranks make for bar bikes.

Crank arms also break very occasionally, generally across either the pedal threads or the spindle hole. This happened to me once, when I was still a courier, coming down off a curb. It is more common—though still relatively rare—that the spider crank or its chainrings will get bent. Using the front derailleur cage or the chainstay as your reference point, some spot in the crank's rotation appears to be out of round. If only one chainring sways, that is your problem. If two or more rings bow out at the same point, this suggests the spider crank itself is bent.

If only one chainring in a set is bent, see if you can slowly lever it straight with a big screwdriver. You want to make sure all its bolts are tight, first. And do be careful not to lever the other chainrings out of round. You tweak it a little and rotate it past the derailleur, to see how it lines up.

This is all easier and quicker up in the vise, of course, and all the more so if you're able to take things apart first. Compare chainring teeth to vise jaws; gradually bend or lever as needed, rotate and do it again. Easy. The big old crescent wrench is useful in this operation, particularly when single teeth are bent out of line. You really get a sense of its leverage, doing this.

You can do something similar for bent spiders, using the vise. Or, if you lack in vises, remove the rings and retighten the denuded spider upon its spindle. It will be one of the bolt tabs that bent; you'll be leveling it against the others with the big wrench. Move very slowly, since it's most likely aluminum; it may snap if you lever too fast.

11: Bottom Brackets

The bottom bracket twists away in the very basement of the frame, bearing the cranks and pedals we stomp on, translating our energies unto distance.

Having dispatched with the cranks, we now enjoy a unique opportunity to check out the **BOTTOM BRACKETS**. Everybody has been secretly looking forward to this, right?

We begin with no less than four distinct possibilities—one-piece bottom brackets, three-piece units, and the sealed cartridge versions of each. The four camps, in turn, are well sprinkled with additional variables tossed in by the different manufacturers over time. Like ideology, perhaps.

All the bottom brackets accomplish the same functions, to varying degrees of grace. An axle, burly enough to support the considerable force created with pedaling, is suspended tightly between two parallel sets of bearings. And while its adjustments were once managed by means of fixed and adjustable cups, on the drive and neutral sides respectively, the stern and uncompromising sealed bearing cartridges have long since risen to the fore. The distinctions reflect our evolving understandings of just what a given bike may be getting up to, essentially.

One Piece

The hoary old one-piece bottom brackets are usually the simplest. Again, we recognize them easily enough, by virtue of the frame's over-sized bottom bracket shell. The crank makes its lazy 90-degree bends, passing through; the bearings' cones rest upon its shoulders. That featuring on the drive side will be in a fixed position; a threaded cone and locknut opposite allow for our adjustments.

You should also spy a thin, keyed washer set between the two, to help accommodate their peaceable settlement. The nut is undone with your 30-millimeter headset wrench, or perhaps the big old crescent wrench, but the cone itself only gives it up for an old-fashioned spanner (the yellow handle, in the Park Tool arsenal).

You may overhaul the poor old one-piecer, if you're feeling generous. Such units do not have much for bearing seals, and they often show up on fairly old bikes.

Remove the neutral side pedal, to start, and thread both the cone and its locknut out of the way. This lets you pull the crank right out through the drive side. The one-piecers run on huge 5/16-inch bearings, set in to retainer cages—the obtuse red dwarfs, comparing to more usual arrangements—and these get soaked in the bike-specific degreaser, if you have the time. The oily rag will do fine for the rest.

The bearing cones are very rarely pitted, on these burly old contraptions; their races even less so. The one-piecers are heavy, but they are also sturdy. At the worst, they are replaced quite cheaply.

The proper bearing adjustment echoes that which we find with the headsets. Things end up just tight enough to prevent any lateral play, with cone and locknut also supremely tight against each other. And as with the headsets, this may find you over-tightening the cone initially, as means to back it out in the final adjustment.

Sealed Cartridge

This has already been taken care of, with the **SEALED CARTRIDGES**. And while we can indeed find sealed bearings to fit with the overstuffed American-style bottom bracket shells—and the newer, slightly smaller Spanish shells as well—this "cartridge" typically refers to the narrower threaded bottom brackets found everywhere else. Their operations are secreted within solitary and impervious canisters, which enter upon the frame from one side. A corresponding hollow cup threads in from the other side, to brace the far end. They are the big no-brainers. They'll either work, or they won't.

Sealed cartridge bottom brackets are removed with various spanners and extraction tools, in accordance with their manufacturers' designs. The particular tool you call upon varies, but it most often is Shimano's BBT-2, which works for many cheap generic bottom brackets as well. It even coincides with some non-sealed bottom bracket cups, just lately.

Campagnolo's Record and Chorus bottom bracket cartridges are installed and extracted with their UT-BB080 tool; the very one we use with the company's cassette lockrings.

Their AC-H, AC-S, and SC-S cartridges are extracted with the UT-BB100. But the tools and their fittings are distinct in every respect; there is no mistaking the one for the other.

The cartridges, like any other bottom brackets, are installed in to a healthy volume of grease. You paint it on to the frame's threadings, prior to installation. An ungreased cartridge will most likely creak like all hell, after a few rides, and you will also just be begging the thing to rust in place, which, with the cartridges in particular, is one fuck of a situation. The torch we reflexively call upon burns away the cartridge's seals, in the course of its work, and this leaves the mechanism loose as well.

You also want to consider whether or not to grease the bottom bracket spindle ends, before installing the cranks. This question has been shrouded in some controversy—respectable sources have taken strong but opposing views—and so it becomes safest to treat each situation individually, proceeding along the course outlined by the manufacturer. Nobody's going to warranty something assembled in accordance with their competitors' philosophies.

Shimano recommends greasing the spindles, so that is what we do, every last time their cranks go on. Campagnolo's technical literature recommends that we degrease the spindle before installing the cranks, actually. And Truvativ, surveying the scene before them, has elected to split the difference. Where we were pointed toward "clean, grease-free" conditions for the company's traditional tapered-spindle bottom brackets, we're encouraged to grease their splined spindles right the hell up. But the strongest words on the topic may have been penned by Chris Bell, in his Highpath Engineering notes. "Anyone suggesting that grease shouldn't be used [on bottom bracket axle tapers] either hasn't got a very good mechanical understanding or has a vested interest in shortening the life of your cranks," he says.

It's best to chase the threads clean, prior to installing any bottom bracket, with a set of the ridiculously expensive bottom bracket taps. You want to get in there with a rag and some lightweight oil, failing this, to clear out any grit.

The cartridge's business end slides in to a hollow place-holder cup, and it is this last that we like to install first. The hollow's interior dimensions will act as a shelf, to guide the heavier cartridge side into place.

Stop the hollow side just shy of its potential, leaving a thread or two still exposed on the outside. The cartridge side gets fully tightened into place, first. You then thread this hollow side all the way in, as tight as you can, to bear down against the mechanism.

The hollow is almost always threaded to fit the frame's neutral side, with the cartridges. But there was a period in the 1990s when Shimano and certain imitators experimented with the orientation, anchoring the bearing mechanism to the neutral side instead of the fixed. And I thought we were all done with this curious reversal, but I notice Shimano's fairly recent BB-7410 Dura Ace canister pulls the same switch as well. So just you keep an eye out.

Imagine the frame is not there, for a second, and look down at the cartridge in question: anything written or etched on its body should be legible, from your vantage in the seat. This is your orientation; it tells you which side is which. Failing that, look at the threads. They're cut at slight angles to the cups, to coincide with those they find in the frame. Excluding the tiny cliques formed by ancient French-threaded bikes or exclusive Italian-threaded racers—neither being especially

relevant to our purposes here—the bottom bracket cups' threads both point just slightly inward, toward the bike's rear end, when said bike is right-side up. (And the reverse is true, of course, when you flip it upside-down.)

Whichever the case, our final test comes with the execution itself. *You should never feel like you're forcing anything through the threads.* A cup's outside edge remains perfectly parallel to the frame's bottom bracket shell, as it threads in to place. This is how we know if it went in straight.

It is possible sometimes to swap parts around, betwixt the sealed cartridges, but it's nothing you can really count on. The hollow cups on 68- and 73-millimeter cartridges are not interchangeable, for one thing. And this measure, as translated across the spindle dimensions, leaves the cranks too close or too far from the frame. It may ram in to the chainstay that first time around or else the top chaining may settle just beyond the front derailleur's reach. It may still try to get the chain out there, just like before, but it won't be able to. Kind of sad.

We should also get in to the details of our new splined pipes, whose story is not without controversies of its own. I believe things started off with Truvativ's Isis Drive, which set ten even splines to the ends of a hollow 21-millimeter pipe. The applied wisdom from the frame tubes—that hollow can be lighter and stronger at once—had finally made it down to the nether regions below. But Truvativ used tiny ball bearings in the originals, defying decades of industry precedents, and it didn't work out at all. Bottom brackets have traditionally relied upon 1/4-inch balls, and it turns out Truvativ's tiny BBs were not up to the task. They can't handle the pressure; the cartridges tend to develop troubles after a while. The pipe was a grand idea, but it had to fit within the same old bottom bracket shell. This was the price paid.

Shimano's Dura Ace neatly circumvented the problem, by fitting trim needle bearings with theirs. It is certainly an intriguing concept, but these first-generation Shimano pipes do not enjoy stellar reputations among those mechanics in my know. The needles are especially vulnerable to road grit. They are sealed away, of course, but you don't want to go trolling through the mud puddles or anything.

And so the next logical step, as so brilliantly demonstrated by the gorgeous new Dura Ace crankset, was to mount the bearings outside the bottom bracket shell. The circle is made wider, allowing for both the pipe and properly sized bearings at once.

This precious new Hollowtech II design has since filtered down to the 105 road and LX mountain groups, for 2006. While Truvativ and others have since copied the newest Dura Ace outboard bearing arrangements, Shimano's original needle bearing adaptation has also enjoyed a fair circulation. It has spawned a child of its own, in fact: where the original V1 spindle will fit some newer DA, Ultegra, and 105 cranks, the longer and wider V2 spindles are meant for 2005 Deore, LX, and XT mountain cranksets.

Some of the better Shimano units are held together with hollow bolts that answer to 10-millimeter hex wrenches. You can see right through and out the other side. Kind of a cool effect, actually. I do need to mention one major caution, with regards to installing cranks on the new pipe-style bottom brackets: A lot of the high-end Shimano cranks meant for such bottom brackets have the clever self-extracting crank bolts, which save us the trouble of tracking down the correct extraction tool. But these need to be removed, to install the cranks on their spindle. It is way too easy to install the expensive new cranks at slight angles to the bottom bracket splines, which will

of course leave them useless. The only way to make sure this is not happening is to turn the bolts out. The SE jobs feature a pair of symmetrical holes across their face; we attack these with a small spanner. It's a pretty common tool these days; any realistic shop will be able to set you up. But the smaller needlenose pliers also work for this; they're often less expensive and always more universal.

Three Piece

We did save the best for last. It is the adjustable three-piece bottom bracket. This is who you really came to see tonight, right?

I probably learned bottom bracket overhauls back at Wheel and Sprocket, in Milwaukee. I think that's what happened; I don't even remember. Complete bike overhauls were already becoming a little easier, clear back then, because the cartridges were just beginning their invasion. But they've at least a passing resemblance to the religious zealots, in that there's just no talking to them. Every last one at least tries to be hermetically sealed; simple adjustments are rarely even possible.

The sealed cartridges, like the wingnuts, are too easily set in their ways. Their silence tempts us to leave them to their own devices—for years at a time, as the case may be—but this very license encourages them to rust in place, which, dependent, may put an end to the frame's useful life. The saccharine comfort of maintenance avoidance, to my experience, can be expected to explain itself through such dilemmas.

Sealed cartridges are capsulated ideology. They represent the easy way out. You can probably get away with relying on them—a good number of people already do—but I have not experimented with repairing sealed cartridges much at all, because I do not expect to succeed.

Ball-and-cup set

That said, I do run sealed cartridges on a few of my bikes. The ideological supermarket, as they say, is only good for raiding. But I still strive to save all the healthy old **BALL-AND-CUP SETS** I come across, because there really is some hope for redemption. The greatest majority of those I've seen can be returned to service again, once they're cleaned and greased. The design is blessedly simple; they were built to last.

A fixed cup, outfitted with bearings, is secured over on the drive side. A sturdy axle, known as the spindle, flies in to pin the balls against the cup's interior. A further piece, known as the adjustable cup, scoops up more bearings and threads down from the neutral side, trapping the spindle between their two sets. A lockring spins down atop the adjustable cup, finally, making official its new position. And you can turn the crank.

Each spindle and cup features some kind of bearing surface. As with the hubs, the better examples have better finishes to the bearing surfaces. The more chivalrous cups also strive to protect their races, with ingenious spindle-sized rubber seals. The older and more basic ball-and-cup bottom brackets are essentially brown metal rods, which happen to coincide with the bearings; their cups lack any seals. But the fancier ones are always kind of a minority. Most of those I've rescued have been of the simpler variety.

The ends to the original bottom bracket spindles were threaded, to be capped by sturdy nuts, but it was eventually decided to simply thread bolts in to the spindles instead. But any of this is vulnerable to coming loose, if the correct adjustments are not applied with due sincerity. That's what it comes down to. I have known far too many of these to hold adjustments for years on end; I've become somewhat less inclined to nourish any deeper suspicions on their occasional failures.

There are no secret bottom bracket demons, craftily upsetting our work in the dead of night. But there are a couple of bad habits we should talk about. Everybody needs to make sure that original adjustment is done just right, and we also need to work on getting both of the cups tightened all the way down. Ok, people? We can do this.

Cleaning and greasing the frame threads, as described earlier, is a very good way to start. You should be able to find replacement bearing-and-cup sets pretty easily, but it may be more of a challenge to find the right spindle. And just as with the sealed cartridges, the old spindles will have their drive and neutral ends. We find the correct orientation in precisely the same way, by reading the etchings appearing across the spindle's mid-section. Were the frame not in the way, anything such is legible whilst sitting in the saddle. The spindle's drive side is often a bit longer than the neutral side, in essence, but each looks roughly similar.

Some nicer spindles may sport a manufacturer's logo, but more basic examples only have a few odd letters and numbers, which reference an ancient mechanical code, the key for which was thrown out long ago. Spindle length is measured end-to-end, minus any threaded sections. The numbers thing was always kind of a gimmick; the length tells us all we need to know.

12: Hubs

The hubs are the stars in the cosmos of the wheels. Their axles' sustained rotation allows our movement forward.

Any non-sealed bearings in our hubs, headsets, or bottom brackets are periodically due for their overhauls. Situations vary, but this should at least happen every couple of years. But the overhauls are not any kind of instant, on-the-fly kind of thing. If you are trying to do it on the road, something has already gone drastically wrong.

The overhauls may be most critical with the **HUBS**. The precise resolution of their various health and maintenance concerns will always factor in to the quality of the ride. There are things we can do to nurse decades-old hubs back toward their health, in fact. But it kind of depends on the situation.

Most hubs operate by means of loose ball bearings. Many newer high-end models feature sealed bearing cartridges in place of these; a much smaller number of cheaper old hubs relied upon simple caged bearings. Where the cages have been able to work out well enough in the headsets and the old school bottom brackets, the classical hubs' consensus has long favored looser affiliations. And here again, the sealed bearing cartridges have sought to replace the question with an answer.

Whatever it is you're playing with, it is important the bearings become adjusted to a fairly precise point. We don't want them squeezed too tightly, nor loosened beyond useful mea-

sure, because either predicament bodes ill for the hub's bearing surfaces. At the same time, we also need to account for the compression of any quick-release skewers.

Hubs with quick-release skewers should be adjusted such that they end up being slightly loose. The axle has a barely perceptible lateral play, rolling it with your fingers, but this disappears when the skewer clamps it to the frame. The wheel is not able to move side-to-side at all in the frame. But the axle binds against the bearings, if the adjustment is too tight, and this is kind of a drag. But you may not even know about it, unless you take the wheel off and check things out.

All but the strangest hub axles are threaded to accept cones and locknuts on either side. Each is further augmented by matching arrays of spacers and dust caps, which together correspond to certain hubs in particular. A few different axle threadings have been used over the years. Cone height and width and race dimensions each present further variables; a given spacer or dust cap may fit just perfectly or not at all.

And still we find a semblance of unity, because almost all the hubs have subscribed to a handy series of bearing protocols. Excluding the sealed bearing hubs, whose numbered cartridges span a fair range of sizes, *nearly* all the rear hubs use nine 1/4-

inch balls to either side. And almost all the non-sealed front hubs, in turn, will sport ten 3/16-inch bearings in each race.

Shimano's axle threadings—9 x 1 millimeter front; 10 x 1 millimeter rear—have really become predominant, by virtue of their monopoly. There are still plenty of exceptions, to begin with Campagnolo. But the bearings themselves have also become more democratized, which is to say really nice ones can be found quite cheaply. The finest grade 25 balls, as used by Campy and other superstars, will cost about a dime apiece. Lower-quality grade 200 bearings may be set aside for the bar bike, or the slingshot. But we always need to get all 9 or 10 up in there, as the case may be, for their manic circle dance to continue.

The working surfaces of both the cones and the bearing races are meant to brace the bearings in one particular orientation. Balls too small—or too few—inevitably tip this careful apple cart. And where a hub spinning smoothly rolls consistently, one whose balls ride the far edges of their cones feel more sketchy. You know it if you have the wrong bearings or cones, in other words, because things do not turn out like they are supposed to.

Better cones and races are polished to finer degrees, before even leaving their warm factories. The races themselves are quite rarely damaged—the bearings' blazing comet tails are streaked across reasonably broad surfaces—but pitted bearing cones are not uncommon. Any maladjusted hub may earn a pair, if it's ridden too long. And any scars remaining on their working surfaces eventually fuck things up! They need to be replaced, before your ride back up the mountains.

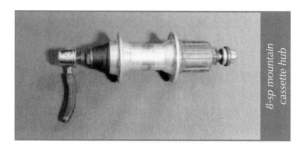

8-sp mountain cassette hub

The various axle widths—9 millimeter, 10 millimeter, BMX's 14 millimeter, and Tullio's 20 millimeter—are expected to correspond with matching frame dropouts. But the pattern is neither arbitrary nor capricious; its evolution merely responds to certain implacable design imperatives. The rear's heftier profile makes it easier to carry all the gears, for example, but the added responsibilities of increased load-bearing ambitions have all but demanded the change. The weight being supported is positively enormous, comparing with the hub itself—imagine the hefty bumble bee, lifting up with such tiny wings—but there is, eventually, a limit. Any serious excess of length translates as increased flex, which can bring its own problems. The window between too little and too much, smartly labeled "appropriate design" or similar, comes to exercise a powerful moderating influence.

This distance, from the tip of one locknut to the tail of its opposite, is known as the **HUB SPACING**. It is very much a known quantity—in the ideal, at least—but it is also quite common that the frames and forks must be spread, just slightly, to accept their hubs. The mild compression works to our advantage, in helping the hub find its place in our world. But there is no need to force the point! Any serious frame stretching can be expected to fuck up the bike's alignment. Pressing a frame together to meet a narrower axle, conversely, puts extra stress on those fixtures mounting the wheel to the bike.

Front hubs are wonderfully predictable. Nearly everything is spaced to 100 millimeters. Many compact folding bikes have 75-millimeter front hubs, but the wheels are also tiny; you almost expect to see it. I've heard of some old 90-millimeter BMX hub measurement, but I'm not sure I've ever seen one.

BMX rear hubs start the listing in back, with the slim spacing of 110 millimeters—one gear; they get away with it. Both track bikes and the old-fashioned 3-speeds share the 120-millimeter gap. But the 3's axle is maybe a bit narrower; its frame dropouts need to be filed down to accept a track hub. That was my friend Amelia's experience, at least. Some really old road or city bikes have also have been 120, but 126 millimeter is the real old-fashioned road bike standard. Fades a bit every year, but we remember.

I have seen only one reference to a 128-millimeter rear hub spacing; I'm guessing it was also an old road bike. Modern road bikes are more recently at 130 millimeters, for many years now. And we can tell the mountain bikes entered production during this time, because this 130 is also the original ATB rear hub spacing; as with 126, ever more rare, on the mountain bikes at least. The big common coin is 135, found with all the modern mountain bikes, hybrids, recumbents, recumbent trikes, and so on. Odds are good this is you.

Tandems may be found with any of the afor mentioned rear hub spacings—except the 110, hopefully—but modern tandems are all using wider hubs. They support the weight better; they also allow a drag brake to slip in on the wheel's neutral side. We're talking 140, 145, or 160 millimeter, dependent upon age and manufacturer.

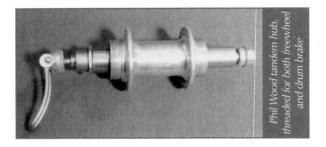

Phil Wood tandem hub, threaded for both freewheel and drum brake

Freewheel

The hub gears either thread on as a complete package or slide down the splines of an existing mechanism. The threaded **FREEWHEELS** are the original coasting champions. (The fixed track cogs, which thread on to distinct track hubs, are discussed on page 217.) Their supreme leisure is too easily taken for granted, from our wizened modern perspective, but of course the freewheels were revolutionary in their time. Our cadence was shifted from perpetual motion to full-on casual, by nothing more than a basic mechanical duplicity. A circle of bearings and spring-loaded palls was inserted between the cog and its fixed base, and away we went.

The freewheel perches upon a stack of wide, flat threads rising from the drive-side flange. These should not be confused with the threadings found on track hubs, which are stepped in two distinct sections, the smaller of which is reverse threaded. The freewheels enjoy the traditional right-handed thread orientation, which in their case means that riding down the road serves to continuously tighten things down.

You may very occasionally come across French- or Italian-threaded hubs and freewheels, but these gems are both endangered like the species. Almost everything you ever come across bears threads cut to the English standard.

Whichever their nationality, the hub threads should always be greased before any freewheel is installed. I've also seen references to another contemporary threading, the BMX Mini, but as yet I've not actually seen an example in real life. My wrenching career shifted straight from the recumbents to the high-end road bikes; there has not been an opportunity to stop and play with the 20-inchers. But my information suggests this Mini is notably smaller, as the name implies; there isn't much confusion. It is associated with the 14- and 15-tooth singlespeed freewheels.

The freewheels are all made of steel or perhaps even titanium, by virtue of their strenuous responsibilities, but the hub threads are typically aluminum. This makes for yet another tedious power relationship, of course; the angry freewheels are only too happy to erase the hubs' more fragile threads. So don't ever install one at any angles, lest you end the hub's useful life. You should *never* feel as if you're forcing a freewheel in to position. It should twirl on like butter, threading into place with the slightest push. Back off if it doesn't, and think about what you're trying to do.

Freewheels are available in a good range of gearing sizes, from BMX singles up to clusters of 7 or 8, which, dependent, may or may not work with a given bike's drivetrain. Neither 9- nor 10-speed freewheels exist. The technology that renders freewheels obsolete came to the world years ago already, back when everyone was still on 7 speeds, and 8-speed freewheels are kind of a fluke this way.

Having played with the freewheels a while, we're given a sense of certain shortcomings particular to their program. The design leaves the drive-side bearings well back from their frame dropout, under the wide threaded section. And the axle is not well supported across their precarious middle distance; it

becomes much more vulnerable to bending. Some high-end examples are able to persist regardless—the old Mavic threaded hubs spring to mind—but their lesser peers simply cannot be trusted with much for weight. No larger riders; no loaded tours.

Cassette

The freewheels also fuse the clutch mechanism with the actual cogs—to varying degrees of permanence—and this makes individual cog replacement either difficult or impossible. But this only means the **CASSETTES** are fucking brilliant. Both our outstanding difficulties are resolved with one smooth move, by fixing the clutch mechanism to the hub itself.

The cassette hub replaces the freewheel threads with a splined cylinder, known as the **FREEHUB BODY**. A gear cassette bearing matched splines slides down around this; a lockring finally secures the cassette in place. Pretty damn trick, considering.

The hub's drive side bearings make the most of the new situation, by migrating down toward the outer end of the freehub body, just under the cassette lockring. Their job becomes much easier; they've no more awkward gap to worry about. The axle is much less inclined toward bending.

The dimensions and requirements of the freehub bodies have appeared in a few different styles, over the years. Most are either rare or obsolete. Suntour had distinct 7- and 8-speed cassette hubs, for example, back when they made hubs. But that was a while ago. Campagnolo has additionally offered various freehub arrangements, for gear cassettes ranging from 7 to 10 speeds.

Shimano's 7- and 8/9-speed freehub body standards are far and away the most common. Both are further improvements on their original 7-speed prototype, which did not have a proper lockring. The top of the original freehub body was threaded on the outside, rather than the inside; the top cog screwed down around it. But it's somewhat easier to shift if the teeth line up just so against the next cog, as it turns out; tightening the locking top cog into place turned this measure into a crap shoot.

Freehub body with fixing bolt

And so the modern cassette lockring was born! It threads to the freehub body's interior; splines around its face click away against those they find atop the cassette's final cog. The cassette splines' profile has also changed: one especially wide stripe has appeared, forcing the cogs to line up in a predetermined orientation. Some number of cassettes have long been available as stacks of spacers and individual cogs; it would otherwise have been easy enough to line them up all crazy and shit. But now this one wide stripe takes charge of the situation; the cogs are made to relate to each other in precisely correct ways.

Shimano's 8/9-speed freehub body is a little longer than the 7, as we may imagine, but this is their only crucial difference. And it is possible to update or replace either sort, with the Shimano cassette hubs at least. A raft of distinct 7- and 8-speed replacement

freehubs has already set sail, in fact. Minute distinctions in dust cap dimensions set many of these just slightly apart; the true scientists among us will note the model number on the hub body before ordering any replacements.

Shimano cassette hubs hold the cassette in place with a big hollow screw; the axle passes right through it. The big 10-millimeter Allen key handily slots into position, once the axle is out of the way, to release the freehub body's fixing bolt. And make sure this last is greased and well tightened on the way back in. They loosen quite rarely, but it makes for an especially bleak and existential problem. This happened to my friend Shelly's bike, on our long ride out to Portland, and at the time I was left absolutely slack-jawed.

All freehubs have just a bit of play, to allow for their mechanisms to whirl, but this is barely even perceptible with the better examples. Shoddier hub manufacturers have insisted on marrying the freehub body to the hub, as one solid package. Cheesy. There are no flats for the 10 to grip, because there's no workable screw in the first place.

Campagnolo cassettes arrive aboard curious plastic decks, which are meant to slot down right atop their particular freehub bodies, allowing us to simply slide the goods down into place. And this is handy, because the cogs and spacers are arranged in a particular sequence: mixing the spacers' arrangements up can well torpedo their careful indexing potential. It would look just about right, but the whole thing would be just a little off.

The cassette's lockring looks quite similar to those we see with the standard SRAM and Shimano products, but they're attached and removed with the distinct Campagnolo UT-BB080 extraction tool. And they made a couple of them, actually: the lockrings supplied with 1998 and older Campy cassettes are not compatible with the more modern freehubs. Different threadings.

Excluding the aforementioned original model, Shimano cassette hub systems are more standardized. The very same Hyperglide tool will fit modern road and mountain gear clusters from 7 to 10 speeds, as well as their imitators from SRAM and Sunrace.

All modern cassettes are removed by the same method. Two tools are required: one presses the cogs clockwise, and the other twists the lockring off in the opposite direction. We have various specialized implements for this at the shop; home mechanics only need a chainwhip for the cogs and the big crescent wrench to hold the lockring tool. (You might re-install the quick release skewer atop the lockring tool to hold it in place, depending.) And whichever cassette you find yourself working with, make sure the thing gets nice and tight, when you put it back together. Grooves carved to the cassette's top cog will match others set to the underside of the lockring; we always want to make sure these ratchet all the way down. Precise torque settings can be found with the various manufacturers' technical data, needless to say, but after a while you just get a sense for what tight is supposed to mean.

A loose lockring allows the cassette itself to sway back and forth on its freehub body, presenting something of a moving target above the derailleur's precise and hopeful clicks. The situation is obvious enough, once you learn what to look for; the cogs can be moved laterally, independently of any play in the freehub body. But you can't be going all ape shit with this, at the very same time, because an over-tightened lockring will in some cases actually bear down too heavily on the hub bearings, enough to even slow things

down. If the hub spins less freely after the cassette is installed, this is why. So you just learn the proper balance, young master.

The hub bodies themselves have also been growing wider over the years. This leaves them marginally more rigid; their wheels become a few decimal points more efficient. Phil Wood has been doing this forever; Shimano eventually incorporated the idea; their myriad admirers duly picked up the scent. Not too big of a deal at all, I only bring it up because these new hubs also have strong appetites for bearings. They don't consume them any faster; they simply hide them. Much as cats do with their toys. The wider mid-sections make for slight shelves, as they meet the flanges; the bearings tend to catch on these. They tip right back out with a small screwdriver, of course, but it's more fun to enlist a small magnet for this. The bearings are all lifted away to safety, like a hostage scene from the movies.

A cassette at rest

Overhauls

All the hub's individual parts can be cleaned up nicely with thin oils, which break down the crusty old grease. You may want to *gently* pry off the dust caps, to better swab the hub's races. Be careful if you do; the old school metal dust caps are bent and dented quite easily. You press it back in place with the side of your wrench, when you are done, to leave it nice and level across the hub.

Any pitted cones should get shitcanned, together with the stanky-ass bearings they rolled in with, OK? Once the bearing races are clean, lay down some nice fat donuts with the grease. The bearings plop right down into this, one by one. Good greases—Rock and Roll's white stuff, for example—hold them in place while you reassemble. I tend to reuse bearings because I'm fast enough already, but we always finish overhauls with new bearings at work.

The cones and locknuts on each side need to end up supremely tight against each other, in order to maintain any worthy adjustment. Again, the measure you're looking for rests at a pretty exacting point, midway along the spectrum from loose to tight, or, if your hub is skewered, just a *hair* to the loose side. Even I, hoary old mechanic as I am, must pause and reflect just a second when I do this. Concentrate, concentrate, concentrate.

Something so simple as a buildup of grease between the bearings and hub surfaces can damn your work! Seat things in place as best you can in the first place, by rolling the axle in a rag. You can also just grab the axle ends, and spin the wheel a few seconds. You will be working in ever-smaller measures, as you tighten down to your finishing point, checking the results after each one. The cone and locknut on one side will be tightened all the way together; the adjustments are made on the other side. Remember from grade school science that jazz about the control and the experiment? Here it is, at last.

I tend to set the side with the most axle spacers as my control, on old freewheel hubs. This means that the cone and locknut's final positioning is translated across the smallest dis-

tance, over on the experimental side, which seems to make things a little easier. The cassette hubs, however, have already made this choice for you: the flats on the drive side cone disappear inside the freehub body, as it's put back together, so you need to make sure that side is completely tight while it's still out in the daylight.

The axle itself helps us determine whether the cone or lockring is being turned. There will inevitably be some scratch or clump of grit or something on the axle threads by the time they're ready for their overhauls; this may be used as a reference point. You can dab on a drop of grease, if nothing else.

You want to check the bearing adjustment, to determine just what needs to move: we either back off on the bearing cone to loosen things up or bear down with the locknut to tighten them down. Position your wrenches such that you're clasping them together between your hands, as you finish; that is enough to get you the goods.

A couple summers ago, I happened to notice that each side's cone and locknut can turn *simultaneously*, for small distances at least. And it seemed really cool for a while because it simplified my work, but our friend Travis warns against this method. It can twist the axles, so don't do it. The science approach enlists an axle vise, in fact, but to my experience we almost always get what we need without one. (But in all fairness, Campagnolo's technical literature confirms that their cassette hub axles are indeed tightened by a very similar method, gripping wrenches at either end of the hub body. You see what I mean about the precise value of definitive statements in bicycle mechanistry? The riddles, they never end. Campagnolo's superior axles better allow for the extra torsion, presumably.)

It is hard not to notice when a hub is too loose, when the wheel is mounted in the bike. You can move the rim laterally in the frame. You set the bike down and it rattles; suddenly everyone knows you need to fix that. But it's more difficult to know if you're riding a hub too tight. The offending wheel has become less efficient in its duties, but it's not likely you specifically notice this. The wind; that damned pizza; all the beer; so many things may slow us down. Pop the wheel out and check on its axle, if you're worried about it.

The benders are also easy to spot, if you know what you're looking for. A sorely bent axle binds at some point, when rotated; the hub's adjustment is on-again, off-again. The situation becomes all the more obvious, re-moving the axle and rolling it on a mirror. The benders may be carefully straightened in an axle vise, theoretically, but that never happens because we have spares, for now. The threading and the overall length needs to match the original.

Checking an axle for bends

Some Campagnolo hubs are still hip enough to incorporate grease ports. Is that cool or what? You can spy the first in its traditional location, shielded beneath a rotating band set around the hub's body; its peer rides midway up one of the freehub splines. Either will open upon only the narrowest of chan-nels, meaning for a bicycle-specific pinpoint grease gun.

The bearing adjustment mechanism aboard Campagnolo's newer Record, Chorus, and

Daytona hubs is pretty happening as well. A solitary 2.5-millimeter Allen key (or Phillips screwdriver, in the case of Daytona) loosens a collar on the neutral side, which in turn is rotated to tighten or loosen the bearing cones. Said collar bears a set of 21-millimeter flats, if you need to do this with the wheel in the frame or something, but we otherwise just twirl the thing closed with the fingertips.

The hubs themselves are taken apart with a pair of 5-millimeter Allens. Each axle end provides for the requisite fittings; the two are simply turned against each other.

The freehub is also excused in a distinct fash-ion. You can spy a lockring of the usual style immediately outboard of the freehub body, which spins off to release it. But this lock-nut itself will sometimes be secured in posi-tion with a small locking screw of its own. If a diminutive bolt-head features along the locknut's side, it must first be loosened with a 2-millimeter Allen wrench.

The unique Campagnolo UT-HU080 tool is required to successfully remove and in-stall some Campagnolo freehubs. Everything simply leaps out and scatters in other cir-cumstances. Our mediating device is only a curious loop of sprung wire, which holds the freehub palls and their springs in place as their freehub is lifted away. We clip it in to place just as soon as the pall mechanism becomes visible, and it occupies this position until everything (or its replacement) is safely back home.

Other hubs make their own provisions in this regard, by incorporating a trim wire band around the palls. Do not bend this any more than you would the dainty HU080! You have to push in on these palls with a small screw-driver or similar, in the latter case, to remount the freehub body aboard its hub.

13: BOXING BIKES

A bike in a box might travel places its peers would never see. And there it might emerge to ride anew, if only we've been careful along the way.

And it is here, with the hubs spinning contentedly in the background, that we may enjoy the leisure to discuss more ambitious pursuits. We learn all kinds of things working at the shops; much of it is simply never put to paper.

Just about every last bike, to take one example, will first emerge from a box. And if we've talked about how things may then go together, the reverse is not also true. But this becomes important, if ever your bike goes on vacation, because the wrong shipment can too easily take it to hell and back.

Bike boxes are quite large, but it's only upon leaving the industry that we find the real excesses. Those bicycle boxes I've seen coming from the airline companies are *ridiculously* huge, beyond all scope or dimension. They are intended for sudden and unexpected disassembly work by anxious professionals. It's way too much space to clunk around in; paint chips and worse are not surprising, unless you pack all your shirts in there, too.

I would skip any of this airline bullshit. No wonder they charge so much, passing out boxes like that. Your bike is more secure if it's not bouncing around the insides of some flimsy cavern. The box and bike should sort of brace each other, to make for a more solid whole.

The safest thing is always one of the hard cases, but shops that sell bikes tend to have a few **BIKE BOXES** kicking around, by default or design. Tandem-sized boxes are more rare; you'll likely have a hunt before you. And while the clever folding bikes may be squirreled away in the suitcases, the recumbents most likely need special recumbent boxes, best obtained from your friendly local 'bent dealer.

The bike may even be shipped to another shop, if you want to avoid all this, but it's still good to head out with those hand tools you need for reassembly. The recipe varies some, dependent upon your mount, but you at least want some Allen wrenches and a pedal wrench. You should also figure out if it's possible and/or necessary to save the box, together with the bits of bike packaging hardware described momentarily.

You want to find some way to stow the bike box somewhere, if a local replacement can not be found. There are not many others that may happen to fit a bicycle. Upright bike boxes are increasingly standardized—one size will probably fit all—but the same can not be said for recumbent bikes. The 'bents often need one for the frame, and another for the wheels and seat (what we call the parts box). The different recumbent manufacturers have also found reasons to use various different-sized recumbent boxes, beyond this point. A set of Rans boxes may be the most universal, in that it should fit both long and short wheelbase bikes. I don't think I've ever heard of anyone charging for bike boxes, incidentally. That would strike me as shady.

The front forks on any boxed bike are almost always flipped around backward, to conserve space. The bars also need to come off, with or without the stem. The box needs to span from the fork to the rear of the back wheel, preferably. Or, if your bike is just huge and you know that back wheel must be removed as well, the box needs to stretch to the tail of the frame itself.

We pull the skewers from any wheels that are removed, to further save on the space. The axle ends are then capped with **BIKE PACKAGING**, to keep them from gouging the frame or its box. And the braces used in the dropouts and on both sides of a mounted rear wheel are just as ubiquitous; any shop that actually sells bikes should be able to set you up.

You want to shift into the lowest gear, if you do leave the wheel on, such that the derailleur is moved all the way toward the bike's interior. It's safest there. More generally it's best to do the absolute minimum, in terms of disassembly, to simplify things at the far end.

The boxing is really not so complicated, once you have the right box. You remove the front wheel, release the air from each tire—and any air-sprung rear shocks, as well—and remove the seat and pedals. You will now discover, if you didn't known already, if the box is big enough. The fork's dropout brace should be all the way forward and most likely down on the box's floor. (Some Rans LWB bikes see it resting on a short stack of Styrofoam pillows, to provide for a more fitting angle.)

You do want to keep the box in its original shape. Don't let it produce suspicious bulges; there can be none of that. Imagine there's a wicked machine at the end of the conveyor belt; any of this shit just gets sheared off. And there's only one trick for this, with the upright bikes, which is with the front wheel removed and the bike kneeling on front fork and rear wheel, slip the front wheel right over that neutral side crank arm. It just slides in between the spokes; you maneuver the wheel up close to the frame.

The drop bars can kind of curl around the top tube; the flatter bars can sneak in wherever their controls allow them to fit. Bar ends and aero bars should probably get removed. The stem and bar control levers may be left loose as well, to better go with the flow. You might even release a cable or two—the front brake, for example—to allow the bars to slide in to a better spot in the box.

The very last thing is to tie it all together. We use zip ties; you can also use your imagination. Crumple some newspaper or cardboard or whatever else is handy to fill the gaps. But do not toss the small parts in this sea, lest they disappear forever. Throw everything in a small box or bag or something; it's much easier to find again.

If you *do* have to take the rear wheel out to ship, go ahead and remove the rear derailleur as well. We assume it will get crushed, otherwise. Just turn out the hanger bolt; there should be enough slack in the derailleur's cable to set it out of the way, between the chainstays. Tape plastic bags or something all around it, as well as any loose chain, if the paint has any art left to it.

You risk damaging your bike, if you try to pack it up too small. The particulars of some Burley recumbents allow the factory to ship them out in one single box—BikeE and Vision both were able to pull off a similar stunt, in their day, but these were oddballs among the freaks, in this respect at least. Excluding Burley, whose boxes are usually wide enough to let 26-inch wheels rest at angles, there is not much variation by box width. Figure around 8 inches wide. Box height is becoming less and less relevant for upright bikes; they're increasingly shipped in taller boxes regardless. Height is only rarely an issue for shipping recumbents.

Bike packaging

14: FENDERS

In defense against the elements, the wisest among the bikes call upon the fenders, which step in above the tires to collect their far-flung abuses.

The **FENDERS** require some means to clip on to the bike—through dedicated mounting holes above the wheels, usually—as well as the clearance to fit in the first place. But these considerations are obvious enough. Scope out the gaps above the wheels. Are there holes up in there? What about the space to shoot some fenders through?

You can manage, most often; it's only a few of the road racing bikes we wonder about, basically. Some of the newer ones seem to think they're too fast to worry about the puddles. The frame and fork close in right around the tire, obscuring any possibilities for more thorough coverage. The effort makes some marginal contribution to the aerodynamics; this may or may not be worth getting your ass soaked. And the brakes themselves also need the clearance, of course; some sidepulls may not have any.

Questions around a frame's fender clearance are sometimes resolved with alternatives. Seatpost-mounted fenders are probably the most useful of these; they fit just about any bike. Suspension forks often lack fender-mounting holes, but we find some to plug right up in their steerer tubes.

The full fender sets—identified by their stainless steel struts—will reliably provide the best protection. The earliest versions of these were made with hard, brittle plastic. They were fa-mously vulnerable to breakage, especially in the deep cold, but they were still a nice update on the original steel bicycle fenders—lighter, adjustable, rust free. The better full fender sets now available also use a far more pliable plastic; it takes hits much better.

The struts end in little hooks, which are joined to eyelets on the frame with screws. You can make your own eyelets with a pair of rack mounts, if your frame doesn't feature them already. The far ends of the struts pass through odd little clamp bolts riveted in pairs to the fender's sides; the fender gets tightened down at some point along its struts. The arrangements allow us to adjust the fender's position, such that it faithfully follows the curve of the wheel, where it provides you the best in protection.

Or, if you feel yourself to be more flighty, maybe you can do better with a set of the clip-on fenders. These are not encumbered with any struts. Their mounting brackets get bolted on at the fender holes; the rear one also clips on to the base of the seat tube. And as the name implies, simple finger-tightened hardware lets us un-clip them in a hurry, which may help with your street cred, if you've been hanging around less interesting sorts of people, in case you and the bike end up going to prom or something. But the clip-on fenders are also good for touring, precisely because they can be taken down like this. All the better to put the bike in the box.

The clips are sold for maybe half what the full sets go for, but their coverage is not as thorough. During winter, conditions occasionally produce a thicker, more adhesive snow that sticks to the tires; the clip-on sets seem to handle this stuff better. The type of snow I reference here tends to kind of build up between the wheels and the full fender sets, until such a point when it rubs upon the tire. But the clips are pliable enough to bend out of the way for a second.

You can also find cheap in-between jobs, the Apex for example, that hover somewhere between full and partial coverage. I don't think too much of the silly wail-tail seatpost mount fenders, because they're supposed to sit too high to do much good at all, and they are continually being knocked out of line with the wheel. So you have to keep an eye on the fender's alignment, which is fucking ridiculous, unless you're able to mount the fender down on the seat tube, such that it shoots out between the seatstays.

I save the full fenders for Grey, my rain bike. Full fenders are really nice, especially in Minnesota in the springtime. But that may approach some kind of universal, right? What sets us apart is the thing about riding in the **SNOW**.

15: WINTER RIDING

The bicycles have never solicited any seasonal restrictions. Their imposition, as too often suggested within the industry itself, betrays nothing so much as a lack of imagination.

Cross-country skiing I kind of relate to—I can remember my neighbors skiing down the middle of the street, after big storms—but I no longer understand the downhill thing. Biking is free; you just go and do it whenever. And the more you keep at it, the better you begin to realize what **GEAR** you need to stay warm and nubile in the frigid.

The first tendency is to overdress … don't. Maybe you want to pack something extra, if your distances are ambitious, but more usually you want to feel a little under-protected as you walk out the door. You're not sitting down with a lift ticket; you're staying active.

The coolest thing about winter riding has to be the clothes you get to wear. It seems best to go as kind of a granola bandit. A lot of the technical sports gear is pretty worthwhile, and you really don't want to leave anything exposed, not on the super cold days, at least.

You always want to start with the black, form-fitting head sock we call the balaclava—a must-have kind of accessory; it goes with everything. The top can get folded so it just covers your ears, on the warmer days, but personally I'd much rather just chop off a sleeve for such purposes. Long sleeves can provide for some happening tails in back; the shorter ones can layer atop these as required, all of which still fit under the helmet.

The point becomes kind of obscure, in tropical climates like San Francisco, but in the snow you do best to have some kind of dedicated cycling jacket. These are shells, cut to better fit the cycling profile, just loose enough to accommodate a few layers beneath. Following on my own fifteen winters' riding, I would say the armpit zippers may be the single most useful things about these. They accomplish climate control, without baring your chest and neck to the icy wind.

Reinforced Carhardt jeans often block the wind just enough, for that matter. And the good old-fashioned choppers or similar may still provide the best choices, for the deep cold anyway. These of course are the traditional two-piece Minnesotan mittens; same things I used on my paper route when I was a kid.

I've taken to riding in my engineer boots, in the winter. I grab the less interesting waterproof hikers as shit starts to melt. I have never had the slightest interest in the form-fitting booties, meant to cover cycling shoes in the cold. Clipless pedals do not strike me as a good idea at all in the snow. I think I'd rather walk.

For special added effect, you might slap a pair of cross-country skiing gators over the tops of your boots. They keep your feet nice and dry, and raise the practiced eyebrow as well. I'll never forget the reaction I got from a couple punk rockers, decked-out to the nines, up by the local art school: "Watch it, space hero!"

I laughed all the way home. And so we proceed; for the freedom of the galaxy … . There's always going to be those who think of bike messenger work as some kind of groovy summer job, discounting the winter months. There was at least one day in my first year when an excess of snow forced downtown to shut down. We got to go home early. And I remember another, over the third winter maybe, when the frigid cold snapped the palls in my freewheel. I had to walk off the balance of my packages. But I can not even imagine trading in for some car that may never start.

Freehubs and freewheels both are pretty famous for failure, in the deep cold. The palls either seize in place or simply come apart. It just coasts in either direction; only technically connected to the wheel.

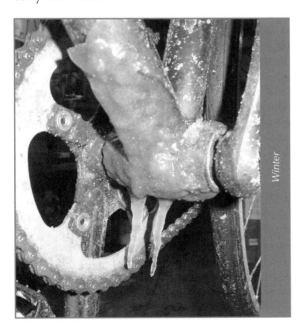

This is the cross you bear, if you insist on coasting through the winter. An ailing freewheel might be removed and revived with a little oil, dropped in to the seam around its backside, but that's about all we could do. Spin the freewheel in your hands as you do this, to work it in; you will hear the difference the oil makes. It's ideal if we can sneak some kind of heavyweight oil in there, but in all likelihood the best we can do is gob on the thinner stuff. It sneaks through the crack. Just douse it until it begins to leak out the far side (the same might be done with freehub bodies, of course, once the hub is taken apart).

I imagine the better-quality freehub bodies hold their own somewhat better, as do some of the new high-zoot singlespeed freewheels, but we're still not in any position to speak of promises.

Derailleurs, too, are vulnerable. They don't actually die; they just stop moving. We expect a vast epidemic of temporary work stoppages, on really cold days, pending negotiations for temperature modification. A confluence of considerations point us toward the fixes.

I'd originally been turned on to **FIXED WHEEL** as a winter thing; it only became more constant with the arrival of spring. Points may certainly be made for its more general worthiness, but as it concerns us here, the fix shines like a star on the cold winter nights.

I managed to go downhill skiing now and again as a kid, and the fix recalls that experience. And just as the skis open to horizons well past the cracked plastic sleds of our childhood, so too the fix carries us beyond the precarious freewheels. Where the ski edges are carved in to the snow to set a course, the fixed wheel's momentum momentarily reverses to similar effect. The comparison does test certain boundaries, I realize—we're holding lines against a circle, from a certain angle at least—but the reflex itself is eventually quite similar.

It gets to the point where you can correct inadvertent skids in motion by pushing back on the pedals. The wheel starts sliding out from under you; you press it in the opposite direction. Any kind of freewheel action, you get none of this. You can't kick the wheel back a little bit; all you can do is coast. That back wheel becomes passive and ambivalent; less of a ski and more of a sled.

These things said, a solid case may be made for wintering aboard the singlespeed mountain bikes as well. It kind of depends on the weather.

The snow tends to be dry—on days cold enough to threaten the freewheels' integrity—and thus more easily tamed by our thin-wheeled fixed gears. But these quiet, crystalline afternoons are bracketed by their opposites, when the heaps of heavy wet snow can never possibly melt fast enough. The fix's trim pizza-cutters slice like swords, scraping for the bottom of the pan regardless, and you find yourself quite stuck. And yet this very softness suggests things are not cold enough to shatter the freewheels' spines, and of course the fat knobbies are more in their element.

It's best to limit the winter's sore abuses to one unlucky bike, if and when possible, but a case may be made for a pair of them. Or you may pick another favorite entirely, contingent only upon your own readings of the wind. The salient point is that it can be done.

But we also expect the story to change, as spring arrives. There inevitably comes a point when the snow becomes too soft and sloppy for the **KNOBBIES** themselves, and it is here that the thinner fixed wheels again step in and take things over. I long assumed that thinner road tires were always the best for the snow, because this was my experi-

ence. Where fat knobbies skidded across the surface, thin tires seemed to cut through the fluff, to better grip the hardpack beneath, much like skis. But that, as it turned out, was circumstance. A few years ago, when I was discovering my thin-tire theory, almost all my winter riding was in downtown Minneapolis. I was a messenger, living in the shadows of the skyscrapers. The lame municipal plow-fucks habitually use any available bike lines for snow storage—I shit you not; it's just insane—but the other traffic lanes were *comparatively* well maintained, which, of course, is quite extraordinary.

It was only more recently that I found myself roaming around outside the precious core, rediscovering the snowbanks deep enough to build forts in to … and it is here, where both traffic and plowing are less intense, that the knobbies can make some sense. For a while anyway, until any serious melting happens, and, of course, assuming you're not in any hurry. The knobby tires will always be slower. But it's the season for it, if ever there was one.

I know plenty of people who take no-brake track bikes through winter after winter, clipless pedals and all; others who swear by singlespeed mountain bikes; at least a couple who dash recumbent delta trikes through the snow. Maybe the useful thing to say is that winter riding best arrives in a range of distinct persuasions. Give yourself time developing the snow legs; trust your instincts and never the cars. You may even start to like it.

Fresh snow is slower going. It does offer a bit more traction—preferable to dancing around on the compacted cookie-cutter snow, perhaps—but the central concern is always for sliding around. Anything reflecting any kind of light can suddenly, easily knock you on your ass. It is best to avoid the slick spots, where you can manage it. We are usually able to.

More generally, you really *don't* want to be relying on any sudden moves. There's no better way to lose it than yanking on the brakes. I do run front hand brakes on my fixed-wheel bikes, but I barely touch them at all in the snow. Staying upright is more about controlling the speed, with your legs.

You should see if you can slow down, before you have to cross any ice. You're probably going to hit the ground if you don't. Once you are on the ice, try to relax. The bike is likely capable of carrying you across, but you must simply let it happen; you cannot be a control freak. Any abrupt gestures only amplify, up to the point of your own downfall. Suppose there is something magical about the two wheels, rolling in line; turning the handlebars or squeezing a brake lever will fuck up the flow. So deal with it later, once you're good.

Winter riding imparts all manner of incidental information, as well. Our scale is more easily understood. The snow reduces roads to tracks and stripes, just wide enough for solitary lines of cars. The average bike suddenly can't do anything close to car speed anymore. And, once in line, the cars are all just endlessly trying to crawl up your ass. Nobody you know, revving the engine on the slick right behind you. You learn to pick up on the engine noise. How close they are; whether they're going to slow down at all. They won't. This all goes down maybe half-blocks from passing lanes and intersections; the problem seems to lie in your failure to be both places at once.

The driving experience provides for fleeting, illusory power, which asks to stand in for a great many things. Nobody wants to slow down those humbling few seconds before they absolutely have to, as this will showcase some special weakness. But you're still right in the way with the damned bike! You can grind off into the snowbanks and stop, or you can wait it out and see if you get hit.

I rarely take shit from drivers … in the summertime. Making the most of those advantages available to me is always foremost in my mind; it is simply part of the experience. But much of this disappears through the winter—I cannot speed, swerve, stop on dimes. So all too often I suck it in, plow into the snowbank, and let pass the trembling, bloodless jellyfish.

There are all kinds of things we can say about the whole process of hurry, as it relates to winter. I think winter is a fine time to inquire after the quiet, to write books and such. There is nothing remotely natural about trying to rush while the world is frozen around you. To call it "counterintuitive" is already too much effort. The cars' evident ambition—to quickly force the bikes in to the ditches—suggests a basic lack of understanding.

16: On-the-Road Repairs

The best bikes of our generation may yet suffer their troubles,
even far from home, because sometimes shit just happens.
But salvation can take a while; you might try initiative.

I'm not sure how best we may smoothly segue toward it, coming in from the cold, but our next adventure comprises solutions for **ON-THE-ROAD**. It skims the top of everything that has come before, taking only what is portable, sorting the crucial elements from the available doomsday scenarios. What's the word? Triage.

You want to put together a basic mobile repair kit, including a pump for your tubes. (Most of the portable bike pumps can be easily switched, from presta valve fittings to those for shraeder; some will even have spouts for the both of them.) Your kit should also have a spare tube, either a Quik Stik or a pair of tire levers; some assortment of the more common hex and box wrench sizes, including anything you need to take a wheel off; a Phillips screwdriver; and maybe a patch kit. All of which can fit in a cargo pocket, were there the need, but it's probably more natural in a bag or similar. The last one of these I put together ended up in an old parmesan cheese container, in fact. (I previously thought these were only useful for carrying sunglasses.) A small rag, quite nice for on the road, mashes down under the lid. So your shit doesn't rattle so much.

Your **FLAT TIRE** is only a pain in the ass if you need to be somewhere. Excluding that small clique of readers with the curious mono-blade forks, you first want to take the wheel off. This is easier if you flip the bike upside-down. Is it raining, snowing, something like that? If all you have is the wheel and your bag, maybe you can go do this inside somewhere—campus-type buildings, back entrances, whatever works. You may want to lock the rest of the bike outside, depending.

Shift down to the smallest gears, if you're able to, if the flat is out back. It's easier to pull the wheel out this way; you also know where to set the chain on the way back in.

Do what you can do to get any remaining air out of the tube. You're not creating a vacuum or anything, but the more the tire can move around, the easier this will be. But the tire may be kind of stuck to the rim, if it's been on there a while. So go all the way around the wheel, first one side and then the other, and get the tire un-stuck. You trace the tire's bead with your fingertips; it backs off as you do so. It is possible to replace an inner tube without fully removing the tire—you can just leave one bead parked on the rim—but you always want to make sure that you check the tire for any damage or debris.

It is sometimes quite obvious just what made the flat—some nail jabbed into the tire, a gash along its sidewall—but it's far more common that you need to mount a search. Pick a point on the tread, above the tire label for example, and run its full circle through your hands. Your fingers thoroughly sweeping the insides for any spikes; your thumbs doing the same on the outside. You should do this a couple of times, actually. Find anything yet? It is best if you can dig any debris out with some kind of implement. A knife or a pick is ideal. You packed a blade, right?

What about the sides of the tires? See any rips? It does not matter how small, the tube still tries its damnedest to sneak through. Sidewalls are much thinner than the treads; it is easy enough to do.

Especially ambitious road debris may sometimes reach up to gouge the tire's sidewall, but the tires would sooner gore themselves on the bike's very own brake pads. They may have already carved balding streaks all the way around the tire, like malignant rubber comet tails. Smaller troubles on the sidewalls can be mended with a tire boot, described momentarily, but of course we never know where the longer comet tails may land. Nor does it make a whole lot of sense to try riding such a bubble at lowered air pressure, because this in itself increases the chances of pinched flats.

Smaller rips and gashes can be mended with a **TIRE BOOT**, which steps in beneath the sidewall to provide moral support. Tear a small corner off that last twelve-pack; back it up with a good piece of duct tape. You can save the scraps from that last roll of Velox, alternately, for use with roadside repairs. The nice thick rim tape? Double up a couple pieces, right over the gash. But you get the idea. And do make sure the booted sidewall is not faced against any generators or dynamos, lest the wee rips tear into chasms.

You got that good inner tube? It wasn't crammed in anywhere it could get popped,

right? Fill it with a little air; just barely enough to make it round.

Clincher tires are held in place by their **BEADS**, which are either wire or kevlar. The one is far and away more familiar; the other is more of a lightweight racing thing. Wire beads are not easily bent; kevlar beads allow for the magical folding tires. And while we like to take the whole damned tire off, in the case of flattened wire bead tires—to better check for damage and debris—you may just keep the one side mounted to the rim, with any popped kevlar bead tires.

Kevlar is best known for its protective qualities—against glass; against the bad guys—and the beads are more of a side project. "Kevlar belt" indicates a tire with this sort of flat prevention.

We like to line up the tube's valve with the tire's logo, in either case, to simplify flat-spotting. If you are shocked to find a Vulcan war dart approximately one-quarter of the way around from the logo, for example, you have some idea at least where the hole may be in the tube. And you do want to start at the valve when mounting either of the tire's beads. Get that in place first; work the bead up and around in both directions. Once one side is in, push it all the way over across the rim, such that the tire ends up centered on the wheel.

And whatever you do, don't even think about grabbing the tire levers again! OK? Imagine they're actually small knives; we do not expect them to work in reverse. And while there is nothing better to remove a tight clincher tire, we just as reliably do better to reinstall tires with only the fingertips. Once the bead becomes tight enough to suggest tire levers, the odds are made steadily better that you merely pop the new inner tube on the way back in. And damn, you're *still* stuck.

Knuckles turning white with anxious fury can be a drag, but you can find a loophole. Most rims feature slight valleys down their central sections, where the bead diameter shrinks just a bit. Scoot the tire bead toward this valley, all the way around your wheel, and go try the damned tight spot again. I bet you have better luck.

Beyond the flat tires, the biggest threat to concern our **WHEELS** is that they're knocked out of true. You packed a spoke wrench, right? Park Tool's basic mobile repair pouch is again recommended, because its clever triangular spoke wrench answers to all three of the nipple sizes we commonly see. You first want to flip the bike upside-down, to see about truing the wheel against the brake pads. The brake's quick release can be left open for the ride home, alternately.

It is also possible the wheel has suffered a **BROKEN SPOKE**. You can account for its absence through simple treachery, by over-tightening those spokes featuring immediately opposite on the rim. This can be neither righteous nor just, from the wheel's perspective, but you'll probably get away with it. The wheel is considerably more vulnerable to further troubles, going this route—you would definitely want to take it easy, until you were able to stop and do the right thing—but that's for later, after the bad apple grudgingly rolls your ass back home.

You need to actually replace the spoke, if you're out touring or something. The spoke most likely broke out back somewhere, and this means that the gears are in the way.

This provides a further reason to tour on the cassette hubs; their design also happens to

simplify spoke replacement. We even have a special tool for just such purposes, courtesy of Pamir Engineering. Recall that we need two levers to remove the cassettes, one for the lockring and a second for the cogs? The Pamir Hyper-Cracker enlists the drive-train itself in the first function, while using the frame for the other. It is an exceptionally clever device.

Pamir Hyper-Cracker

You slip the Hyper-Cracker on to the lockring and replace the wheel in the frame, with the tool's arm catching on the chainstay. Turning the cranks pry the lockring loose. Is that cool or what? Pamir even provides hollows for 14- and 15-gauge spoke nipples at the end, to true up the wheel when you're done.

We find no such luck for the old and tired freewheel hubs. There have already been far too many distinct extraction tools to consider. You want to pack the freewheel remover specific to your equipment, if you go out touring, because its twin may not be found down at the five-and-dime.

You also need some serious leverage to operate your freewheel's extractor, and this is the bigger issue. Some of us are able to remove freewheels by means of a large adjustable wrench, but this does not mean I want to run around with one. Freewheels can also be removed by means of a bench vise, alternately, but you have to go and find one. And you never know, that farm house up on the hill may have one out in their barn or something, but it also sounds like they have some dogs ... . Replacing the damned spoke can too easily become some kind of existential quandary, which is ridiculous, given the alternatives.

We carry spare spokes by attaching them to one of the frame tubes, naturally. Some of the finer old tour bikes did this quite well by wearing pairs of diminutive spoke bridges atop the chainstay, over on the drive side, if they're sharp. It was a nice enough detail in its own right, like the old chain hangers or the front derailleur tabs, but the spokes would also protect the paint from the chain. They really thought things through, back then.

You can tape a few to some quiet and out-of-the-way place, alternately, like inside the neutral chainstay or something, but don't forget the nipples!

The oldsters provide slots for three spokes—the drive pull, drive neutral, and front wheel sizes—but you might just stock up with the drive side pull replacements. These are the most likely to fail; they can usually fill in for the other sizes.

With regards to roadside brake repairs, you should see if you can get used to the occasional squeak. And so long as the roads are wet, odds are best you can't do anything about it in the first place. The rims need a good bath at the least, and their pads a sound filing; neither easily happens on the sidewalk.

The **RUBBING BRAKES** are sooner dealt with. You first want to make sure the offending wheel is properly centered and secured in its dropouts, by sighting down the center line. This is quite often the only problem, actually. The road calipers and centerpulls are knocked slightly out of adjustment often enough; make sure the nuts securing their tail bolts are totally snug.

Most cable-driven braking systems incorporate methods to manually center the brakes; most usually a small screw pointed in laterally toward the wheel. Dial anything such in small increments, and keep an eye on the pads as you work. Some centering arrangements execute quick decisions; others take their time about things. And remember to wiggle any linear pull or caliper arms a bit when you finish, to help the adjustment settle in.

Modern dual pivot sidepulls have their own distinct centering screws, worn up top on one shoulder, like rank or something. Press hard; their faces will want to strip. The older sorts don't know about any of this; they are best centered manually. Grip both the mounting bolt and its nut; reaffirm that they are indeed fully tightened; gradually turn the both of them simultaneously. Disc brakes typically bear large dials outside the pads, turn with 5-millimeter Allens or the fingers to modify the pad positions. Recall that the disc tolerances are mindlessly exacting; move with careful deliberation.

Are the brakes getting a bit too loose? Every honest braking system should feature at least one barrel adjuster, at some point along its cable. Turning them out increases the cable tension; the reverse is also true.

Many barrels wear distinct knurled collars about their necks, which may be twirled all the way down, to affirm a given adjustment. But the barrels may also run empty, once they're turned all the way out, in which case it's best to spin them all the way back home. The cable itself can be further tightened down at the component's binder bolt, before fine-tuning again. You should always remember to fill the barrel again, whenever it runs empty.

The barrel adjusters are also our best hopes in dealing with the derailleurs, on the road. It's not likely that turning any of the small and more conspicuous screws featuring thereupon will meaningfully improve upon the situation. Their diminutive threads hold adjustments well enough; they will not rattle loose. Any random adjustments can be expected to fuck things up. The more, the better.

There are only a couple of occasions where it may be useful to mess with the limit screws. We can compensate for a busted chain link by dialing the low limit in a few rotations, as mentioned previously; just enough to block the derailleur from trying to embrace the largest cog or two—it eagerly stretches itself to death, otherwise—and we may also use the low screw to account for a sorely bent derailleur hanger. The bend may leave the derailleur's cage riding perilously close to the spokes, in the largest cog; turning the L screw in keeps it back at a safe distance. The shifting accuracy itself is more about the shift cable's tension, which is enforced by means of the barrel adjuster.

As we're riding around, the most common complaint we hear about the drivetrain is that the chain "skips out of gear." This condition most likely descends from one of three conditions, depending: either the drivetrain parts are worn, or the rider is less familiar with the bike's shifting system, or the shift cable has fallen out of adjustment.

You first want to make sure the rider is fully comfortable with the shifting process, before checking on the cable's tension. If both considerations are as they should be, I then start to wonder about the wear. It is famously difficult to recognize a worn chain by sight, but the toasted hub gears may be more obvious. We expect the two to feature together.

Attempts to force the shift levers past their natural stopping points can not be expected to do much for anybody. Shifters respond poorly to force; it's the easiest way to ruin the plastic ones. Older or more stubborn bikes may ignore our work with the barrel adjusters if they're hiding rust in the cable housing, any of which need to be overhauled or replaced, to improve anything. Adding oil to the chain can make shifting smoother—up to a point, at least—but it remedies neither worn parts nor poor cable tension.

17: SCAVENGING

When the fittest really do survive, the clever will know to scavenge. The bikes provide us with ample opportunities, in this respect.

Broken chains are quite rare, but they are easily repaired with a chain tool. You need to carry the correct-sized Hyperglide pin to safely repair any Shimano chains. It is always good to have a few spare links of the *right* chain in your kit.

The darkened corners of any active bike shop, needless to say, are cluttered with an abundance of abandoned chain clippings. Most chains are cut to fit the individual bikes; riders rarely ask after their remainders. And such is this world of ours, in an innumerable attrition of small and incidental ways. I'd originally thought to include a much broader chapter on the fine art of scavenging, but our time is precious and enough has already been said. The curious reader should know what to look for by now.

The one point that may be usefully highlighted concerns the **WASHERS**. You will keep coming across all kinds of washers and spacers. Harvest them. Take a short section of chain completely apart, to start: the rollers, between the links, fit perfectly around our usual 5-meter bicycle screws.

These may lend your rack or fender just enough clearance to avoid dragging on the chain. Keep an eye out; this problem is neither rare nor quiet. Rear derailleurs themselves will sometimes shift into top gear a little easier if you slide some kind of thin spacer on to the fixing bolt, to rest between the derailleur and the frame's hanger. It happens that either the larger (rear) chainring bolt spacers or 10-millimeter (standard rear) hub spacers fit this bolt just fine. You probably have to play with the limit screws and the cable tension a bit to get this going, but the spacer occasionally makes a positive contribution where other approaches fail.

A new cartridge bottom bracket, for that matter, sometimes leaves the spider crank hanging just *slightly* too close to the frame—old and new spindles might have been measured differently; the chainrings may suddenly press against the frame—but we just slip a common freewheel spacer betwixt cartridge and frame shell, to relieve the pressure.

You want to keep as many threads anchored inside the frame shell as you can, so you only want to use really thin spacers here as well. I would be especially careful doing this on bikes with aluminum bottom bracket shells. And it's best if the cartridge's hollow cup does not feature a lip around its exterior, in such situations, because this lets you tighten it farther in to the frame. This compensates for the spacer you put in on the other side; it prevents the cartridge from shifting around under the pedaling pressure.

It is more common to use a stack of the wider, plastic spacers found between cassette cogs to line up a particular cog at a specific point along a freehub body, as when switching a bike over to singlespeed. You want to line up the cog with the chainring as best you can; the handful of spacers makes this easy enough.

Older 7-speed Shimano HG cassettes are often built around three tall and narrow screws, which answer to a 4-millimeter socket.I don't know if anyone actually makes a 4-millimeter socket, but you can also make your own, by locking a couple of nuts against each other over a 5-millimeter screw. Our 5-millimeter bike screws commonly have 4-millimeter heads to them; these are essentially upside-down sockets. (More modern 7-, 8-, and 9-speed cassettes are usually built in accordance with a much cheesier plan; pressed together with fancy rivets basically. You can still get at the individual cogs or spacers, but you must drill them free.)

18: Rust

Rust is the great equalizer: any of our steel bikes or components, no matter how precious, are vulnerable to its ravages. We'll do best to protect them.

Any older bike, salvaged or no, inevitably squares off against the dread specter of **RUST**. There are things we can do to forestall the confrontation, but the days are long and Earth still spins, and the simple truth is a lot of bikes never get the help they need here. Excluding the carbon fiber rocket ships—none of which have yet grown too old—you want to make sure the frame's seat tube is thoroughly greased. And the bottom bracket threadings should always be greased, whether poured from concrete or carved from balsa wood. Other smaller problems sometimes arise, but as the rust concerns our bikes these two areas will provide for our most pressing concerns.

If something is frozen, the classic solution in either case is some kind of a torch. Heating the metal expands it, briefly creating the sort of red-hot scenario in which things may go free. But not everybody has access to that kind of firepower, and experience suggests we rarely ever actually need it. Massive blasts of heat fuck up the paint and can weaken some frame materials as well; our search for more peaceable alternatives is a meaningful one.

You do best to flip the bike upside-down on the floor, to start, because even the mightiest Park shop stands absorb some portion of your energy. You also need some means to make sure the tool does not slip from its target, even after the tool's tail end disappears up inside some kind of massive pipe, because things up front get to be pretty damned intense.

The modern bottom bracket cups have been thinking ahead, in this respect, in that their arrangements will be much easier to wrangle upon. Current goods from Shimano, Campagnolo, Truvativ, and others each feature broader and deeper splines, to better greet their various extraction tools. And we find a few different ways to hold these last in place, from purpose-built shop adaptations to the carpenter's ubiquitous EZ-Grip clamps, but the simplest home method incorporates nothing more than a washer or two. Run down to the hardware store, grab a broad flat washer just wide enough to pass the spindle bolt through, and also one to cover the tool's body, and finger-tighten the both of them atop your extraction tool. And go get your wrench; reef away to your heart's content.

The only trouble comes with the damned plastic cups, as used by Shimano and a few others. You wouldn't think that plastic can rust itself in place, but it sometimes manages to. And you ask them nicely to step the hell out of the way, with your monster leverage, and sometimes they simply crack instead. You have to pry out the remainder with a screwdriver or similar, once the cartridge is removed from the other side. It's been my experience that a torch is inclined to melt the plastic cups in place rather than start them on fire, but anything's possible. You should check on a given cup's material before you get all heavy and shit, if you aren't sure; see what a knife or a file does to its edge.

This was all even *more* complicated, back in the day. The pin spanners are particularly tough to torque with, but there's a couple other arrangements that are almost as bad. It's probably best to start with the fixed cup, with the oldsters. It is often possible to convince a fixed cup wrench to stay on top of the job until the mission is complete. (The 1 1/8-inch [36-millimeter] headset wrench also does well, in a pinch.)

Where the sharp modern extractors are disciplined enough to retain a useful focus, the clumsy old fixed cup wrench is too easily distracted. It trends off to angles and drops angrily to the floor, left to its own devices. Maintain a slight pressure on the wrench, in plane with the offending cup's threads, in order to prevent this. You usually need a wider pipe to fit the ends of such implements; hold the face in place on its cup as you slip the tail up the tube.

You first want to try moving the lockring, over on the adjustable side. This and the adjustable cup simply move together, a lot of the time. And if your lockring tool only features the one tooth, make sure you keep this pressed firmly in to position. It slips free and strips the lockring, otherwise. The various multi-toothed lockring tools are more useful, in this respect, but you find they're also somewhat more picky as to which of the rings they deign to grasp.

The adjustable cup spins out or at least loosens with the lockring, if you're lucky, but it's at least as likely the fucker won't even budge. The cup will have been adjusted in one of a few different ways. Back in the olden days,

each of which required either a conspicuously flat wrench or a wispy little spanner. Any of these needs to be clamped in place with an EZ-Grip or similar, which of course is why we do the fixed cup first: much easier to clamp down flat, once the spindle has been pulled out the far side.

You will likely want to enlist the help of a couple loose door hinges as well, to provide the clamp with useful pressing surfaces. One fits over the empty cavity where the fixed cup once squatted; the other jams the wrench or spanner firmly in place atop the adjustable cup. And the omnipotent EZ-Grip climbs over both and squeezes together a supremely tight sandwich, which gradually loosens as soon as the frozen cup begins to move. You only need to break the original rust bond; the struggle becomes much easier just after that.

It is quite rare that such methods fail to yield results, properly executed, to my experience at least. But we may try one last thing, before lighting upon the torch. Do you have access to a die grinder? Open an elongated box into the cup; something just big enough to stick with the open end of one of your wrenches. A nice big strong one, like 16-millimeters maybe. You just made your own personalized custom spanner! Grip it right up there by the head with a big old crescent wrench; slide the Jesus bar over the end of this; and push.

No dice? A simple propane burner is fine; oxy-acetylene is overkill. Heating metal more than you need to can damage its relative strength. You heat up the area around the problem a while, then go. But see if you can get anything plastic out of there, first, because it either melts or burns or both. The jaws on the EZ-Clamps are vulnerable this way; you should set them aside and just use the tool's skeleton for this. Have a blast!

Seized seatposts are even more fun. The last time I did this, for a nice old Santana road tandem in the Calhoun Rental fleet, I found myself stripping the bike down to the frame. This allowed me to flip it upside-down and clamp the seized post in a vise, whereby I was eventually able to begin swinging the frame back and forth, to finally ease the fucker loose. Just about toppled the damned workbench, but it worked.

Seatposts really don't provide much for useful surfaces, the old-style straight ones in particular. The modern laprade units provide a pair of flat-sided surfaces up top, once the mounting hardware is removed; these can be lined up to your advantage.

Drip as much penetrating oil into the frame/post interface as possible, and then let it sit a couple days. Try to rotate the post in the seat tube, to get it moving, while tugging it upwards as well. You kind of screw it up, I guess.

The worst thing you can do is to try and chop the post out. See if you can track down a friendly local machinist; maybe you can pay them lots of money to drill it out for you. An old friend presented me with just such a project not so long ago, actually. It was a nice old Bridgestone XO-1, unfortunately, and I could not do a thing for it.

RUSTED SCREWS are a smaller pain in the ass. They attack anywhere it's not hot and dry, which is to say they're somewhat passive aggressive. You don't have to be doing anything at all; eventually they just come around to fuck with you. It sucks.

They are also our Cassandra figures! When you see rust in the screws, you want to check the rest of the bike for similar problems. Metal threads are especially vulnerable to rust. It is rare that both a screw and its fitting are both

born with any intrinsic rustproofing; the microscopic gaps they require to move against each other are just wide enough to slurp up any spare water that comes along. They just gulp it down; it's as if the bike wants to set aside little rust sanctuaries or something. But that should not appear on any kind of endangered list! Or maybe the good Doctor Lomborg found a place for it. As repeatedly suggested by his closest peers, that clown is way too much of a poseur.

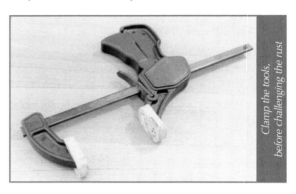

Clamp the tools, before challenging the rust

Rust is in fact taking over, everything and everywhere, because it is inevitable. The most we may hope to do is rally ourselves for heroic rearguard actions, hoisting our clever opposable digits in defiance and all that, but it's necessarily a touch pathetic. The sum of our skills is still nothing to nature.

As it relates to the bikes, rust is always easier to deal with on a preventative basis. Trying to bust it up after the fact is like forcing managed care on top of a health care crisis; your very fate is reduced to a shell game. It takes all of a few seconds to dab some grease on the threads, to prevent the rust, and that is all you have to do. Stems and seatposts and steerer tubes, same thing.

There are only a couple exceptions to this. Spoke nipples are discussed on pages 190-191; they may go for some more specific compound. And the fixing bolts securing brake components are traditionally slopped with some kind of thread-locking compound, in place of the grease. This holds them firmly, but also prevents their corrosion. Some manufacturers also put thread locker on bottom bracket fittings, as means to counter these parts' very occasional tendency to back out on their threads, but I can't say I understand why. To my experience, it is far more likely the bottom brackets will rust in place. Just use grease, and make sure everything is really tight.

It is good to strip everything down for a thorough lubrication, every now and again. Make a ritual of it, OK? I leave the details to your imagination.

But let's get back to that little screw, shall we? The first thing to ascertain is that in fact it has seized. Drop some thin penetrating oil around its base, the T-9 for example, and let it sit for a bit. Holding the tool quite firmly, to prevent slippage, check one last time to see if the screw can be moved at all. It just may turn itself out nice and slow, if you take your time, squeaking ever so slightly through the dust.

Use your best tools, when the time comes to turn it on out, and push down really hard. Worn-down edges on the Allen wrenches in particular are inclined to slip off target. But this may not end the world, even if the poor screw does begin to strip, because it's possible you can modify the situation just enough to earn a second chance. File a pair of parallel flats on the sides, for a wrench, or see if you can cut a new slot for the screwdriver with your hacksaw. Either of these would fill out the aforementioned pathetic rearguard gesture; there are no guarantees at all.

Worst case scenario sees the poor screw's head up and snapping off—a brilliant, spontaneous commentary on the value of overbearing force. Everything should just flow,

you know? Any remainder needs to be drilled out, which itself may or may not be possible; it really depends on the situation. But you always want to give the penetrating oil every opportunity to soak in, first. See if you can arrange for the rusted threads to be more or less level and facing up, such that gravity helps ooze the oil down where it's most useful. Can you let things sit for a couple days? Even better. You might even build up a small oil reservoir, with heavy plastic bags and duct tape, immediately around the affliction we're concerned about.

Flip the project over and do the backside a few times, if applicable, but make sure the bike is very still indeed before you grab the drill; up in a stand, preferably, or at least somewhere it won't get kicked. You shoot your smallest drill bit directly down the center of this dead screw; getting bumped and breaking the little bit midstream is vastly counterproductive.

It is kind of a trick, getting started. You just barely push on the drill, only enough to keep it on target, and play with the angle to keep it centered. I encourage you to take your time with this. You aim for dead center; the drill bit gets distracted and wanders off to the side; you angle the drill such that it's back on target. It's as if you're carving out a tiny bowl, scraping its sides only when you need to, always aiming back to the broadening pit.

The purpose of this tedious little exercise is merely to blaze a trail for one of the various easy-out bits, which reverse-thread backwards into the stump as means to corkscrew it back out. But the original drilling may well loosen things up by itself, given enough time, oil, and good fortune.

19: LOCKS

The world could never be truly wicked, irrespective of the cynics' droning tedium, but all the same it's good to lock your bike. More to the point, lock it well.

Rust can reduce all the tanks to dust, given the time. It is only when attacking the bikes and such that the rust may appear reactionary. Such is our course, in fact, that the bikes are far sooner seized by the **LOCKS.**

Locking the bikes, for quite a long time, was a fairly straightforward proposition. The standard-sized cable locks, which can all be cut quite easily, failed to deter even mildly ambitious thieves. The cheaper U-locks were something of an improvement, if not a solution, because the lower prices indicated lesser grades of steel, which, given that nearly all were at least wide enough to accommodate a hydraulic car jack, became a more immediate problem. And so we always tried to steer people toward **KRYPTONITE'S EVOLUTION LOCKS,** at the least, which bend hardened steel into smaller and more useful profiles.

The trim Evo packages leave our wheels exposed—unless you pack a spare or something—but various remedies may be applied to the situation. Kryptonite had just introduced an excellent locking skewer system, in fact, when everything suddenly changed. The tubular cylinder key-ways, as used throughout the industry for three decades, were suddenly found to be worthless. Any of them defeated quite easily, it turns out, with the plastic body of a ballpoint pen.

This had previously been discovered in the United Kingdom in 1992, as contemporary articles indicate, but it took the Internet and some wingnut in San Francisco to bring the whole charade to its screeching, acrimonious end. But rather than tell those who may have been able to help about his discovery—if only to save everyone concerned a whole mess of trouble—said loser indulged every last juvenile fixation and posted the news to a website. And just like that, predictably enough, all kinds of people began losing their bikes. Some peoples' kids, you know?

The similar looking but more complex disc cylinder locks, as used with Kryptonite's legendary New York series since 2000, are not known to be vulnerable to ballpoints or anything else. The company had planned to introduce such a kit with its less expensive equipment at the industry's annual trade show a few weeks later, as it happened, but this clown just needed to get his ego fix instead.

Kryptonite's response to the crisis, as outlined on their website, has been all we may have hoped for. Other reputable lock manufacturers, such as On Guard, have also provided us with useful alternatives. And the new laser-cut keys are not known to be vulnerable to any regular household items, as of this writing at least; both companies produce such goods.

The cylinder lock keys do wear down, over extended use. They'll still work for a while, just not as smoothly. It's far easier to simply lose the keys, of course. You may order replacements from the manufacturer. They need the number etched to the key; you should write this down somewhere. Some locksmiths have the means to produce duplicates, alternately, but they need a working original to copy from. You need to hang on to at least something, in other words, lest you earn yourself another grand paperweight.

But I don't need to tell you to use your head, do I? You're best to stick with well-lit and well-trafficked sorts of places, whatever you happen to pack, and posts that can neither move nor be disassembled. Imagine the thieves have wicked tools extending from each of their digits, but they're a little self-conscious about actually firing up the metal-cutting implements, if only for the commotion they make. The less you leave to chance, the happier you'll be at the end of the night.

The 5/8-inch shackle extending from my super-bad New York 3000 is rated to resist 5 tons of pull strength. What is that, a tugboat? But still I'm not worried, because the guarantee was free, for up to $3,000 in coverage. The guarantee is a lock's plume of feathers. The more it covers—and the less extra you have to pay for it—the better the lock is thought to be. The small print invariably suggests you need the dead lock and receipts for everything, to collect the cash—we're trusting the thieves to leave us the evidence, presumably—but the package has been able to sneak past all the lock's lawyers regardless, and this is the point of interest. I do not necessarily expect to see any compensation, in the event of troubles, but I do appreciate the gesture. And things being as they are, nobody's really able to do better.

We also need to consider the legions of bummies and aspirant crackheads low enough to rob your bike of its useful parts, far too few of whom actually stick around for the grand boot party. The awesome new Pinhead locking skewers—first offered by Kryptonite, and later by On Guard—provide the wheels their best defense, but of course we may worry after some of the non-skewered components as well. Don't lock a bike in public overnight, if you live in a fucked-up place like San Francisco, if it means anything to you at all!

If the thieves have any trouble stripping our bikes to scrap, they need only look for the **QUICK-RELEASE SKEWERS.** Our forebears began with legitimate purposes, when first inventing the technology—they only wanted to save time and frozen finger-fumbling, whilst out racing—but the hardened drug fiends were also less of a problem, back then.

Cyclox Locking Skewer

And how have the intrepid designers interpreted developments, in the many years since? The Q/R lever's persistent fixation upon the wheel axles suggests an unfortunate choice of emphasis—that compliance with automotive roof-racks is more important than parking safely, whenever you're out riding around town—and its association with the seatposts is fully conspicuous. With the rare exception of our rental bikes, I struggle to imagine a scenario in which this feature becomes less than a liability. The metal Allen key sets are right up there with the damned ballpoint pens, in terms of their ubiquity; the seatpost quick release clings on by the very fingernails of convention. The few seconds' foresight and figuring the seat bolts would cost a thief could easily save us so much in hassles. The clever road bikes already expect such rudimentary cautions, when first they're born no less; why are their wider-tired kin so consistently dumbed-down? The seat height is critical to the comfort level, which keeps all kinds of people out there riding; how is it even possible we want to turn this measure into some kind of crap shoot?

The popular and quite reflexive response to the situation—to just pull the damn thing and bring it inside—carries consequences of its own. The rain and snow rushes right down the seat tube, eagerly rusting the bottom bracket in place. It's the fucking snakes again, chasing the damned mongoose around.

The cheapest theft deterrent wraps common hose clamps around the quick-release levers, clamping them to the frame. They are undone in minutes, but experiences suggest this may be just long enough to soothe a perp's panicky impulses. The bolt-on skewer sets hold a similar promise, on bikes without disc brakes at least. Neither these nor Pinhead's new locking skewers should be charged with securing disc brake-equipped wheels, up front in particular (see page 30). And as with any other skewers, make sure the threads are greased and tightened quite thoroughly.

The open bolt heads on wheel skewers or other useful components may also be paved over with Shoe Goo adhesive or crumpled tin foil, if you really want to damn the torpedoes. But either can be scraped out with a small screwdriver, given the opportunity.

20: BUILDING YOUR OWN WHEELS

If learning bicycle repair provides us with a real degree of autonomy, learning to build our own wheels offers a further extension of the same joy.

The best wheels have always been built by hand, and they always will be. We sometimes lose track of this—as when shady-ass American manufacturers force underpaid laborers in the global south to rush through the process—but as with education and even democracy, the original impetus is at least worthwhile. Absent of any other considerations, an understanding of wheelbuilding makes the process of evaluating and repairing injured wheels quite a bit easier.

A truly fine wheel begins with double- or triple-butted spokes, primarily to take advantage of their increased resilience. The thinner mid-sections flex a bit more; riding stresses are not simply shot directly to the vulnerable elbow bends, as with straight gauge spokes. Aluminum nipples are also favored, by some people at least, because their weight savings is more meaningful— the lighter the stone, the easier to twirl the slingshot—but this doesn't necessarily balance against other considerations, such as the durability. We may even slip tiny brass washers beneath the spoke heads, to account for hub holes that have been drilled a bit wide. The outer spoke intersections can be tied and soldered, as well, to further strengthen the wheel. And this hasn't yet considered the spoke lacing pattern, let alone the major components. Wheelbuilding quickly becomes about as intricate a science as we have use for.

Several books have been dedicated to the subject. Gerd Schraner's *Art of Wheelbuilding*, for example, is quite good. My only real quibble with the author's studied treatment appears on page 59, where he calls out, "some well-known manufacturers of compact wheels, who apply radial spoking to the rear wheel." By this he suggests BikeE, presumably, who were always most interested in radial neutral lacing on 20-inch rear wheels. The company sucked ass for many reasons, not least the scale and frequency of their warranty recalls, but the neutral rear spokes were not one of these.

Well-built wheels should not lose any spokes at all, so long as their component parts remain intact. It just should not become an issue, if you know what you're doing. But the machines presently charged with building most of the world's wheels are famously short on patience, to make a long story short, and it's not at all clear we'll ever be able to teach them much of anything. Industrialization's manic momentum has only added to petroleum's myriad economic distortions; this is simply what we've been left with.

The wheel's building is not necessarily an emotive experience in itself, strictly speaking, but the further refinement of the craft draws upon certain essentially human sensibilities.

And what about the spoke tension? The machines' famous on-again, off-again consistency is too easily impressed upon a rim's profile, after a season or two. Appreciable subtleties in this regard are less easily grasped by the furious mechanical digits. But their crowning misstep ignores any pre-tensioning on the spokes, as described momentarily, the omission of which essentially releases a meaningful but random variable upon even the most carefully laid plans. Machine-laced wheels are more likely to find themselves in trouble, no matter what you paid for them, because they simply know no better.

The easiest and most successful wheels are always built by the book, needless to say—shiny and perfect hubs; new spokes and rims—but things being as they are, we may do well to consider other contingencies as well. I've built dozens of wheels with used rims and spokes, for my friends and myself and the rental bikes as well; you learn to work with what you have.

So what's up? Did you finally save up for some kick-ass touring wheels, or have you only just dumpstered enough parts to start maybe talking about some transportation? You want to begin with a good truing stand, either way, and hopefully a **TENSIOMETER** as well. A wheel's fortunes in our times are largely contingent upon the strength and uniformity of its spoke tension; these curious devices translate this measure to mechanical verse. They really bring Elvin magic to mind, in the noble purity of their purposes; we'll revisit their unique charms as we finish our work.

You're sure the spoke wrench is of the correct size, together with all its nipples? Fit a small binder clip to the stand somewhere, to use as a bookmark on the spokes, if ever someone happens by to ring the doorbell. And what about the hub; are you sure it's

worthy? It needs to match against the number of holes you find on the rim. Put a thumb over two spoke holes on a hub; cover the two opposite holes on that same side with your other thumb; count the holes between your thumbs. Seven indicates a thirty-six-hole hub, six means thirty-two, five is twenty-eight, and so on.

The spoke holes on the hubs are offset against each other, across the two flanges. This effectively divides the rim's holes between the two hub flanges, as with even and odd numbers. The hubs need to enjoy the appropriate axle spacing for the frame in question as well, and they must also coincide with the drivetrain. Clear up any wild ideas before you start, OK? You probably don't want to do a damned thing with a Suntour cassette hub, for example, because your odds for finding any useful cassettes were long ago shot to hell.

Your choices with the rims come shrouded within their own layers of mystique, as well. There are better and worse grades of aluminum, for one thing. Where reputable manufacturers like Mavic reliably provide us with sturdy alloy hoops, the aluminum rims found with department store bikes have more in common with crumpled soda cans. The distinction becomes readily obvious, whether building a wheel or simply trying to regain its truth. The crap rims can't take shit for a hit; they're far too easily swayed by the suggestions of wayward spokes.

More realistic rims enjoy double-walled construction—the spoke nipples only sprout from a distinct terrace set above the tire bead's ground floor, in other words—and we may also look for a flawless seam, machined braking surfaces, and stainless steel eyelets around the spoke holes as well. We earn a marginal weight penalty with these, but they are quite useful in sparing the rims some stress. The spoke nipples roll their hard shoulders heavily forward as we tighten them toward the truth, executing strenuous circle-dances upon the softer alloy floor; the trim squad of eyelets flies in and takes the edge right off. The disc brake-equipped hubs shoot far more stress at the rims; we always want to build them with eyelet-equipped rims.

The disc-specific rims don't strike me as nearly universal enough, though I can appreciate the logic of the various off-center rear rims. They minimize the wheel dish, which can only be good news. But the carbon rims really strike me as useless pretension, in terms of their cost and utility; I can't imagine the world will ever find much use for them. A more diplomatic colleague advises against hanging carbon-rimmed bikes from our ubiquitous bike hooks as well; the lilting new frisbees cannot support even the racing bike's weight from such angles! But we already can't clamp the carbon frames in our stands, or clean its surface with solvents, or even salve its inevitable creaks with any grease at all. The murky epoxy resin may well be allergic to any such agents. Of course the new speed freaks will lose some weight, in other words; it's about all that may reasonably be asked of them.

Counting the holes in a hub

What are you thinking about, anyway—day trips, serious racing, just kind of everything? Wheels built with 36 spokes take more of a beating; those with a trim 28 are somewhat lighter. The 32 has really become standard. Every other spoke hole may be offset to ei-

ther side of a central line, but this in itself doesn't really say anything about its quality.

Bicycle spokes have traditionally been harvested in the non-butted "straight" 14-gauge size. The thinner and lighter straight 15 has really been fading out; the 14/15/14 double-butted spokes are just that much more reliable. And we like any of these to be stainless steel, needless to say. The tired old zinc spokes become only more brittle, as time goes on, and they are far more inclined to rust to their nipples all the while. But this is old news; even the garbage wagons flash stainless smiles these days. Wheelsmith and DT have both long provided the world with decent spokes, but Campagnolo and other reputable parties have moved on to the Sapim spokes. You may be mounting a search to track these down though; I understand they're only sold in 500-piece allotments. How democratic!

Lesser sorts of "double-butted" spokes are easily spotted away from the better ones, in that their defining features are machined rather than drawn out. Our wheels are well-served to pick up on the distinction, because spoke quality—together with the wheelbuilding skills and the swarms of potholes underfoot—fills out the unholy trinity of wheel damages.

Those spokes unlucky enough to break almost always snap right up at the elbow, because this is where they are under the most pressure. Everything kind of comes to a head up there; it's crazy. The aforementioned brass washers may well ameliorate the situation, if the hub's spoke holes are distinctly wider than the spokes themselves—as with recent Shimano Deore mountain hubs, for example—but none can be asked to compensate for a lack of building skills.

The straight-pull spokes swing things from another angle, charging straight out from their burly straight-pull hubs. But the direct approach is still fairly rare, things being as they are in our world. The flattened aero spokes, which often need specially slotted hubs of their own, are about as unlikely. (Some aero spokes are simple hooks, which can be inserted backwards into a regular old non-slotted hub. These may make for workable spares, on a tour, but I wouldn't build a tour wheel with one.)

Nipples are most often brass. If there's an argument with steel spokes, the nipple is meant to lose because it is cheaper and usually easily replaced. The aluminum nipples fill out the same argument more forcefully! Their weight savings is considerable—from the view of tiny bits of metal, at least—but you also find they're more easily damaged. So what gives; are you winning the time trial or only beginning a heroic bar tour? Does a derby seem likely?

The round Spokey nipple biscuits make it easier to bring the spokes to higher tensions, by gripping their nipples on all four sizes, but I'm not at all sure they're necessary to the process. Just hit the base of each spoke nipple with a drop of oil, as with any other serious wheel-truing process; the more comfortable and ubiquitous Park spoke wrenches should do you fine.

Sapim provides us with curious T-handled 5.5-millimeter socket wrenches, with which to dial the bases of their elite racing nipples; the long-necked giraffes, among the spoke keys. But the hub-mounted nipples featured with Shimano's annoying and evidently somewhat more marginal new wheelsets are instead adjusted with miniature flat wrenches, in patient and wholly counterintuitive measures. Try this sometime; you may well see what I mean. And as with any other blade-spoked wheels, make sure to grip the spoke

right above the nipple, to prevent wind-up. Various implements are available for just such purposes; you can use a fourth hand pliers if nothing else.

There is also some chance you may come across the Spline Drive system, which uses bizarre starfish-shaped nipples, to prevent us from even thinking about stripping things out. These clogged with mud far too easily, of course, and so it was they went extinct. I'm not even sure the tiny metal starfish was ever properly studied as a distinct species, actually. Maybe somebody should alert the good Doctor Lomborg, with a starfish pie perhaps!

As with the rim eyelets—or the hub's tiny brass washers, as the case may be—we also want to install an enlightened intermediary between the spokes and their nipples. Riding's endless vibrations can cause the two elements to become distracted from one another; our judicious diplomats are charged with preventing this.

There exists some debate as to what is best for our purposes here. I caught some flak for advocating the use of blue Loctite, a removable-strength thread-locking compound, in my first repair manual. My recipe came courtesy of this guy Dave, a mechanic of twenty years, but its reception suggests the Loctite thing is a minority view. (I am not sure! I have no survey data.) Blue Loctite easily holds the spokes in place; the concern is that it does so too ambitiously. A spoke compound is no help if it prevents further tensioning and adjustment.

I no longer use this method myself, as it happens, but I'm not necessarily convinced it's a bad idea, *because I have never, over the course of my own decade, had any real troubles with it.* I have not yet seen a wheel built this way that can not be trued, upon oiling its spoke threads. I may be a freak, but that is my story. The only exception I can imagine is some dumpstered wheel so thoroughly corroded we can't do much for it in the first place. But that's rust, not Loctite.

It is far more common and even *accepted* to hit the tops of the nipples with a lighter, thinner thread-locker such as the Threebond, once a wheel has been built. This may be done on one side or both, depending on whom you speak with. It makes the most sense over on the neutral side, where the spoke tension is lesser; those on the drive side are tight enough to hold their own.

A distinct theory holds that some sort of lubrication is best, for wheel builds. We soak the nipples in oil, or dab a little grease on the threads, or maybe even both. The effort manages to keep the rust under wraps, but the goal is to let the spokes achieve a higher tension. Lubrication has that effect; it often convinces metal fittings to get just a nudge tighter. I know those who swear by this method, but it has always been a minority position, among the mechanics in my know at least.

I'd only begun experiments with Rock and Roll's Nipple Cream spoke compound this last summer, on the advice of persons I find reasonably credible, and things seem to be working out pretty well. And this is actually too bad, because I just invested in a couple tiny buckets of Wheelsmith's staid Spoke Prep compound, the ample remnants of which will inevitably seethe and glower in my general direction whenever I step away from their practiced glow. But old chum Joel Greenblatt also hipped me to the classic old-school spoke compound, in the interim—linseed oil, of all things—so the whole excursion is arguably pointless and existential in

the first place. Linseed is very toxic, cheap, and flammable; it has also been aptly salving the spokes for decades.

Any serious excess of the linseed oil will likely gum up the works, so you want to set up some kind of rationing system, such that only the bottom thirds of their threads are dosed, something like that, at least. Designate a spare spoke as your paintbrush; dip its threads in the goo and slide this across the working members.

The Loctite or Nipple Cream arrives within convenient dropper bottles. Wheelsmith Spoke Prep comes in tiny plastic tins; you barely dip the tips of half the spokes' threads and roll them against their peers. Wheelsmith is also unique in asking us to let their pastel pastes dry thoroughly, before beginning our ministrations.

You also want to decide upon a **SPOKE LACING** pattern, before getting started. It's nothing especially complicated, only specific. Each pattern requires a particular spoke length, for every distinct hub-and-rim combination. Full-sized wheels may use spoke lengths from about 250 to 310 millimeters; the smaller recumbent and folding bike wheels make far shorter demands of their own. Shops tend to stock the sizes their bikes use the most; a few may have the absolutely brilliant Phil Wood spoke-cutting machines as well.

The spokes on the inside of the wheel are installed first. Those outside the hub flange come along and cross them. Excluding one cross and radial, each lacing pattern finds these outer spokes going over at least one of its peers, before finally passing underneath one last spoke. You temporarily bend the crossing spoke out of line, to make it fit. But that's cool; they should each just spring right back, excluding the humorless carbon fiber spokes, of course. The wheel's plans quietly adjust in compensation.

The more resilient crossing spokes, in contrast, are made stronger when they're able to lean on each other. Tying and soldering their intersections codifies this solidarity, essentially. But we also want to avoid making any especially sharp bends in the spokes, as these draw in and concentrate the inevitable stresses of riding. And so we shoot the crossing spokes right over their most immediate peers until the very crossroads in their trajectories, at which points they briefly tunnel beneath.

Three cross, the most common lacing pattern, sees each of these passing over two and under one. Four cross, the burliest lacing pattern we really like to use, goes over three and under one. You can probably guess the two cross, right? Over one, under one? Speaking of pairs, there are only two exceptions. One cross, as you may notice, does not easily bend under anything at all. And this is fine, for them, so don't be trying anything obtuse. But the radial lace is the great free radical, the super-trendy zero. Its spokes don't even want to touch each other. They only happen to be sharing the same wheel.

Radial lacing, sexy as it is, has always been more controversial. This is a function of their curious convention, to a large extent—radial wheels typically set all the spoke heads on the outsides of the hub flanges, and this indulgent streamlining upsets the carefully balanced stress loads associated with more conventional lacing patterns—flanges have been known to break right the hell off, across the spoke holes. Imagine the poles, losing their magnificent ice shelves.

Many hub manufacturers, such as Surly and Campagnolo, discount radial lacing outright.

Mavic discourages all-out radial lacing as well, but they also acknowledged a back door of sorts, in referencing the use of alternating spokes to build radial wheels. The spokes simply meet the hub flanges as they would on any old cross-laced wheel, with every other spoke head faced to each side. And I can't encourage anyone to violate the protocols outlined by any particular component manufacturer, of course, but I imagine the Mavic alternating-radial project may enjoy a broader utility.

Does the wheel dish call for two distinct spoke lengths? Lay the ones perpendicular across the others, to avoid mixing things up, which is counterproductive. The cross-lacing patterns appear comparatively more complex, at first glance, but any of them may be broken down to four groups of spokes. The wheel's right and left are more properly known as the drive and neutral sides; each feature what we call the pull and push spokes. These last consider the wheel's forward momentum: where half its spokes appear to be pulling it along, the rest may be seen to push it from behind.

A truly fine wheel will stand by virtue of its construction. This may or may not be accented by the quality of its parts, as the case may be. And it does not matter where on the flange your first drive side pull spoke is deposited—technically speaking, at least—but this original should always hook up with the second spoke hole from the valve. (There once was a rim-drilling pattern that disputed this, by drawing the first drive side pull spokes to the first hole past the valve. But we see these very rarely, in America, at least.)

A given rim's spoke holes are often angled and positioned to accept spokes coming in from the drive or neutral hub flanges, with every other turn, and the spokes' trajectories become relevant as well. The cross-laced spokes together form greater and lesser triangles, before lighting upon their rim. Our simple cautions with the first spoke's flight path allow for the greatest possible space to appear above the valve.

This done, we can be confident our brave volunteer becomes a positive role model for its peers. It becomes our attentive lieutenant, marshaling the others toward their rightful positions. The rest of the drive side pull spokes occupy every other hole on their flange, before descending with uniform precision to fill every fourth hole on the rim.

For the moment at least, thread the nipples like halfway up the threads. And we can take a quick break, if you like, to better understand this concept of "pull spokes." Take hold of the rim with one hand and the hub with the other, and twist the hub clockwise. The spokes all draw into the rim; you can imagine their lot trying to drag the circle forward. Pull spokes. We make this very twist permanent shortly, when installing the opposing push spokes, but we can leave things nice and loose for the moment.

The neutral pull spokes—the first half of the slightly longer ones, with the dished wheels—shadow the pioneering drive side pull spokes all the way around their circle. Peering straight down upon the wheel's neutral side, these newest spoons in its collection fall one hole back on the rim, and half a spot back on the hub flange.

And the first set of push spokes do indeed begin with the aforementioned hub-twist, such that all the spoke nipples sink down through their rim holes. (It's common enough that a few may get kind of hung up, like they're afraid to make the plunge or something. Shake the hub around a bit; they'll go and do their thing.)

I'm in the habit of beginning the push spokes where we left off, over on the neutral side, if only to spare a little hassle in switching the two piles around. But the very first lends the pioneers' noble intentions a meaningful legitimacy, whichever the case, by setting a course for its peers to follow. If the wheel was a bolt-action rifle, this first push clears its breech with an audible satisfaction.

Push spokes begin inside the flange and exit outward, such that their lengths drape down off the flanges' cliffs. And you only need to recall our aforementioned precepts, to chart their proper course. Neutral spokes occupy every other hole on the rim. The push spokes take every second hole on a flange; a given example crosses over any pull spokes in its path *excluding* the very last in a sequence. In the case of our three cross, each spoke goes over two others before ducking beneath the third. Over two and under one, in a straight line, points to one open hole in particular. The remainder of neutral push spokes follows the very same pattern, of course.

And lo, the gentle reader is left with only one last set—the drive side push spokes, in our story so far—and the hub and rim, by fine coincidence, each has just as many holes available. These finishing touches only trace those you last installed.

Did that work out? Cool. Go all the way around the wheel and tighten each nipple, to the very last of the spoke threads. Everything becomes somewhat easier if the spokes all begin from this same basic adjustment. It's worthwhile to take your time and get this right on the money.

The heads capping regular newborn spokes are offset to 90-degree angles, but the rim beneath asks them to bend just more than this, so you want to **PRE-TENSION** the spokes before you do anything else. And this is not complicated at all, for the grace of our precious opposable digits, which easily press flat the wayward spokes. This is most important with the push spokes, on the outsides of the hub flanges—they bow way the hell out to the sides, when first they're laced—but it does not hurt to do the spokes inside as well.

Were this pre-tensioning left undone, as with the machine-built wheels, our further tensioning may only accomplish this original leveling very slowly and unevenly. But we're cool like that now; it's all good. We next want to take the wheel up to a **WORKING TENSION**, at which point the spokes are tight enough to impact upon the wheel's overall trueness. The spokes become only just suspended within the web; they're no longer rattling loose between hub and rim. This condition typically arrives after five or ten half-turns on all of the spoke nipples. Something on that scale, at least. The details are necessarily left a touch vague; their circumstances settle for nothing less. The important thing is to be doing the same for each one, to start things off nice and level.

Any drastic confusion in reaching a working tension suggests the spokes are of the wrong size. Lengths far off their marks are occasionally, inadvertently redeemed by switching up the lacing pattern itself—spokes too long for three-cross lacing may have just what it takes to become four cross, for example—or by switching the parts around. Maybe they'll work with that one other hub in the drawer there, you know?

When truing the new wheel, your first concern should be with any hops or flat spots you find on the rim. But you first need to develop a rudimentary lateral true to really see these, which itself draws upon the question of wheel dish. Are you with me here?

The hops and flat spots are most crucial in the long run, but ultimately everything really does matter, and some of it may well be happening simultaneously.

Each of these steps is only a more dramatic rendition of the wheel-truing techniques first described on page 48; the same principles apply throughout. Hops and flat spots are often more challenging than the lateral true, and this is why we deal with them first. The final rigidity we're working toward kind of presses any hops and flat spots in to place; the build affords us a unique opportunity to take advantage of the softer working tension. Lateral truth is revealed to be a function of roundness, in this respect.

The more true your wheel becomes, the smaller its corrections will need to be. The spoke nipples' benchmark half-turns slim down to quarters; these become less routine and more exceptional. And it is here, with the round and lateral true accomplished, that you want to get serious about sorting out the **WHEEL DISH**.

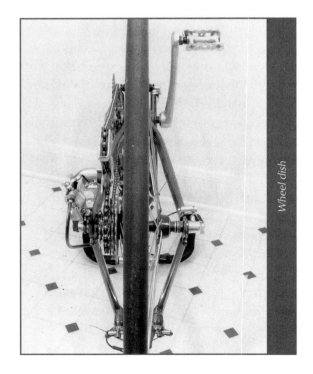

Wheel dish

Excluding a few dedicated innovations, such as Ritchey's Off Center Rim or ATP Vision's offset rear triangles, the spokes themselves are charged with centering the rim in its frame. Their improvements are more pronounced on 8-speed road wheels than 7-speed mountain wheels, by virtue of the distances involved—the slightly narrower gear cluster fits easier into the 135-millimeter axle spacing—but you find the compensation tends to translate as about 2 millimeters' spoke length in either scenario. This rough estimate is likely refined with further adjustments, needless to say.

You may simply split the difference, alternately—using 299-millimeter spokes to cover for both the 298 and 300—but it's best to use double-walled rims with any such projects, lest you find yourself faced with the supremely annoying task of filing down over-long spoke ends. Or the neutral spokes may be loosened by quite a bit, conversely, if their common spoke length is off toward the short side.

You may even get away with leaving a spoke thread or two exposed, so long as their nipples are formed of wholesome brass, but any serious excess beyond this point may well collapse the whole damned cave. I'm thinking of this backyard science experiment of a wheel someone passed me the other day. Its neutral spokes were all way the hell too short; a good half-dozen popped free of their nipples as I tried to true the damned thing.

Shops have dedicated dishing tools, which measure a rim's relative position against the hub's axle ends, but the wheel dish may also be sampled by flipping the wheel back and forth in the stand. Its calipers may well be less than perfectly centered themselves, as the case may be, but at least one should appear equidistant to the rim in either orientation.

I'm in the habit of measuring wheel dish in the frames, myself, because I worked as a rental mechanic for a few too many summers. The dishing tool lived eight blocks away, at the main store; I did not always have the opportunity to pursue the textbook methods. Once the wheel dish has been dialed in, any further tensioning should be applied equitably to both sides of the wheel.

Singlespeed or fixed cog wheels are not supposed to require any dish at all, but this really depends on what you're doing. A 135-millimeter-spaced mountain bike frame is not easily realigned to accept a 120-millimeter track hub, for example, so we find ourselves adding 15 millimeters worth of spacers to the hub's neutral side. This most likely ends us up with a good chainline—which is all the more crucial, with fixed gear projects—but of course the hub flanges also have taken a few steps to the right. And so the wheel arrives upon a **REVERSE DISH**, with its steeper spokes scaling the neutral side. But this, too, is fine. Wheel dish and wheel strength have an inverse relationship; the reverse dish yanks the rug out from beneath their tedious conventions.

The responsibilities associated with actually supporting the mass of a cyclist can be expected to settle the spokes a bit farther than simple truing had been able to, and so we finally want to **PRE-TENSION** the spokes one last time. First, grab them in pairs, all the way around each side of the wheel, squeezing each together with conviction. We then press the wheel flat to the floor—or to the door jamb, if you're feeling more cautious—and bear down upon its rim, hard enough to laterally stress the spokes. You may or may not hear them creak. Rotate and press the rim a few more times, regardless; flip the wheel and get the other side as well.

The pre-tensioning is best accomplished in dusty basements and the like, lest the wheel's axle grind ungainly divots from the priceless hardwood, but its fair pursuit presumes a judicious use of our strength in the first place. Old and tired spokes will very occasionally snap, beneath this lateral pre-tensioning—better in the patient basement than out in the wild world, needless to say—and there also exists a far smaller chance we'll taco the rim. But this is extreme sport, finishing upon the wheel builder's quiet and studious ballet. So don't go being a hard ass; think in terms of a nice firm shove.

This lateral tensioning business will sometimes highlight the differences between drive and neutral tensions, on multi-speed wheels at least, and distinct rims respond in their own ways as well. Where the delicate road rim may *barely* begin to buckle beneath a healthy pre-tensioning, a burly old Sun Rhyno Lite easily remains stern and impassive. But you get the idea.

Set the wheel back in the stand, once you're done, and check things over. There may be a spot or two that goes slightly out of true, and this is the point of the exercise.

The spokes together form a carefully balanced collective. The poorly tensioned member is not able to do its job; it secretly fears everyone else may be let down. And so the sum of their tension is totally crucial; the average needs to be pretty high. I used to habitually stop shy of an effective wheel tension, before I learned better, and I further venture that this is a common mistake.

We can get a *general* feel for the spoke tension with the hands. I built this way for years, actually. It becomes obvious if some spokes are far tighter or looser than others, at the least, and these appraisals should *ideally* be confirmed within the truing process. We like to find ourselves tightening the overly loose spokes and loosening the exceptionally tight ones, in other words, bearing the drive side's tensioning privileges in mind.

Deviations from this rhythm first suggest some problem with the rim, if it already has some miles on it, but I would also wonder if I wasn't missing some problem with the spoke tension, like an exceptionally tight spoke somewhere.

A useful final tension is not easily described with mere words. Its approximation quickly becomes too many horseshoes, not enough hand grenades. And where I once suggested the drive side pull spokes may be tightened until they "barely" move, further observations reveal that relative hand strength is of course another wonderful human variation. See if you can't track down some wheel of upstanding reputation, which can be relied upon as a reference. The carefully seasoned hand-built wheel is the best choice, needless to say. You squeeze its spokes, and transfer this feeling to the ones you're building with. Or you may simply pluck the spokes, if you're musical, tuning the new wheel to the original's precise resonance.

Where either of these tests are preferred to the open voids of space, the tensiometer speaks with real authority. Its soothing presence hits a dead bulls-eye at fifty paces, blindfolded. The spoke tension is measured out in millimeters of pressure or kilograms of force, dependent on the particular tool's manufacturer. Any of them will essentially balance a pair of dynamic points across a spoke, such that a carefully calibrated spring may translate from their third dimension to our second.

Park Tool's tensiometer arrives with a handy reference chart, outlining the successive tension levels for different spokes—the straight and the various double-butted sorts become tense at slightly different rates, basically—but the final reading itself is left to the viewers' discretion.

I worked briefly with some humorless technocrats at an exclusive Berkeley "pro shop" who sought to follow this final orthodoxy quite meticulously, but these particular clowns also happened to be shady as all fuck; I was left seriously disinclined to consider any of their advice too seriously.

I have instead relied upon an old and faded note posted above the truing stand at the original Hayes Street Freewheel, which recommends 130 to 135 millimeters of pressure as a good average, for the nearly ubiquitous 14/15/14 gauge double-butted spokes. The bland Berkeley technocrats' tedium is likely more accurate, when negotiating tensions with the obscure ultra-thin racing spokes, but the world has precious few uses such unlikely wires. The simpler average balances the wilderness beyond to the potentials for selfconscious obscurity; it also seems to work out well enough.

Building a wheel with used parts can be more challenging. All the parts involved have enjoyed the opportunity to really let their hair down. The spokes have picked up at least a few minor bends; their holes in the hubs have been carved out by various microns; the rim may have scored the odd flat spot or two.

Any of this may make for greater or lesser problems, needless to say, balanced against your circumstances. But you should strive to begin with components that are at least reasonably worthwhile, lest their project waste your precious time. The hub, for example, should either spin well or not. An overhaul may improve a given situation; it's a good

thing to know either way. Everything else about them—their spacing, spoke holes, and gearage options—also need to jive with the program.

A rim's merits can be more difficult to appraise. Its vulnerable role in our world nearly invites calamity; there's all kinds of things that can happen. A given rim's troubles may fill out the distance between numbingly routine maintenance and just riding along, depending. The lateral dents that sometimes afflict older and softer rims may be carefully resolved with a rag and some pliers, for example, but the corresponding flat spot we normally look to see in such situations will only continue to cause problems.

There exists an odd tool meant to press out just such kinks, by leveraging against the hub, but its actual purpose has always been more ornamental. A rim straightened by such means is left with a weak spot; nobody can put a warranty on something like that.

Things are such, in fact, that my first inclination is to assume the second-hand rims cannot be usefully redeemed. It's good to be skeptical of any used bike gear, pending its thorough inspection, but the rim's troubles can be especially damning. Hold it lightly against a more worthy example, carefully comparing the sum of their profiles.

You also want to make sure there are no cracks around the spoke holes or their eyelets—older wheels that were built too tightly will occasionally crack—and you should check out the brake surfaces as well. The brake pads will patiently carve substantial channels in to the sidewalls, given the time, and eventually they break on through to the other side.

The productive half-life of the spokes may be the most contentious of all. The question is very subjective. Elite racers in the first world are better to avoid any used spokes at all, so long as the requisite industrial capacities are maintained, because the tarnished wires gain various barely perceptible stresses and damages. The very notion bridles against that old and precious competitive spirit, in fact.

But what if you're full-on *busted*, and the wheel needs to roll regardless? I reuse spokes all the time. It works out just fine, for my purposes at least. You do want to avoid using damaged spokes—those ravaged by tossed chains in particular—but that's probably obvious enough. And the zinc spokes begin with damages of their own; I try not to mess with them as well.

More worthy spokes can recover from anything less than sharp bends, and those as well if they really need to. You just ask the big old box pliers about this; they'll know what the hell's up. My biggest concern, when reusing spokes, is what the threads look like. They may need to soak a night or two in the straight citrus solvent, to get rid of any dusty grit. And if the nipple feels all gritty against the threads, I usually let this stand in for any spoke compound. It's the opposite of scientific acumen, to be sure, but it's not likely at all you'll be getting the things clean.

A wheel built with used parts comes together in the same way, in terms of our techniques, but the truing process may draw more heavily upon the imagination. The final adjustments vary more than those found with a new wheel; our techniques need to develop broader tolerances for variations.

21: SINGLESPEEDS

The sure-footed singlespeed bike rolls evenly past the derailleurs' frantic condominium tower, grinning bemusedly, to pitch a camp beneath the stars.

No muss, no fuss

The **SINGLESPEEDS** have really come in to their own, these last few years. Having finally fit ten cogs to a wheel—and fourteen gears within a hub—it's as if the industry has at last noticed all the tinkering that was going down out back.

Stripping down to a single gear may seem counterintuitive—and it may well be, for certain applications—but the tendency's presence among us remains constant and reliable. Says Steve, a seasoned singlespeeder friend in Minneapolis, "I got lazy and stopped using my gears."

I still equate singlespeeds with the Surly name myself, because they were among the first manufacturers to take the idea seriously, as I was coming of age in Minneapolis. Surly's famous 1 x 1 has long been ubiquitous within the local cycling scene. But it's no longer so much of a fringe phenomenon; big old warhorses like Bianchi have also chanced upon the scent.

You might check in with the good folks at *Outcast* magazine, as mentioned in the resources section, for the latest and greatest in singlespeed glory. Any decent purpose built example features track-style horizontal dropouts and the clearance to run some seriously fat knobby tires. Dedicated SS bikes tend to be built pretty well; your time isn't so wasted with disposable crap. Sometimes, 180-millimeter cranks are used, as they offer more leverage, and the frames are starting to have the extra ground clearance these need to spin. Riser bars, slightly wider than regular flat ATB bars, are favored for similar reasons. You're not relying on any complex little devices to help out with the gear reduction; you want to take full advantage of the available leverage. Up to a point, at least! Steve in Minneapolis was always calling out the barend extensions as "tree hooks." They are marooned out there pretty far, on the riser bars at least; the trees probably find them more interesting than any riders might.

Chain adjustment is simple enough, on bikes with horizontal drops. You pull the wheel back in its frame, and you tighten it in place. But the SS chains should not be quite as tight as fixed-wheel chains. The shadowy mechanism that allows for the coasting needs a little breathing room, to throw its mojo.

Excluding some of those unfortunates afflicted with the rear suspension, it is always possible to convert a working multispeed bike to singlespeed. Any such project makes the bike quite a bit lighter, of course. It is central to the singlespeeds' charm; one of the first things you notice. The mass of derailleurs, shift levers, cables and cable housing, spare chain links, and chainrings adds up. (But you should save one of the old shift cables, if your bike does not have the horizontal drops. Just trust me.)

Singlespeed conversions carry their original fundamentals forward, in terms of their relative qualities—a nicer geared bike makes for a nicer singlespeed—and this becomes evident as we strip things down. The lame riveted cranksets associated with crappy mountain bikes, for example, cannot be asked to surrender their extra rings. The same creatures often arrive bearing multispeed freewheels, rather than cassette hubs, which necessarily makes for complications of its own.

In terms of the gearing, it is most natural to simply split the difference, by using the middle cog in back and the middle ring up front. This gives the average hybrid or mountain bike something in the range of 32/16 for gearing. The 2 to 1 ratio is pretty standard for 26-inch SS off-road bikes; city-going steeds may do better matching the middle cog to the top chainring.

Absolutely shiftless

Many gear cassettes are easily disassembled; others will have never been bolted together in the first place. But you should hang on to

the spare cogs—and your extra chain links, for that matter—until you're sure about the gearing. The chainring bolts featuring aboard a double or triple crankset are too long to properly embrace a solitary ring: an extra chainring may be kept in place, if need be, but a pack of the shorter track/singlespeed bolts should only cost a few bones.

Whichever chainring you're using, the urgent prerogatives of a proper chainline will most likely find it mounted on the crank's inside shelf. This same consideration may find you opting for a different-sized bottom bracket spindle as well, as the case may be. I can only tell you a good chainline is very much worth the trouble, mechanically speaking, with the fixes and singlespeeds in particular.

And the cassette hubs again become particularly useful, when arranging for a singlespeed chainline. A solitary working cog is mounted to the freehub body, between stacks of the ever-more ubiquitous cassette spacers, and you simply arrange the elements to your advantage. Press a ruler to the chainring up front; see how this lines up in back. Easy. (We've only one important caveat, in fact! You will want to hang on to the top cog the cassette came with. Use it just under the lockring, such that the serrated faces of each line up and groove, just as they're suppose to. This helps keep that lockring nice and tight, of course.)

Things were somewhat more arduous, back in the olden days. We had to re-space the hub and re-dish the wheel, to align a BMX-style singlespeed freewheel beneath the warm glow of the healthy chainline. Both these operations made the wheel marginally sturdier—by moving the dished spokes and the unsupported axle segment to the neutral side—but their execution surely occupied a small piece of time.

A hub's cones are sometimes particular to the drive and neutral sides, so you should make it your business to only swap the spacers themselves over to the neutral side. (There's probably a thin washer over there already; it can hop over to the drive side instead.)

This becomes an opportune moment to overhaul the hub, but the cones do not necessarily need to leave their bearings to complete the change. You'll do well to at least shoot some grease down in there, so long as the opportunity presents itself, but all you really need to actually *do* is roll the axle from one cone to the other, such that the long end moves next door.

Re-dishing the wheel is an equally straightforward project. All the spokes on the drive side are loosened by a few turns; those on the neutral side are tightened by a similar measure. But we just discussed wheel dish, on page 194-195.

The singlespeeds will always prefer horizontal dropouts, but their theory in itself does not necessarily require them. The raw luxury of coasting leaves the chain idle and free, whenever its services are not in demand; there is no need to keep its lower length under any tension at all. And so we arrive upon the **CHAIN TENSIONERS**, which crawl in to the clumsy old derailleur hangers and playfully invite us to go ahead and take a load off.

There have already been a few examples, but Surly's Singleator may be the most famous. It sets a derailleur pulley under some serious spring tension, in such a way that it may be aligned at any particular point beneath the freehub body. And as with any other chain tensioner, it's best if the chain ends up as

short as we can possibly make it. This should maximize the available spring tension, reducing the chances you'll ever dump the chain.

T's chain tensioner

Lacking such conveniences, of course, you can actually get what you need by stretching out a rear derailleur. It must only be convinced to sit still, under the one cog. This may simply be done by dialing the high limit screw all the way in, if you're lucky, but odds are you probably can't: limit screws tend to bottom out before their cage arrives upon any useful chainline. But listen, did you save one of the derailleur cables? Shoot it straight in to the derailleur, with the head landing where the cable housing has otherwise ended, atop its so-shortened tail. Push the cage in, such that its pulleys line up directly beneath the cog, and fix the binder bolt right then and there. And if your derailleur does feature a barrel adjuster, you can even fine-tune this measurement.

But the world still spins and its days are long, and as it turns out there's an even simpler way to do this. White Industries' eccentric ENO flip/flop hub introduces an offset pivot around the hub axle itself, allowing us to fit either a track cog or a freewheel to a frame with vertical dropouts. Is that cool or what? Better still, it's available in 126-, 130-, and 135-millimeter spacing. The wheel slots in to the drops, just like before, but the offset effectively lets it sit a little forward or backward in the frame. Nice one, folks.

Every singlespeed freewheel I've come across has been installed and removed with the same mighty four-toothed BMX freewheel extractor, but you'll find that some examples hold up better than others. And as with any other component part, the singlespeed freewheels have been available in a broad spectrum of quality levels, which to my experience generally correspond to their respective price points. And while the wider 1/8-inch BMX chains can work with the narrower multispeed chainrings, in the singlespeed conversions, it goes without saying that the reverse is not also true. The slim 9- and 10-speed chains only shrink away in fear, when set upon the wider singlespeed freewheels.

22: RECUMBENTS

The manifold charms of regular bikes aside, a curious few have opted to sit down on the recumbent bikes instead. Their numbers grow every year.

It was in my livelihood to rent a number of **RECUMBENT BIKES**, the first four summers of our millennium, and I can tell you that a good many people are fascinated by them. Anyone walking in the door may or may not have been interested in the 'bents; they were just part of the program. This was all so many days in the life, at the time; it only became remarkable once I'd moved on. The strange truth is that a lot of cycling industry people seem to nurse persistent hang-ups and suspicions about the recumbent bikes, of all the odd things, and to this day it still just baffles me.

The Fautenil Velociped, considered to be the world's first recumbent bicycle, showed up in 1893. A basic recumbent bike was put into production in France in 1914. Charles Mochet's more advanced Velocar became quite popular in the early 1930s, but the design's intrinsic advantages in speed were already controversial by 1934. Racing officials at the UCI Congress that year voted to refine the definition of "racing bicycle," to exclude the recumbents. And so we see our world today. In terms of the frame geometry at least, the simple truth is that there is precious little left to experiment with, on regular upright bicycle frames. This cuts both ways, to be sure, but really it is the crux of the matter.

You use some different muscles when riding a recumbent. It's not like you can stand up on the pedals and crank up the hill. You just lean back into the seat and jam, instead. There is a learning curve, but as with the fixes, I'm not sure I've ever known anyone to go back.

The recumbent frame, seat, and handlebar features are indeed distinct—from each other, as well—but the bikes themselves are bound together by the same sorts of components we find elsewhere in the bike world. The cables do tend to be longer; cable lubrication is more crucial. But this very consideration is not helped by the way the cables are too often routed, unfortunately. Bike E made it a trend to zip-tie cable housings down to the longer recumbent stems, as means to help the 'bents fit in to the upright world or something—they were once the largest recumbent manufacturer in America; their missteps tend to cast long shadows—but the zip ties' death-grips necessarily make the cable sneak through unlikely angles, which is only asking for trouble.

The solution, as demonstrated by the heroic Rotator Pursuit and its fine friends, is to zip the cables to each other. They quite naturally form one solitary and graceful arc. Freeing up a Bike E's cables in such a way can only help things along. It got to the point where I'd just reflexively do this to Bike Es entering the rental fleet, back when we rented them; it makes that much of a difference. Looks cool enough, too; more forthright, less artifice. The awkward stem-tied cables suggest some cheesy suburban bondage scenario; the graceful arc of those bound only to each other brings to mind the reigns of majestic steeds. So do what you need to do.

Where the upright bikes accommodate us with adjustable seatposts, the recumbents turn toward horizontal solutions. And Bike E, in its day, again aligned itself with the cheesy suburban approach. The seat slides back and forth on its frame, allowing a range of different-sized persons to fit the same bike, but that's about it. Certain other, more happening recumbent manufacturers like Rans, Bacchetta, and Rotator have before and since also considered the seat's *angle*. Which, for longer rides especially, becomes especially helpful. Bike E was more of an investor abstraction than a bike company; the heart was never there in the first place.

Rans may have the best system overall, with its excellent Rad Lok. As with an upright bike, you want only a very slight bend to the knee at full leg extension.

The alternative is to just leave the seat put, and make the pedaling axis move back and forth. And this is quite common, actually. But the adjustment may not go as quickly, because it necessarily squares off against the bike's chain length. This can be an important detail—the chain cannot be made to stretch in accordance with our whims; forcing the point is going to break something—and so various remedies have been applied to the situation. The most successful of these, as developed by Vision and Inspired Cycle Engineering and likely others as well, will incorporate a pair of pulleys: one fits to the frame, while the other hangs from the more transient boom, with the chain slack forming a fluid "Z" between them. The efforts allow everyone to sit at the same point, on

a given frame, which allows its geometry to become more specific.

The ever-expanding recumbent canopy already shelters a good number of curious tendencies, but we may at least discern a careful chasm betwixt two established factions, the long wheelbase and short wheelbase bikes (LWB and SWB). The first shoots the front wheel out in front of the feet; the other tucks it in under the knees.

LONG WHEELBASE bikes disperse riding vibrations better; distance rides don't beat you up so much. Their head tubes have traditionally been set at mellower angles, which widens the turning radius, but also provides for a mellower and more intuitive steering experience. An especially long and slender stem rises from this distant nose; basic steering is accomplished more with leaning.

Vision and Burley, in contrast, have both produced LWB bikes with steering linkages. A steeper head tube is connected to a parallel steering tube, set farther back on the frame; the handling becomes sharper.

Steering linkage

The long frames are usually a bit heavier than the **SHORT WHEELBASE** bikes. This affords the shorter 'bents some useful advantages in climbing and accelerating. The head tubes are necessarily steeper, comparing to those we find with the traditional LWB bikes—the long stems would skewer us, otherwise—and so the geometry lends itself toward city riding. But I've met plenty of people who take LWB bikes around town, and I've probably known more to tour on SWB 'bents. Our grand acronyms only fulfill the most general of descriptions.

The **COMPACT LONG WHEELBASE** bikes are the grandest compromisers, amongst the 'bents. Theirs is the syrup Cannondale and other most upright manufacturers have tried to push, when entering upon the coveted recumbent market. The front wheel is downsized to 16 inches, which allows the fork to be moved back in toward the rider; we're left with an approximation of the more stable LWB handling, in a more convenient SWB-sized package.

Bike E did fairly well with this format, needless to say, but theirs was always a more ponderous enterprise in the first place. The company weathered an unfortunate number of warranty recalls—the failing welds on the seat struts, to take one example, were simply notorious—and their obsessively timid efforts may have marked the friendly CLWB in unfortunate ways. But the design was already taking the easy way out on another of the 'bents major controversies, the bottom bracket height. Its relatively low pedal height is somewhat familiar from the upright bikes, and thereby somewhat easier to get used to—over those crucial first few minutes' riding time, at least—but it is also somewhat less efficient. The riding position is almost conspicuously casual; it does not easily provide much for leverage.

Taller bottom brackets are associated with increased speed, among the recumbents. We're better able to push off against the seat back. I've seen some bikes with seriously high-ass bottom brackets—my first home-build, Hellbent, kind of accidentally ended

up with one of these—but most are more reasonable. The pedaling axis does not need to be much higher than the seat base, to earn worthy advantages.

How tall are you, anyway? A well-fit recumbent leaves you sitting no *higher* than about where an especially intuitive chair sets you, with the feet easily flat upon the ground, and it is fair to say that different 'bent manufacturers have better considered the shorter and taller riders. Your best option in exploring such questions, needless to say, is to visit your friendly local recumbent specialist for some test rides.

And what about your riding style? Are you going for straight speed, or are you riding in traffic? Most riders are able to find mounts bearing at least a *general* range of seat heights, regardless of their stature, and this allows for certain other considerations. Where an especially low seat enjoys pressing advantages with the aerodynamics, the taller profiles provide for improved visibility in traffic situations. Most 'bents produced for the American market enjoy relatively high seat heights; a fraction of the more European-based designs feature distinctly lower seats. It is only a sprinkling of hardened zealots, known as the low racers, that really hug the ground.

The recumbent drivetrains generate questions, together with momentum. The chain is going to be at least twice as long as that strapped to an upright bike, and it's likely run through at least one chain pulley. "Chainline" begins to reference both the horizontal contours, as well as the lateral alignment—snaking under the seat, or perhaps over a fork crown—and so the pulleys are typically lent important roles in the decision-making process.

Those featuring along the chain's top run need to be considerably stronger than those lifting its lower length, to better accommodate the pedaling torque. Cheap pulleys are simple plastic biscuits on metal bushings; better ones mold rubber wheels built around sealed bearing cartridges. But neither should need any teeth, in this application; they only slow things down and make some noise.

We also have the **MID-DRIVES**, which move the front shifting to the middle of the frame, some distance back from a separate drive crank up in front. The extra-long recumbent chains can make the shifting process a bit sluggish; the mid-drive snaps this problem neatly in half.

The technology itself might best be described as reasonably spontaneous. None of the reputable component manufacturers has yet explored the idea—the 'bents are too often dismissed as some fringe group, or perhaps a special interest lobby—and so the fanciest mid-drives ever made have only been cobbled together with whatever was on hand. You lop off the arm on a spider crank, perhaps, or figure out how to mount some kind of freewheel midway up the bike frame.

The mid-drives also introduce a multiplier effect upon the gearing, and this becomes especially useful when matched with smaller drive wheels. Lacking such conveniences, decreases in the drive wheel's size are best answered with commensurate increases in chainring size. The 20-inch/406 drive wheels found with many recumbents might be matched with chainrings of 42, 52, and 63 teeth to approximate a standard touring crank, for example. And if you're not hip to the small-wheel thing, it makes them look totally bad ass. *What kind of monster, pushing Olympic gears on such a mount?*

The **RECUMBENT STEMS AND HANDLEBARS**, like the bikes themselves, have grown and flourished in novel ways of their own. Their curious energies have already gathered something of a bouquet, in fact, and the bikes eagerly pick their favorites.

The placement of a bike's head tube, together with the particulars of the stem, will tend to favor one style or another. Bacchetta's cool swept-back bars can look nice anywhere, to take one favorite example, but they really work best with the forward-thinking stems and head tubes we find on their own bikes.

The extra long LWB stems are sometimes built light enough to allow for a small degree of flex, to further dampen riding vibrations. Your hands only happen to be sitting there, rather than supporting your weight; they can totally get away with it.

The SWB stems are more solid—their head tubes are going to see more weight and torque, by virtue of their position on the frame—but it's still minimal, compared with the upright handlebars. Many pivot forward, in fact, to allow for easier mounting. These **FLIP-IT STEMS** have become nearly ubiquitous among the SWB bikes, actually. There should be some provision to move the handlebars up and down, as with the LWB stems, as well as a set screw to adjust the bar's resting position. LWB flip-its are quite uncommon, but I've put a few together, for purposes of storage and the like.

The flashy under-seat steering handlebars are likely the most famous, but the more pedestrian above-seat handlebars have always been far more popular. ATP Vision's underhanded wingspan dominated the diminutive USS kingdom, in its time: a goofy alloy trapeze was fixed to a stem extending from the rear of the fork; control levers were mounted to its flailing ends. And these very features were the first things to smash themselves, if ever the bars ran aground. Repair bills tended to be far-reaching.

These sorts of USS bars might or might not be variously safe or comfortable, dependent on whom you speak with. They swing out pretty far, on the corners. This makes for a bumper-height truck lure. I do not recommend USS bars for commuting. (Yes, of course I realize the damned truck might also be the menace; I'm only offering suggestions on how best you might defend yourself.)

You may have better luck with side stick steering, if only for the sake of this last point. Side stick bars also begin from beneath, but they only shoot out and then straight up, to provide for handy joysticks. The side sticks will not flare out on the turns, however, because they are built around a steering linkage: the axis of motion is made lengthwise, to coincide with the bike frame, and this helps you stay out of trouble. The bars still arc out a bit, twirling around their steerer tube, but it's nothing like the mad abandon we associate with the USS bars.

Some of the nicer recumbent **TRIKES** incorporate a slick adaptation on the side sticks, linking three pivot points with steering rods. Of all the 'bents, these championship turtles are surely the most flamboyant. Theirs is an experience unto itself!

There are exactly two configurations possible, of course. The tadpole design, which runs two wheels in front, is the daring and adventurous young chariot. The delta trike, with the two wheels in back, is our earnest and hard-working proof that another world is entirely possible. Where the one might take us to exactly where we're supposed

to be, its mate might well bear anything we may ever need. Their presence forms a delightfully odd, truly specialized far corner in the bicycle universe.

Trikes of either sort cast wider shadows, in comparing with their simpler peers. The lower and wider a given example becomes, the more stable it will be. The tadpole design finds riders seated only inches above the ground—somewhat lower than is the case with most other recumbents—but the vantage lends well to the experience; it relates only marginally to anything that has come before.

The relative height and width are together enough to impact upon deployment considerations. It makes for a paradox, perhaps. The trikes are the closest to replacing our "need" for cars, by some measures, but by some readings at least their very characteristics can discourage their use in traffic. But for this we do not blame the trikes! Hats off to Mark and Gary and all the others, triking on through the Minneapolis winters, right there on the city streets.

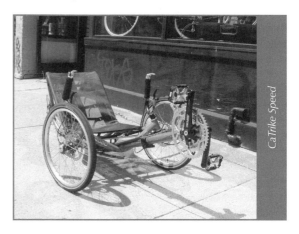

CaTrike Speed

The trikes, like the regular 'bents, accept just about any bike accessory you'll find use for—fenders, lights, bells, whistles. Every tadpole trike I've worked on has also featured an adjustable boom, to fit different-sized riders. The remarkable Trice has even taken this one step beyond, by incorporating a second boom at the frame's tail end, with which to dial in the seat's particular angle. But there are so many especially cool things about the Trice.

The new Catrike Speed machines are also quite impressive, to take another favorite example, but for different sorts of reasons. A number of crucial improvements have allowed for an exceptionally simple and lightweight design, to put it in a nutshell; as with ICE's Trice, we can see they've really been putting the time in. Suffice it to say that if you do find yourself lucky enough to be looking for one of these, you'll be greeted with a range of fantastic choices.

It was only upon moving on from the recumbent shop that I began to understand just how maligned the poor creatures have too often been made to be. Ask around some; you may well see what I mean. The industry's broad bias against the 'bents has to be flatly ridiculous, given what I've been able to see of the public's broader sentiments, but more than that it's disappointing. The mish-mash of guesswork, suspicions, and worn-out anecdotes comprising the industry's prevailing dismissal of recumbent bikes is conspicuously vapid. It does coincide with certain more practical concerns—the 'bents very presence challenges decades' worth of traditions, essentially, from all the damned marketing on up to our very repair stands—but this still leaves the great knee-jerk lame and reactionary. It can only grow more tired.

I don't ride a recumbent. I may or may not in the future; I have absolutely no idea. Any of it assumes I keep waking up in the morning! But I have already met all kinds of people who just love the things, including many who would not or even could not ride conventional diamond-frame bicycles. And I do strive to be serious about seeing less cars on

the road, so of course I'm happy to help as I can! Who would I be, to impose an uncomfortable ride on an eager cyclist?

Taking care of business

23: The Fixed Wheel

The fixed wheel is the simplest bicycle, and yet its ride can be fully sublime: in removing our common mediations, the world is presented as it really is.

The **FIXED WHEEL** is the original bicycle. It will outlive all the others as well, without so much as an effort, because its drivetrain has no use for their fragile abstraction. A cog is paired to a chain: your legs move faster to accelerate, or slower to do the opposite. There is no coasting; no gears to shift. It is a ripe peach, set against the churning fruit salad.

The original riders are all long dead. And the last ones, with luck, have yet to be born. The cadence itself may go on forever. It is timeless and immutable, like the stars and the cold.

What is it you're looking to do, anyway? This is no stale "better or worse" dilemma; it has far more to do with the situation at hand. *Soyez realistes*, the fix breathes! *Demandez l'impossible!*

I want to tell you the fix delivers the best advantages in both speed and control, for this was my original experience, but it's not quite so simple. Too much of my time has been shot through short dashes across the flattened asphalt, burst out within the heavy traffic; the geared mounts may likely do better in other arenas. But the performance in itself is only one part of it, right? Our question is more substantial.

You will find that opinions tend to be strong, with regard to the fixes. You can dig them, or maybe you just can't. People may tell you the fixes cannot be controlled, and that they wreck the knees; their full enjoyment becomes so much risky behavior. And these very worries are easily supported by anecdotal evidence—however redundant, unique, or shopworn each example may be—but none of it necessarily reflects anything intrinsic to the experience.

This basic pessimism is also buttressed by more incidental concerns. And yet at the very same time, working cyclists all over the world lend the fixes their implicit trust every day, in situations many people would rather not face at all. It is patently stupid to presume any sweeping statements about messengers more generally, but I have known quite a few to ride the fixes. Some stick with it, like partners; others do other things. What can I tell you? It is all very subjective. The local weather and terrain may be the most important considerations. Fixes often do far better than geared bikes in the snow, for example, but they have more trouble with steep descents.

The fix can provide for quicker, more intuitive acceleration; the freewheel bike's hand brakes will likely stop you sooner. And where the gearing range easily earns its keep over the course of a distance, the solitary fixed cog arguably provides for a tighter degree of control. The fixes' maintenance is all bread and water, but their coasting kin are more prone toward various surgeries. The one rockets straight up the hills; the other gives us a special leisure through their descent.

The inventors may not have given a rat's ass about any of this. Their enduring platform began as the best and only one of its kind, but the abstraction artists and their deconstructionists eventually managed to catch up, and soon enough it was merely the cheapest. And there, as we know, opens the exhausted playground we see before us today.

The technology itself is known as fixed wheel or fixed gear, depending who you talk to. Its purpose-built machines are known as the track bikes. And the principle itself can become possessed of a certain orthodoxy, balanced against the mad clamor of its newer peers, but this is not necessarily such a bad thing. There are a few important ground rules—the bottom bracket needs to perch at a certain height, for example, lest its endless pedals catch to the ground—but they've also been shadowed by the greater forces of habit. These patterns only emerge from so many years of practice, rather than somebody else's bourgeois marketing schemes, and this affords them a peaceful dignity.

The extravagantly stylish *pista* handlebars are traditionally taped only across their lowest reaches, for example, to encourage the cultivation of more aerodynamic riding positions, which, lacking the splendid extravagances of gearing reduction, become a more important consideration. Speed implies discipline, in its essential form; the track bikes have traditionally assumed we'd rather go fast.

But the fixes' established tendencies are only their convention; they may or may not have anything to do with you. I'm thinking of my friend Jim's bike, a sleek purple-and-white gazelle of a fix, topped with bright yellow hand grips on some big honking high-rise handlebars. He mounted an old-fashioned horn up there, you see, with the rubber squeeze-ball? Jim and friends have an amazing punk band called Ass, back home in Minneapolis; you should check them out.

Others I know have followed the prescribed dogma more carefully, with that killer brakeless image and the half-taped track bars and all that. The classic rock still enjoys substantial air-play! But if you do go for the old rock star crunch, I only ask that you do it up proper. No, I'm kidding. I really don't care what the hell you do.

I've gravitated toward the hooker bars, myself. They are triathalon bars turned backwards, to suggest more likely angles. Like the old city bars, but meaner. Rounder. Narrow enough to sail right on through the tight spots, but also considerate enough to lend the hands some fairly intuitive options. And of course they're a natural match for one of the soup spoons, as described on page 92-94.

Hooker bars

Hard-rocking fixers are often more inclined toward the seamless and romantic Brooks saddles, but these elegant shelves are something of an acquired taste. Wherever it is you happen to sit, it is positively crucial that you're left at a precisely correct distance from the pedals. This in itself can make or break your appreciation of the whole experience, actually. Poor saddle positions inevitably encourage the development of knee problems; it's the difference between a natural rhythm and a relentless pace.

If the saddle is not set to a good position, any further troubles echoing up from an outsized gear become all the more meaningful. And skidding the oversized gear, as we might well imagine, can too easily melt away the rest of our ice cream.

I don't skid so much myself, for various reasons, and this allows my fixes the leisure to sport regular old rat-trap pedals. Which, in turn, affords a certain discretion in establishing the seat height. My weary soles are left free to scoot around just enough; they tend to gravitate toward the best positions. We still like the pedaling axis to spin beneath the balls of the feet, needless to say; raising the saddle effectively pitches it toward the toes, and the reverse is also true.

If this footloose abandon presumes a judicious balance between intuition and common sense, the professional frame fitting session actually does the math instead. But a good fitting's sublime precision really anticipates the appearance of shift levers and their kit; the jackrabbit pulse of urban fixed gearing may well stretch and fray its careful answers. But the fitting details are crucial, with any bike, in terms of doing well and staying healthy over the long run. It is not supposed to hurt, to ride the fix.

My favorite rat-traps notwithstanding, most other fixed riders in my know have gone with either toe clips and straps or the clipless pedals in their stead. Each makes skidding the bike a hell of a lot easier, of course, and the clipless at least also answer questions around the fitting far more definitively.

We once had something of a hunt before us, tracking down a decent track bike frameset—the originals were only produced in velodrome-sized batches—but our fortunes have steadily improved. Certain more happening manufacturers such as Surly and Bianchi have offered worthwhile track bikes and frames for a few years now; the curious reader might well do best with one of these gems. Their relative qualities range from pretty decent to really hot; expect to drop a few bills.

The cheap way to get into fixing is to convert an old road bike. Anything with horizontal dropouts may be up for the task, actually. I'm thinking of my friend Jordan's first fix, a born loser of a decrepit old mountain bike whose peeling decals identified it simply as the Mud Slugger. It was one of the earlier fixed wheel conversions to roll out of our old spot down at Calhoun Rentals; later projects became somewhat more refined. Our friend Xara's bike Detail, once another dusty and anonymous Bauer frameset, springs easily to mind.

The typical geared bikes' bottom bracket shells are more down-to-Earth than those we see with the track frames, to better coincide with the more leisurely freewheeling worldview, so we want to use shorter 165 or 170-millimeter cranks to compensate. This is important! The effort helps you avoid catching the pedals to the earth, which will likely capsize your ship, quite suddenly in fact. The cranks are made a mad whirl, by virtue of their fix; any contact with the ground below essentially challenges them to a fight. But the ground is much bigger; it wins every last time.

The crank length ideally suits its own needs, rather than the bike's, but our shortcut here is necessarily bereft of such luxury. I've caught pedals a couple times and gotten away with it, somehow, but my old friend Morgan broke his collarbone this way. The danger is quite real.

Fixed gear pedals are always supposed to be short, for similar reasons, but the dedicated track pedals' tranquil velodrome profiles arguably leave them less useful in our manic world of today, in the weather, especially. They have no real teeth to speak of; your wary soles will too easily slide off into the void. But many of the clipless pedals are short enough already, and the aluminum cages on better mountain bike pedals are trimmed down easily enough with tin snips. Cut flush with the axle's end, and file down the ensuing dog-ears, lest you pop your shins.

The rental shop is a project of Calhoun Cycle, recumbent and folding bike specialists, where flourishes a careful but genuine appreciation for advancements in the cycling arts. The owner Luke had arranged a decent arsenal of metalworking equipment in the basement, for just such purposes, and so it was there that I got curious about building a fixed gear recumbent. He'd shown me a picture of a fixed long wheelbase from the 1960s somewhere, once I'd ventured my theory; there even seemed to be some kind of precedent.

I was staying at my friend Christina's house at the time, and her boyfriend Gino had gathered a respectable pile of abandoned bicycles out back in the yard, to build an altar for the Burning Man or something like that. And I believe this might have been where I found an old 24-inch chromed BMX frame, which seemed an ideal candidate for my newest ambitions. (BMX, of course, is the traditional platform of the homemade recumbent bikes.) A boom tube was brazed to its snout, once the chrome had been scuffed away, and Hellbent was born. The name honored Christina's wonderful black cat, Hellbat.

But I hadn't asked nearly enough questions, prior to beginning my experiments. My principle design prerogative—to the extent that I had any at all—was to avoid putzing around with any chain pulleys. And I did get the pure and direct chainline, but this left the pedals jabbing angrily toward the sky, with the seat nestled in the frame's valley far below. The riding position was left untenable: too much accordion, not enough flute.

The War Bike meant to improve on this. Its own snout extended a good foot forward off the bottom bracket shell, ending in a thick square of sturdy metal, to make for a battering ram. The whole thing was pretty well overbuilt, actually. And it did fare better—I rode all the way to Saint Paul and back, at least once—but this fortune only revealed a more damning contradiction. I'd only meant to bring home a nice jug of water, but it seemed I'd managed to capture some volume of oil as well.

The whole body essentially presses the back wheel to the ground, on a recumbent: this means, in the case of fixed gears, that one cannot simply hoist up the tail and kick a pedal in to starting position. It is a small point, and I might have learnt my way better with time, but I found myself tipping over to the side in the interim. And this got to be a drag, in traffic especially.

The War Bike was propped menacingly in a corner somewhere, to glare angrily at passers-by so long as it might be useful. I was left with my 20-inch fixed gear wheelset, which had begun to seem quite interesting in its own right: the smaller circles are spun and stopped quite a bit easier. This very tendency becomes a famous liability for the small-wheeled folding bikes—they spend their momentum all too easily—but the fixed wheel's centrifuge sooner approximates a metronome. And where all things are equal, the small wheels are stronger and lighter as well. The brilliant new verse fully screamed for a better translation.

I went and found another dejected old BMX frame, buried within Gino's rusted cornucopia out back, and eventually chanced upon methods to raise the saddle and handlebars to more useful elevations. Luke had rafters full of cromoly tubing at the shop; a couple pieces happened to fit. And so the airship rose yet again, at which point it became clear the rusty old chassis I'd begun with had been scrapped for good reasons. But my old friend Chuck was cool enough to flow me a better BMX frame, upon realizing my unique predicament, and the Street Cleaner was born.

This new beast was *fast*. Lovely acceleration; nice handling; the traffic profile of a hungry door mouse. And so a dedicated 20-inch fixed frame, bike #3, was pieced together in the basement that fall. The assembly was concluded just in time for winter, whereby I discovered the 20-inch front wheel was not really the thing for pushing the snow around, not with the handlebars way up in the air, at least. It was like shoveling the sidewalk with a soup spoon.

So I threw together another quick experiment, piecing together tubes from three dead frames—the Yokota, Gitane, and Mongoose decals were each left visible, actually—and this time matched a 700c road front wheel to the 20-inch rear fixed wheel. And soon I realized Patches here was finally what I'd been looking for! But I'd been in quite a hurry, given all the snow, and so wasn't too surprised when the rushed construction failed some weeks later.

The tail section was clipped from another dead road frame, once Patches had been dispatched, and reconfigured to accept a 20-inch rear wheel. And bike #4, as well,

became the finest in all the world! But the guesswork comprising its attempts toward frame geometry might have been more carefully considered. The frame's carefully rearranged seatstays ended up reaching about midpoints on the original seat tube, and this seemed to generate a reliable creaking, which announced itself anew every last time I hit a bump. And the ride was also pretty damned harsh. But this is one reason the small-wheeled folding bikes avoid full-sized frame triangles in their designs; their combinations tend toward a stern and uncompromising testimony of the pavement below.

Bike #5 might well have been pulled from some grand magic hat, given its willingness to learn from the past. I'd rescued the battered Cannondale Pepperoni mountain fork from Patches' tomb, largely for aesthetic reasons, but also for its fender holes: they could fit a road caliper brake, which allowed me to run a 700c road wheel up front. This was a more whimsical decision, to start; the outsized Pepperoni's grip around the wispy thin road wheel suggested boastful cartoon characters more than anything.

Bike No. 5

And that was finally it; at last I'd really won! The resulting effect wouldn't necessarily have meant too much on a prom night, needless to say, but it did manage to draw in the best from disparate elements: where the larger front wheel handled and held speed well enough, its smaller companion was positively ideal for urban fixed gearing. And I was seated atop a reasonably flexible pillar, leaning back nearly above the rear wheel; the traction would obviously be good. And at last—that next summer, at least—I had myself a proper *art school* bike. After the hairstyle; long in front, short in back?

I did fit the Pepperoni fork with its proper knobby mountain bike wheel, come the following snow. My travels began on Oakland Avenue in central Minneapolis, at the time, which was not plowed as thoroughly as uptown or downtown; this was just the natural course to take. The fat 26-incher also coincided with the fork's original brake bosses, allowing its tired old caliper brake to be replaced with a righteous Deore LX cantilever set, which was cool, because this was about the time I started riding downtown again. Old chum Brad Emery needed someone to cover his shift, on the days he went hunting, and it happened I was looking for employment.

I did find myself switching back to a thin-tired fixed gear at some point, but only because the knobby tire was way too slow for courier work. The art school bike did just fine, in every other respect. Mid-winter, downtown Minneapolis? None of these new 16-pound carbon fiber math experiments can say shit to that. My friends within the proper cycling industry, needless to say, have typically been somewhat less convinced of my successes. If nothing else, my odd new duck might exemplify the precise antithesis of a solid marketing plan.

All the fixed gears enjoy a common lineage, fortunately, regardless of any distinct inclinations. Their great shining star is the **TRACK HUB**. It is the quiet monk, to the cassette hub's neurotic executive. Where the boss man strives to coordinate external gear re-

duction *and* manage the internal parts organizations simultaneously, the patient scholar only meditates its surroundings.

Basic track hub

The track hub might be mistaken for an old school freewheel hub, but for its threads, which are stepped in two distinct sections. The wider stack below is for the cog itself; the narrower range above is meant for its lockring. This upper deck is also reverse threaded, such that the cog is made to struggle against its lockring to spin free, and it is this endless conflict that generates the possibilities.

The zealous convert: track wheel in a road frame

The **TRACK COG's** English, French, or Italian threads are indeed the very same ones we find carved upon their respective freewheels. But none of these others can ever presume toward fixing glory, because there is no reliable way to secure a regular track cog to a freewheel hub. It eagerly spins free, the first time you really press backward on the pedals. You *were* running some kind of hand brake, right?

The wrong answer provides for illuminating insights, in the ideal, but even its imagination may suffice for inspiration. It is not my point to be doctrinaire—I am but your intrepid interpreter—my cautionary tales are offered only for the best reasons. Can you feel me?

Nor can we expect the thread-locking compounds to provide for any meaningful salvation, in this respect at least. Their application only postpones the inevitable, until some more precipitous moment. The cog might not spin off on that first ride, in other words, when you might have expected it to; it might just hang out, until your first attempt toward a panic stop.

Our parable might have ended there, but circumstance lends a further duplicity, lurking within the dusty and forgotten parts box. It happens that most of the lockrings associated with the traditional ball-and-cup bottom bracket sets can be threaded on to their respective freewheel threads as well, by fine coincidence, and people sometimes guess that these may stand in for fixing purposes as well. But they don't.

A bottom bracket lockring perches on the very same threads used by the cog itself, were the pair mounted aboard a freewheel hub. The cog still yearns to spin free, every last time you push backward on the pedals, but suddenly the misplaced bottom bracket hardware is all up in its face: the endlessly patient hub becomes an incredible white-hot crucible, concentrating the full strength of your legs against the bike's momentum itself. Those few threads caught in the open are suddenly thrust into an adversarial position, antithetical to their very purposes; they would really want to just strip out and be done with it.

We might find ourselves brazing seals across the old freewheels' backsides, once the collapse is finally realized, before thread-locking them aboard regular threaded hubs—such might cautiously approximate a fixed gear, after it's been pedaled up a big hill a few times—but given the raw luxuries of our passing present, anything less than a proper track hub is somewhat conspicuous.

Crossed against the spectrum of human endurance, the relative size of contemporary cogs and chainrings and wheels tend to favor something just less than a 3 to 1 gearing ratio. Where the full-sized bikes are concerned, in other words, the city-going rider likely does best with a chainring nearly three times the size of the cog. This typically provides for a useful average; if nothing else we find a good reference point. My art school bike runs a 4 to 1 ratio, to compensate for its diminutive 16-inch drive wheel, but fixers in hilly cities do better with ratios smaller yet.

Bigger gears will likely be faster, when paired with the coasting option—on the descents, at least—but they don't provide much of an advantage with the fixes. Their slower cadence is more stable, riding across the icy roads, but it is always easier to spin faster, than push harder.

A given combination's particular fortitude may best be described in terms of the **GEAR INCHES**. The name codifies the old imperialist valuation system, and I've even heard it is not entirely accurate, but this is just how people tend to talk. When everything rolls forward by precisely one rotation, the gear inches describe the distance gained across the floor. Their sum considers the cog, chainring, and wheel sizes, together with the crankarm length. City-going riders may do best between the high sixties and the low seventies, generally speaking.

The **TRACK LOCKRINGS** typically provide but a pair of openings, for our lockring tools. It is way too easy to strip them out. Our professional lockring tools handily circumvent this dilemma, by gripping the north and south poles at once, but the single-toothed consumer versions need a finer touch: you need to hold the tool firmly in place with one hand, while bearing down with the other.

The track lockring threads have been broadly standardized, with the notable exceptions of those from Campagnolo and Mavic, each of which employ their own distinct standards. You should never feel as if you're forcing any of these parts in to position! And make sure you grease the threads, OK? Some people I've met more recently use mild thread-locking compounds on the lockring threads, but I've been riding greased lockrings for about five years now. I grew up riding through the winter road salt, which happily rusts through anything it may touch; the supplementary thread-locking redundancy just would not have occurred to me. But whatever it is you find yourself doing, make sure everything is tightened securely. Manufacturers' websites should list their respective torque recommendations, if ever there is confusion on this last point.

The cogs beneath are traditionally attached and removed with a chainwhip. Its flail should be 1/8 inch wide, to better accommodate any wider cogs it may encounter. The more completely the cog is gripped, the more comfortably you can lean on its chainwhip. You might even loop a rubber band around the top of the handle, to better catch the flail's swinging tail.

My friend Christian once showed me another way to install and remove track cogs, using the very chain that drives the bike. Loosen the wheel and loop the chain around the frame's bottom bracket shell, then double the chain back over itself, such that it wraps twice around the cog, and spin the wheel to move the cog. Picture the wheel rolling forward, to install a cog, or backwards to remove one. It becomes a massive lever, in this application; you're able to tighten or loosen the cog with less force. (The old chainwhip might be augmented with a Jesus bar, alternately, if leverage becomes an issue.)

Hennepin Avenue, Minneapolis

As with the singlespeed freewheels, the cogs themselves are either 3/32 or 1/8 inches wide. Proper track components have traditionally taken the wider road, in this regard—the broadened shelves of their mythical 1/8-inch glaciers take more heat to melt—but our slim pretenders are more common and less expensive. And it is best if all the parts can be made to match, to minimize their wear, but for the 1/8-inch chains at least this is not necessary to the project.

The tensioned master links supplied with SRAM and conneX chains really are awesome for derailleur-equipped bikes, in comparing with the lame Shimano or Campagnolo master pins, but they're not meant for use with the fixed gears. Neither manufacturer provides such connectors with their track-specific chains, actually. The sudden changes in momentum associated with the fixed chains inevitably threaten to loosen any tensioned master links, especially if the chain is loose. Loose chains suck, on the fixed gears. They always threatening to fall off; their cogs and rings wear more quickly; the slop punctuates your decisions with an unfortunate hesitance.

The track chain is tensioned when you can't get more than an inch of play, pushing up and down upon its length. We accomplish this by walking the hub backward in the dropouts. You shouldn't be able to pull the axle all the way back to the end of the dropouts, when the chain is mounted, because this tells us the chain is too long. The axle can only be pulled back to some mid-point along the dropouts' horizon, if things are as we like them to be. Go ahead and tighten down the neutral side axle nut, at this particular point.

Grab some spokes up behind the crank and pull the front of the wheel toward the drive side chainstay: the drive side axle end edges backward in its dropout. Tighten its locknut down in this new position, as you're holding the wheel taught, and this new tension will project itself onto the chain.

You might find yourself repeating these steps, or switching their polarity to the opposite side, as the case may be. Just keep your eye on the prize. And be sure the wheel is perfectly centered in the frame, when you do finish, by sighting down its tail end. Once the proper discipline is achieved, you will do well to enforce it with a BMX chain tensioner.

I've not yet managed to wear out a fixed drivetrain, but it is at least theoretically possible. Travis T. tells me the chain's rollers start breaking away, eventually. The chain might sooner lose a link, once the wear stretches past a certain point, but by then at least it's best to replace the whole of the drivetrain simultaneously. A new chain applied to a toasted old cog grinds and makes lots of noise, at least until the weary cog convinces it to shut

the hell up, but by then the eager new chain is just as burnt and cynical itself.

We can reasonably expect the bonafide track chainrings to be nice and round, but many of those arriving from multi-speed systems are slightly ovalized instead. The chain's tension is on-again, off-again, were the derailleurs' timely interventions slipped from the scene. Yet the ovals' lazy smile is only immediately obvious with the old Biopace chainrings; the more common sloppy grins are less easily discerned. You need to actually set things up on the bike, to get a sense of the situation.

The obtuse Biopace eggs are counterintuitive in any situation—by most accounts, at least—but the minor ovals can work it out fine with the fixes. You only need to position them correctly upon their spiders. There tends to be a very small degree of play across the crank's bolt shelves, when first a chainring is mounted; this may be turned to our advantage.

First loosen the chainring bolts to finger-tight. Then get the chain tension as high as it needs to be, and spin the crank through a few rotations: its chainring tends toward the most central location. And that's it; bolt the ring down while everything is still perfect.

Dedicated track frames are spaced to 120 millimeters. Their hubs usually reflect this, but the threads are mounted closer to the axle ends to provide for a better chainline. Surly and other manufacturers have also produced track-threaded hubs of 130- and 135-millimeter spacings, for use with the road and mountain frames.

Many of the old traditionalists can be convinced to appreciate new environments as well, given a few millimeters' worth of axle spacers, but it's more common these days that we just use a **FLIP-FLOP** hub instead. Most are already spaced to 130 or 135 millimeters, but any of them allow us to burn twice as quickly, by threading both flanges at once. You are able to blast up the hill on a fixed cog, before flipping the wheel around to leisurely coast back to Earth.

Most such cosmonauts balance the track threads to freewheel threads, but they sometimes end up doing the same thing for both sides; their role in our world is simply to provide for the option. Your gearing choices need to be of at least roughly similar sizes— within a couple teeth, at least—in order to use the same length of chain.

Like most of my friends, I began my own fixing experiments with the Suzue Junior loose bearing track hubs. They're obscenely cheap; the wholesale cost approximates a night out at the bars. I'm always broke, and at first I wasn't sure I would enjoy the fixing; the Junior set just seemed like the way to go. And the things do work, strictly speaking, but the cones and dust seals and axles are all crap. You can buy a realistic track hub, or you can keep replacing the cheap ones.

Campagnolo and Shimano both still produce fine loose-ball track hub sets, as of this writing at least, but the various sealed bearing track hubs have also become somewhat more popular. They're simpler to deal with; many are quite good. I've had fine luck with the Surly track hubs—through the Minneapolis winter, no less—but the Suzue Pro Max and Phil Wood products are likely more famous.

Where shift levers presume to regulate our reactions, the fix instead trusts our instincts. Our decisions to walk, trot, or run are enforced directly upon the drive wheel; there is no need for translation. The plan is also supremely efficient, in that nothing is lost. The

coasting itself draws away a portion of our energy, just as grandpa's big clock eventually winds down, but the fixed wheel hasn't heard anything about this. It rolls as it pleases, until it grows tired.

The fixed wheel's journey might also be ended by other methods. The classical approach merely pushes backwards on the pedals, to counter their sustained momentum. But this may take a few seconds to work, so people sometimes skid as well, and you hear about threading the needle or finding the hole or going for the opening: the actual distances required to stop at speed are still significant. So the bike might be trusted to stop with its wheels alone, given the faith or perhaps circumstance suggests a more conventional approach.

Surly flip-flop hub with chain tensioner

Any brake mounted to the front wheel is spared a good deal of the ground fire the tail gunners face, given their strategic positions, and this supreme leisure allows their pads to wear somewhat more slowly. Their cables are also quite a bit shorter, in comparing with the others, and so they happily subsist with only a minimum of lubrication. And of their pair, physics awards the front brake with 80 percent of the stopping power. The sum of its characteristics, in other words, does not easily provide any rationale toward mere brakelessness.

You're able to run a fix with its hand brake, in fact, but this becomes counterintuitive. Its use gets to be entirely superfluous, in normal conditions. The lever becomes so much lawn furniture, perched atop the handlebars; it might be obligingly pulled out to accommodate the occasionally serious downhills and panic stops. All things being equal, you should be able to get what you need with the legs.

The smaller your gearing choice, the easier this is to do. You might even learn the skid. This erases the tires, just as it did when we were young, but then we quickly find more pressing considerations. Think about that, skidding a fast bike to a stop! It's as if the butterfly has sprouted wheels. If only we could slip some flint in the tires, to make for a proper comet-tail effect … . What was it we were talking about?

The easiest way to learn is to start on the snow. For our purposes here, it's best to find a reasonably fresh patch, something compacted but not quite solid. The traction isn't nearly what the outside world would like it to be, but this very consideration bends handily to our own nefarious purposes. We're more easily able to lock up the knees, at level points in the pedals' rotation, and this is basically all it takes.

You skid just fine on the ice, needless to say, but the odds are good it'll be ass-first. That's what the snow is for; it gives us just enough of a grip on reality. The aspirant skidding artist certainly does well to enlist toe clips or clipless pedals, at least as soon as the snow melts, because the abrupt appearance of improved traction forces our return to the boring old rules of physics. The dry pavement seizes upon the passing tire; the locked knees buckle and threaten to give way.

The toe clips were once the only way to deal with this, back when trials first began, but most fixed riders in my know have long since moved on to clipless pedals. I've known a colorful few to rock the curious Power Grips in their stead, but the anecdotal evidence suggests these don't work as well for skids.

In my life I've only known one person to enter a sustained skid at speed, lacking such benefits. This was Chuck Cowan, as best demonstrated at the 2001 North American Cycle Courier Championships in Minneapolis. He has a shop there called Behind Bars. You should go check it out.

Grey, the rainy day fix

If you don't run clipless pedals or toe clips on your fix, I would *strongly* encourage a front hand brake.

The forks associated with dedicated track bikes typically avoid making allowances for anything so obtuse as brake hardware—the bikes traditionally relegated to the worry-free confines of indoor velodromes—but caliper holes may be carefully installed to the crown. Or maybe you can search out a front hub with a drum brake, alternately, which is positively ideal in the winters.

Any front brake delivers the majority of a pair's stopping power. Used in combination with the legs, your shit can slow the hell down in a hurry. Sidepulls can work out just fine, once blessed with realistic brake pads. Cantilever or linear pull sets are even better. A disc or hydraulic system likely presents a fix with certain damning contradictions, however, in that either may actually work a bit too well. The legs tend to move more slowly; we expect a meaningful learning curve at the least.

And that's it; we're done! The razor-sharp disc brake has at last been crossed against the endlessly patient fixed gear; I can barely imagine what else we need to talk about ... with bicycles, at least! But I've only been able to notice a small portion of all the amazing developments transpiring all around; my treatment here only contributes to an ongoing and far broader discussion of a great many topics. And the very next words—let alone the last ones—will surely belong to other parties entirely. So go on, get out there and ride.

RESOURCES

A to B Magazine
19 West Park
Castle Cary, Somerset
BA7 7DB
UK
www.atob.org.uk/home.html
atob@onetel.com
Telephone/Fax 44 (0)1963 351649

Car Busters Magazine
Kratka 26
100 00 Praha 10
Czech Republic
www.carbusters.ecn.cz
Telephone (420) 274 810 849
Fax (420) 274 772 017

Cars-R-Coffins
17 Russell Avenue South
Minneapolis, MN
55405
USA
www.carsrcoffins.com/welcome.php
crc@carsrcoffins.com
Telephone (612) 203-0914

The Centre for Sustainable Transportations
Suite 309, 15-6400 Millcreek Drive
Mississauga, ON
L4N 3E7
Canada
www.cstctd.org/english/index.htm
transport@cstctd.org
Telephone (905) 858 9242
Fax (905) 858 9291

Critical Mass Hub
www.critical-mass.org/

Detour Publications
590 Jarvis Street, 4th Floor
Toronto, ON
M4Y 2J4
Canada
info@detourpublications.com
Telephone (416) 338-5087
Fax (416) 392-0071

Encycleopedia
www.encycleopedia.com/index.cfm

**International Federation of
Bike Messenger Associations**
P. O. Box 191443
San Francisco, CA
94119-1442
USA
www.messengers.org/ifbma/

The Outcast
www.yesweareontheweb.com

Surface Transportation Policy Project
1100 17th Street, NW
10th Floor
Washington, DC
20036
USA
www.transact.org
stpp@transact.org
Telephone (202) 466-2636
Fax (202) 466-2247

Velo Vision Magazine
York Environmental Centre
St. Nicholas Fields
Bull Lane
York
YO10 3EN
UK
www.velovision.co.uk
peter@velovision.co.uk
Telephone/Fax 01904 438 224 (from UK)
or 44 1904 438 224 (from outside UK)

Victoria Transport Policy Institute
1250 Rudlin Street
Victoria, BC
V8V 3R7
Canada
info@vtpi.org
Telephone/Fax (250) 360-1560

63xc.com
www.63xc.com

The Guest Book

INDEX